The Big Top on the Big Screen

The Big Top on the Big Screen

*Explorations of
the Circus in Film*

Edited by
Teresa Cutler-Broyles

McFarland & Company, Inc., Publishers
Jefferson, North Carolina

This book has undergone peer review.

LIBRARY OF CONGRESS CATALOGUING-IN-PUBLICATION DATA

Names: Cutler-Broyles, Teresa, 1962– editor.
Title: The big top on the big screen : explorations of the circus in film /
    edited by Teresa Cutler-Broyles.
Description: Jefferson, North Carolina : McFarland & Company, Inc.,
    Publishers, 2020. | Includes bibliographical references and index.
Identifiers: LCCN 2019054067 | ISBN 9781476671185 (paperback : acid free paper) ∞
    ISBN 9781476637754 (ebook)
Subjects: LCSH: Circus in motion pictures.
Classification: LCC PN1995.9.C512 B54 2020 | DDC 791.43/6579—dc23
LC record available at https://lccn.loc.gov/2019054067

BRITISH LIBRARY CATALOGUING DATA ARE AVAILABLE

ISBN (print) 978-1-4766-7118-5
ISBN (ebook) 978-1-4766-3775-4

Front cover image of circus backstage © 2020 Dm_Cherry / Shutterstock

Printed in the United States of America

McFarland & Company, Inc., Publishers
  Box 611, Jefferson, North Carolina 28640
  www.mcfarlandpub.com

Acknowledgments

This book was made possible in large part by the many friends and family members who continued to ask about its progress and encouraged me as it went through a number of iterations, dramatic shifts in direction, and a few shaky moments. I cannot thank the authors enough for their hard work and dedication, and for continuing to believe in the process. Thank you as well to the peer reviewers for their incredibly helpful and thorough notes that helped make this collection a more cohesive and far better work.

In addition, thanks go to my husband Robin for supporting this and all my endeavors, and my team of beta readers. And a special thanks to Brent Stypczynski for his editing help at the last minute. You all helped to keep the fires burning under my feet and in my heart, and your thought-provoking questions in this and other arenas continue to make me think in ever-broadening ways. I can't wait for the next adventure.

Table of Contents

Introduction

Since the early 19th century and the initiation of the canvas tent—later to become the big top—and its merging with animal menageries, the circus has been a form of entertainment familiar to American audiences. The attractions are many and varied, and include visual, physiological and psychological pleasures. The circus and the medium of film would seem a suitable match; they both present a visual attraction that draws the gaze while it asks audience members to suspend disbelief and enter a world of wonder.

Indeed, films of all genres utilize the circus as setting, background, and even character. Unlike horror, romance, western, suspense, coming-of-age, adventure or fantasy, and simultaneously potentially partaking of them all, the circus film crosses genres easily, becoming a hybrid creature—in one sense, becoming a freak[1] as surely as those beings often contained within their celluloid stories. It is no surprise that a good percentage of the films which feature circuses tend toward the horror genre, or at least films that have a particularly dark element, and a number of the authors herein seek out that darkness. The circus is, after all, a place in which the natural order of things is overturned, where expectations and social norms are thwarted, and unforeseen alliances are formed. It is a place where anything could happen, encompassing a broad spectrum of relationships, family units, power dynamics, sociological and labor-related hierarchies, and a range of people with different physical appearances and abilities.

In exploring this space, the authors herein utilized a number of approaches that run the gamut from psychology to gender to film theories. They examine non-human animal and freak bodies; circus labor, equality and stratification; film and circus history; "monsters" both human and non; and the power of the circus to shatter and change lives. One element seems to hold as a through line: the liminal space created by the circus itself often becomes a place for/of *transformation*.

Transformation can manifest in a number of ways. P. A. Wilder, David Blanke, Whitney S. May, and Lisann Anders, in the first four essays, explore

1

the way the circus in film can function as mirror, mentor, abyss, and harbinger of things to come, ultimately all liminal spaces in which characters within them, and by extension the films' viewers, are forced to reflect on and challenge their understandings of self, of other, and of the world in which they live.

In the next two essays, Jessica L. Williams and Fernando Gabriel Pagnoni Berns examine the darker side of the circus (film). In these pieces, human freaks, para-human, paranormal vampires, and terrifying clowns become spectacle. The dis-abled and non-human body acts as a site of horror, enticing both characters and viewers to step close. These essays ask us to examine our fears of these "unnatural" creatures as a way to understand the artificiality of boundaries of otherness.

Kylo-Patrick R. Hart and Michael Charlton address the circus and the concept of childhood in remarkable and very different ways in their essays. These examine the way nostalgia, memory, trauma, and healing can be generated by the circus if we learn to see and embrace its carnivalesque nature and sometimes unsettling reality.

The essays by Rachel L. Carazo and Ayal C. Prouser investigate cultural constructs such as animal-human relationships and gender binaries, and ask its filmic characters and viewers to take a step back and recognize that their assumptions of various forms of others are culturally bound, entwined, and mutually created. In this, these authors use the circus space to show us our own, often unacknowledged prejudices.

Finally, Teresa Cutler-Broyles examines the role of the circus as mirror, one that reflects, conceals and sometimes distorts the concepts of identity and knowledge of self.

While each essay is unique and powerful on its own, the overlap of ideas is evident throughout, reinforcing that the circus is a place of power and is singularly separate from everyday life. It is this separation, this liminal state, that allows it to function in such magnificent, entertaining and significant ways.

This book can be read straight through, or piecemeal. Each author's work offers a new window into how and why the circus element in their chosen film matters. Any list of circus films certainly far outreaches the extent of this volume. Our intent is not to make a claim for an overarching examination of circuses in film, circus films, or circuses in general, but to begin a discussion of where and in what ways circuses have featured in a few films through the last century. It is my hope that later volumes will find a vast realm of possible starting points from which to broaden the scholarship of circuses in film, in a wider array of genres, and for this to be one moment in such an array.

Ultimately, circus films are more than they appear to be, amalgams that ask us to examine our expectations and question our limits as we immerse ourselves. These films draw us in, recreating the liminal circus space on screen, and we become a kind of doubled audience. We watch the performance unfold on screen in all its magic and spectacle; we enter the circus space and become for a while a flying trapeze artist, a strongman, a horseback-riding diva, a lion-tamer. A freak. An outsider/insider with the ability to see clearly the divisions between us and them, animal and human, normal[2] and abnormal—and we see that they are all the same. And so are we.

And when the film ends and the credits roll, we return to ourselves with renewed understanding of the journey we have taken on the way to ourselves.

NOTES

1. The term freak here is used as it would have been used to describe those people whose bodies were outside the norm, who were displayed or displayed themselves in the circus sideshows or freak shows during the late nineteenth and early twentieth centuries. While not commonly in use today in the same way, and seen as a derogatory term, it still occasionally crops up, most often by self-described "freaks" who perform in carnival side-shows.

2. The term normal here is used to denote those people whose bodies are seen as the norm. These terms and the understandings of what they mean are culturally- and societally-based, and time- and context-dependent. Today the term normal is not an acceptable mode of discussing human bodies, or behavior for that matter.

(Re)Producing the Circus

Defining Circus Cinema

P. A. WILDER

In 2017 Ringling Bros. and Barnum & Bailey Circus announced its final tour and subsequent closure after 146 years of business (Feld 2017), but while the American circus—at least in that incarnation—appears to have newly ended, cinema has long depicted its demise. This essay first touches on a few historical developments of the American circus and American cinema, then moves toward an outline of the new term *circus cinema*, following a discussion of circus-fan films and studio-produced circus cinema to construct a working definition. Circus cinema is distinct from the live spectacle of circus, as well as being unique in a film history context. Firstly, circus cinema transmutes circus acts into aesthetic compositions of light and color, replacing the physical spectacles with psychological dramas. Secondly, circus cinema by necessity displays, and centers its dramas around, the labors of circus, spending considerable screen-time on working people and the interaction of labor and power relations in a capitalist system. Finally, circus cinema designates the backstage as a carnivalesque space, which allows for the imagining of equal relations between workers and owners.

Circus studies is a fairly new field of discourse, but the literature has been multiplying steadily since Paul Bouissac's 1977 *Circus and Culture: A Semiotic Approach,* and Janet Davis's 2002 *Circus Age.* While many circus studies texts focus on the labor of circus, be it done by human or beast, classic film studies texts often champion film as the democratic art form most capable of raising class consciousness. This essay brings the two fields together under the term *circus cinema.* This new field of discourse relies in definition on two foundational texts of cinema studies: Walter Benjamin's "The Work of Art in the Age of Technological Reproduction," and Tom Gunning's "The Cinema of Attraction[s]: Early Film, Its Spectator and the Avant-Garde." This essay connects the ongoing discourse of Gunning's "cinema of attractions" to Benjamin's "here-and-now"-ness. This framework explains the impossibility of reproducing circus *essence*, and how circus cinema mediates this lack with a substitute. The work of Janet Davis to chart the culture and history of circuses in America informs this essay's historical overview of circus labor, and this essay analyzes three films: Victor Sjöström's 1924 *He, Who Gets Slapped*; Charlie Chaplin's 1928 *The Circus*; and Henry Hathaway's 1964 *Circus World*. These three films should in no way be considered canonical, they merely serve as examples of circus cinema as outlined above. It is the focus of this essay to attempt a working definition of the term circus cinema, and produce some of its long history, beginning with the histories of circus and cinema themselves.

As a modern spectacle, the American circus depended on advancing technologies like the railroad which facilitated a disavowal of nostalgia for the mud caked wagon wheels and the uncertainty of overland travel. The railroad applied a disciplined concept of time to the space it crossed through, and the bigger circus could arrive on schedule into highly populated cities. The train-bound circus required roustabouts, workers who could perform any number of tasks with no skill-set, as well as more skilled workers and more diverse performers, all groups performing labor more dangerous than before. Train cars allowed for larger exotic animals like elephants and tigers to be brought into the circus, and the side-show and the fairgrounds were also incorporated into this larger circus. Essentially, with train travel the American circus was brought into modernity.

With its expansion, the modern American circus faced the possibility of bankruptcy as well. The larger the circus, the more start-up capital and investment it required. The Ringling Brothers Circus was known as the largest American circus at the turn of the 20th century, and its buy out of the competing Barnum & Bailey Circus in 1907, combining shows in 1919, constituted the first major entertainment merger in American history (Davis 40).

The circus was an easy way for a spectator to view wild animals, witness an exotic performance from unfamiliar cultures, marvel at people marginalized by polite society, and more. Other popular forms of entertainment like the World's Fair, amusement parks, and vaudeville competed for the attention of the urban population. And cinema posed an existential crisis. Movie palaces, like the big top, "Created the illusion of compressing the world into one sparkling amusement where the world could be easily consumed 'at a glance'" (Davis 293, note 6). Cinema has the ability to bring the unfamiliar closer and regularly to the viewer. In "The Work of Art in the Age of Its Technological Reproducibility" Walter Benjamin notes that "the scope for exhibiting the work of art has increased so enormously with the various methods of technologically reproducing it" (Benjamin 25). Motion pictures could be found almost anywhere, whereas one needed to wait for the circus to come to town. And because it is a live act, there is no guarantee that the circus will deliver the same spectacle that thrilled the viewer the last time they experienced it. Cinema, on the other hand, provides the same visual experience each time, albeit the environmental conditions are variable, and as it moved out of the laboratory and into the nickelodeons and later the movie palaces, it began to attract the same mass audience as the circus, and eventually came to dominated the public realm of mass entertainment. Soon, improved cinema technology made the theater more comfortable and the pictures more alluring, and Hollywood began employing circus talent (Stoddart 80).

Circus-fan films are documents made by amateur filmmakers and circus fans, and far outnumber circus cinema films. The Circus World Museum archive holds somewhere between 700 to 900 of these films. Most of these 700 or more films were cataloged by Bill Metzger, who during the 1960s and through the 1980s was a magician at Circus World in Baraboo, WI, during the summer performance seasons, then worked under Bob Parkinson on the off-season at Circus World's Robert L. Parkinson Library and Research Center in the film archive. Interestingly, circus-fan films are rarely documents of circus shows, but rather provide a documentary look into the construction of the circus, thereby sharing with circus cinema a look backstage at its inherent labor. *Circus Parades and Old Times*, for example, filmed by Paul Van Pool between 1928 and 1939 of the Seils-Sterling Circus, shows the machinery of circus that is often overlooked. It features various shots of men erecting the big top, performers and animals from outside the tent before going into the show, and back lot sledge gangs hammering in tent stakes among the caravan of trucks, cars, and wagons needed for transportation (CWM FM 206).

The sledge gang is a particularly interesting group to focus on in a discussion of circus labor and reproducibility on film. The boss of the caravans divided the workers for an 85 man crew called a "big top gang" into two main groups: the men who laid the tent stakes; and the men who pounded them into the ground with sledge hammers, who "stood in a circle and took turns hammering each stake into the ground, singing rhythmically as they worked" (Davis 47). In the Van Pool films, a circle of men stand around a stake while the leader taps it into place. Following this set rhythm, another man swings his hammer down on the leader's off beat. This pattern is repeated by each man in turn, until the whole gang is swinging hammers in a round. The movement of their upper bodies and the hammer heads flying through the air creates a blurring of action that resembles a flower blooming at a rapid speed.

Like the Ford assembly line model, circus labor was segmented and divided along class, race, gender, and skill level. In one of Van Pool's later films, the 1940 *Behind the Scenes with Ringling Brothers and Barnum and*

Bailey Circus, a group of black men make up a sledge gang. In a wide shot, the segregated sledge gang is shown hammering away. The film then cuts to a single white man operating a sledge machine, a large device that requires only one person to pull a lever that drives a stake down (CWM FM 28). The stake driver machine came into being around the turn of the 20th century, give or take a few years. According to Peter Shrake, the Head Archivist at Circus World Museum, the Gollmar Bros. Circus was an early innovator of the device. Depending on the circus, the machine was commonly used by the 1920s, although human sledge gangs continued well past the circus's adoption of the technology (Shrake).

Davis notes how some circus bosses segregated labor along race lines and one in particular, James Bailey, was perhaps "reluctant to hire African Americans as workingmen because white workers interpreted the presence of blacks as a threat to their own social and economic standing" (Davis 70). The Van Pool film demonstrates how this segregation resulted in black men continuing to perform hard labor, whereas the white worker was allowed to handle an expensive machine that could do the work of many.

Segregation in the circus reached past labor and into domestic areas as well. Performers and the owners ate, leisured, and slept in areas away from the workers, who were often given numbers rather than be addressed by name. Davis notes that circus owners "often treated workers as anonymous cogs in a vast production machine" (Davis 41). These "cogs" were paid the lowest wages in the show. Many circus-fan films include long takes of the circus trains entering town, and animals being unloaded. Again, the Van Pool film provides a strong example of the significance of this moment, with camels, elephants, horses, and zebras being led out of the dark cars into the light of day with local townspeople standing by to watch the tent go up (CWM FM 206). Van Pool seems to be quite skilled at navigating the busy work environment of setting up the circus, grabbing multiple angles of a task and traversing large areas of land to record the various assemblages of the circus tent and side shows.

A film made by Walter G. Heist documents the Ringling Bros. and Barnum & Bailey Circus in 1944 at Madison Square Garden in New York City. This film demonstrates that the integral scale and dimension of the circus can be captured on film only at the expense of the immediacy of the live act, and then partially. For moving pictures, it is a one-or-the-other choice: scale and dimension, or immediacy. Shot from the stands, this film shows choreographed aerialists performing fantastic stunts high above the ground without a net (CWM FM 621). The camera must tilt down to show the distance and the danger. Although this reproduces the real space and presents it without an edit, the presence of the act escapes the camera. The film holds no danger for the viewer, even though it is taken from the audience's point of view. What is missing is the "here and now"-ness of the stunt, which is unreproducible.

Circus Cinema Theory

Live circus can't be reproduced because it is a spectacle that occurs only in view of a live audience. It is constituted by its here-and-now visibility. As Benjamin theorizes, even with the latest technology, reproductions lack "the here and now of the work of art—its unique existence in a particular place," exactly what makes circus spectacle possible (Benjamin 21). Without an audience, stunts are only so much rehearsal. Anyone who has spent time on stage or in the ring understands that although a performer brings with him or her to the performance all his past rehearsals, something fresh occurs and makes special the act when demonstrated for a live audience, and this cannot be forced, learned, or rehearsed. Conversely, and rightly sterile, the camera reproduces only what occurs before it. The realism perceived by cinema audiences is related to things; objects on-screen are recognized for what they are, while concepts and complex interactions are only inferred and grasped at by the viewer. According to Henri Lefebvre, visualization "serves to conceal repetitiveness. People *look*, and take sight, take seeing, for life itself" (Lefebvre 75). *Seeing* unfairly becomes *knowing*. Lefebvre, like Benjamin, believed that "repetition has everywhere defeated uniqueness, that the artificial and contrived have driven all spontaneity and naturalness from the field" (Lefebvre 75). Three-dimensional stunts viewed from a circular arena cannot be accurately reproduced on a two-dimensional medium that mimics three-dimensional space and is viewed in a face-forward presentation. The spontaneity and naturalness of a live act is not transmittable via audio/visual recording equipment. The dimension cannot be reproduced accurately because the spectacle is a mass itself of people, animals, the tents, the high-wire, and other props and various locations. To take it all in requires an in-person view. The circus is not simply one act, one space, but a fully immersive event with side-shows, Circus Days, menageries, performers in the stands and behind food counters, etc., that creates what Davis calls a "frenetic placelessness" that "helped hasten the nation's move toward a mass consumer culture," rooted in a "disembodied modern media" (228). The two-dimensional screen of motion pictures flattens the sublime extravaganza.

Perhaps counter-intuitively, distance is key to circus audience experience, which cannot be reproduced with a camera. Without an in-person experience of the stunts, the circus cinema viewer has no connection with a performer but through their face, relying on photographic mediums and close-ups. Yet, to feature the performer's face the camera loses the scale of the stunt that live circus spectacle is reliant on. This is mediated by a transmutation of the stunt's components—gravity, force, speed, and the human body—into the filmic components of shapes of light and color in an aesthetically pleasing two-dimensional frame. Rather than the marvel of a human body flying through the air high above the audience to grasp another's wrists or fall to certain death, cinema can only produce the sensuous image of moving light and color. To simulate the tension of the live act, danger is replaced by narrative progressions in which circus workers, performers, and the circus as an organization face the many dangers of live circus, and the thrill of witnessing interpersonal dramas these dangers provoke.

Circus cinema thus depends on the transmutability of circus arts and labor into aesthetically pleasing compositions. When not producing these compositions, circus cinema discards the live circus raw material of bodies, scale, distance, and gravity, and instead reproduces the human countenance in narrative form; the raw materials of live circus contain no psychological interiority, which narrative cinema is dependent upon. As circus cinema transmutes circus acts and labor into narratives, it produces a glimpse and discussion of labor not seen by live circus-goers through its unique backstage access. The studio films that make up circus cinema avoid the "here and now" of live circus spectacle. Instead, the on-screen circus is relegated to the space of cinematic "attractions" punctuating the narrative with moments of stalled cinematic time to present stunts that remind the cinematic audience that all of what precedes and follows is happening in the realm of circus.

Early films that often predated narrative integration have been theorized by Tom Gunning as a "cinema of attractions," a form of spectatorial address that produces a "visual pleasure in the act of display" (Gunning 33). "Attractions" itself is a term coming out of the circus. Gunning brackets the dominance of the "cinema of attractions" between 1900 and 1906, writing that the term refers to an "approach to spectatorship that I felt dominated early cinema from the novelty period until the dominance of longer narrative films" (36). Gunning's seminal essay, "The Cinema of Attraction: Early Film, Its Spectator and the Avant-Garde," introduced the term to the field of new film history developing in the 1970s and 1980s. Gunning describes the "cinema of attractions" as having "the drive towards display, rather than creation of a fictional world; a tendency towards punctual temporality, rather than extended development; a lack of interest in character 'psychology' or the development of motivation; and a direct, often marked, address to the spectator at the expense of the creation of a diegetic coherence" (36). The address to the audience is still being utilized by contemporary commercial cinema, and action films often borrow punctuated temporality from the cinema of attractions as well. On the other end, a circus displays stunts, animals, trapeze artists, etc., without narrative through-lines. Performers display their bodies and an ability to defy gravity with it, and contort themselves, seemingly all without fear. In the circus, unlike cinema, the face of the performer, with all its emotions, is too far away to focus on, restricting the audience from projecting any psychological interiority onto it.

Yet the methods of display adopted by cinema in its early years came from vaudeville, theater, and the circus. While transitioning to a storytelling approach, early film often employed a lecturer, whose job included "cueing and preparing the audience response to a powerful attraction," just as the ringmaster does for the circus audience (37). Discussing Fellini's 1970 television movie *Clowns*, Helen Stoddart reports that the circus "traditionally avoided arranging its acts in any kind of narrative form," calling any integration of narrative into spectacle a "cross-generic corruption" (Stoddart 81). However, the circus, like cinema, was never static or pure. Its development ranged from the dog and pony show to the most recent Ringling Bros. stadium show on ice.

The early development of montage is one of the historical turning points for modern cinema and one of the elements that keep circus un-reproducible. Only via montage is the work of art, i.e., the film, brought into being. The act of pointing a camera toward action and recording it is but one stage in the longer filmmaking process. If what was recorded doesn't suggest to the viewer what the filmmaker intended, subsequent stages in the filmmaking process can redirect the viewer toward those intentions, improving the resultant film along the way. With film, performance is recorded then assembled later, i.e., improved (Benjamin 28).

With circus, the performance is linear and cannot be reassembled to mean something anew. Live circus can fail, and when it does there are no means to replace failures with successes. On the other hand, circus cinema plans failure and success. Narrative film draws on emotional attachment to character in order to improve successes or heighten failures of those characters, i.e., the psychological interiority projected onto characters' faces. The success or failure of an on-screen character is causal. That is, it moves the narrative along a path that will culminate in the end of a story. Although success and failure are still causal in circus cinema, there is an additional element in the moment of action that is non-causal. Circus acts are non-narrative. When these acts are depicted on-screen they produce an attraction for the viewer different from live circus, but achieve the same dazzling effect. Live circus acts amaze by defying nature. Circus acts in circus cinema amaze as sublime compositions, pictures of the act rendered expertly and closely to show the human form in tension. Furthermore, circus cinema reminds viewers of their own bodies and their place in the world, their place in the (capitalist) apparatus that upholds society. Benjamin notes that "To witness the film actor taking revenge on their behalf not only by asserting [their own] humanity (or what appears to them as such) against the apparatus, but by placing that apparatus in the service of [their own] triumph" reminds the viewer that the machine can be made subservient to the worker (31).

Cecil B. DeMille describes the circus in his 1952 film *The Greatest Show on Earth* as, "a massive machine, whose very life depends on discipline, motion, and speed. [A machine] that meets calamity again and again." DeMille adds that "disaster and tragedy stalk the big top, haunting the back yard, where death is constantly watching" (DeMille 1952). This machine depends on disciplined bodies. In capitalism, the flesh and blood body serves the apparatus, be it material or conceptual, rather than the other way around. Circuses often experienced calamities, and it was the workers who suffered while circus owners bounced back, often to begin new risky business ventures. In circus cinema, the interest of the masses cannot be recovered in one fell swoop. However, what is unique to the genre can begin to remind the masses of their interest as a working class, as the moments of attraction in circus cinema return focus from the face to the body, from narrative to spectacle. These narrative breaks have the potential to unite the mass audience in their shared experience as flesh and blood workers who must daily confront the apparatus of capitalism.

As film conventions moved from a cinema of attractions towards narrative forms, filmic spaces of drama, rather than spectacle, emerged. The focus moved from a fascination with the body to the face, from bodily stunts to psychological interiority. Labor defines this space in circus cinema. The modes of relation of such a cinematic space are ones of precarity and expression, i.e., dramatic labor relations. The interpersonal relationships that develop backstage among workers and bosses find expression in the stunts and gags performed by workers in the ring. Likewise, the precarity of the labor is visible when faced with the threat of circus closure or loss of employment and wages, prompting performers to attempt ever more dangerous and extraordinary stunts to attract new audiences and keep regulars coming back for more. The on-screen circus performers and laborers—often portrayed as criminals—although hidden for a time from external policing, are constantly under threat of discovery and so must mask their identities. This results in narratives of mistaken or hidden identities. As such, the on-screen circus has been produced as a fugitive space, one to flee *to* as well as from. As a refuge, the circus is host to narratives about freaks, criminals, and men, women, and children of loose morals, all aligned with the stereotypes of actual circus folk. Accordingly, the circus is a passive refuge, i.e., having no direct purpose of sheltering, yet providing partial coverage to its members.

Circus cinema predates the era of what many film historians dub *early cinema* and continues on today. In 1897, J. Stuart Blackston and Albert E. Smith made a Vitagraph Co. stop-motion film called *Humpty Dumpty Circus*, using a circus toy-set with movable figures (Dobson XXIV). Circus cinema continued to develop slowly over the next decades, coming into its heyday in the 1920s. Tony Sarg's 1921 *The First Circus*, another animated film, is a short comedy set in prehistoric times that looks quite like the shadow plays that predate cinema. The 1924 Sjöström film *He, Who Gets Slapped*, staring Lon Chaney as Beaumont, tells the story of a scientist who retreats to the circus where he assumes the name HE and disguises himself as a Pierrot clown.

In *Problems of Dostoevsky's Poetics*, Mikhail Bakhtin describes carnival as "the place for working out, in a concrete sensuous, half-real and half-play acted form, a *new mode of inter-relationship between* individuals, counterpoised to the all-powerful socio-hierarchical relationships of non-carnival life" (Bakhtin 123). Following this, the on-screen circus space of *He, Who Gets Slapped* allows HE, a performer considered to be of one of the lowest working-classes, to laugh in the face of a Baron, and be excused as an eccentric artist—but only backstage. While Bakhtin's "carnivalistic life" makes no distinction between performers and spectators (122), in circus cinema the performers, when not in the ring, watch the acts in the ring from backstage—they are themselves spectators. In carnival "all distance between people is suspended," a clown and a Baron are on opposite ends of a hierarchal spectrum, yet "enter into free familiar contact on the carnival square" (123). In other words, backstage in the on-screen circus is where the Baron and the clown meet outside hierarchal social structures. Circus cinema produces a carnival space behind the curtain, delineated by the circus grounds, where societal refugees of any class can meet as equals.

Charlie Chaplin's 1928 *The Circus* imagines the big top as a fugitive space, a refuge, and a site of precarious labor, providing a glimpse of the labor supporting the extravaganza, allowing for a view of the spectacle, its inner workings, and the audience. Such a view, exemplary of circus cinema as a whole, is further complicated by the interpersonal dramas of performers and workers. Chaplin's iconic character of the "Tramp" always comes in from the periphery of society. He is a human figure on the margins, just as the traveling circus is full of outsiders entering an existing society.

For much of circus history, the performers were unprotected by unionization and the state. The human body of circus labor and performance was thus objectified as something abnormal, existing only within the tent and removed from the stationary social fabric of the town through which it travelled. As industry grew and workers revolted against exploitation, live circus lagged behind other labor organizing efforts (Davis 81). Roustabouts had no union and their bosses often withheld pay until the end of the season (80). Chaplin presents this reality in *The Circus* with a group of roustabouts who demand back-pay. When denied their earned wages, the men walk out in protest. The circus owner demands of his property manager to "get anybody," demonstrating that anyone and everyone is exploitable in the service of profit, as well as exemplifying the eternal precarity of the circus. Just as the cogs of machinery are replaceable and can be used in various different functions, the Tramp is continuously made to work in different positions by the circus owner. All to no avail, as when the circus leaves town, he is left behind.

Circus World, the 1964 John Wayne vehicle directed by Henry Hathaway, provides a view of precarious labor and the refuge space of circus cinema in a wide-screen Technicolor disaster-drama narrative. Wayne plays Matt Masters, a circus owner and wild-west showman who is trying desperately to keep his business going. All of his performers, whether Italian, French, U.S. American, or Indigenous American are safe in the refuge of the circus. One character of note, Aldo "Tojo" Alfredo, part of a high-wire and trapeze act rediscovered by Masters in Germany, is exemplary of a particular trope of those who populate circus cinema: characters who have escaped society. Tojo seems to have escaped a sordid past behind the clown makeup and costume, like Stewart's Buttons the Clown and Chaney's HE, landing in the refuge of the circus.

Most screen-time in *Circus World* is utilized representing the construction, transportation, and take-down of the Masters circus—emphasizing labor once again. When not concerned with the apparatus of the circus, the film focuses on the rehearsal of shows and the business of recruiting new acts. Showing the grand scale of the circus machinery, the Masters circus travels across the Atlantic Ocean on its own steam ship named "Circus Maximus." Docking in Barcelona, the circus advertises its arrival with a show for the city, a sort of nighttime Circus Day at port. When a high ladder stunt goes awry, the entire crew and porteños of Barcelona rush to the starboard side of the ship to see the performer in the water. The weight displacement capsizes the steamer, mimicking another spectacle of modernity: the sinking of the 1912 RMS Titanic and subsequent 1958 British film *A Night to Remember*.

Disaster being a constant in circus and circus cinema, the penultimate scene of *Circus World* is dedicated to a tent fire.[1] A mother-daughter aerialist duo save the circus by using their acrobatic skills to climb above the flames and cut away burning tent canvas. They put their bodies in danger to save the company that employs them, performing what the prior narrative showed as near-impossible feats. Although complicated, this moment demonstrates the cinematic focus of both the circus in constant threat of complete failure as a business venture, and the dependence of industry on labor at every stage, and not the other way around.

Whether left behind unemployed, like The Tramp; written off as a buffoon, like HE; or nearly burnt to death, like the Masters circus workers, the workers in circus cinema are central to the narratives by necessity. As such, when discussing the aspects of circus cinema explored by this essay—the transmutation of circus acts into pleasing visual compositions, or the carnivalesque space of backstage—a focus on labor must remain central to the discourse.

Conclusions

Live performance dazzles by its very presence, its immediacy. Circus cinema, on the other hand, dazzles through a combination of light and shadow, image and motion. Circus acts are experienced live within a shared space, while the imagined circus—moving images that this essay calls circus cinema—does not reproduce circus but rather produces new images that dazzle in their aesthetic compositions and punctuate the narratives of labor they are embedded in.

In other words, circus cinema utilizes circus space as an arena to explore the labor behind the spectacle. Rather than record the stunts of live circus the way circus fan films do, circus cinema produces narratives that take place backstage and reveal the underlying mechanics and the capitalist labor relations occurring within those mechanics. In circus cinema, the ring spectacle is replaced by backstage dramas of labor relations, relying on psychological interiority-dependent narratives. Because the circus is such a labor-heavy machine, on-screen circus space becomes a site to discuss labor relations as they are reproduced for a mass audience.

Circus cinema is therefore the genre par excellence for discussing industrialized labor. The circus and film production are both mass endeavors, and both address a mass audience. However, circus cinema (unconsciously) produces labor narratives, never allowing the worker a moment of leisure. Even while sleeping, the worker is traveling (in train cars or wagons, for example). All personal goals are entwined with and dominated by the circus owner's desire to keep the show going at all costs. Circus cinema thus presents labor relations, albeit sometimes in simplified form, as primary to the narrative rather than secondary or not at all.

NOTES

1. Due to nitrate film stock, fire also ravaged early movie houses and studios. Chaplin's studios were destroyed by a fire during the filming of *The Circus*. Chaplin biographer David Robinson notes in his DVD booklet introduction to *The Circus* that not only was Chaplin beset by fire, but "the huge circus tent which provides the principal setting for the film was destroyed by gales," in addition to Chaplin losing an entire four weeks of filming to poor laboratory work (Robinson).

WORKS CITED

Bakhtin, Mikhail. *Problems of Dostoevski's Poetics.* Translated by Caryl Emerson. U of Minnesota P, 1999.
Barnum and Bailey Circus Street Parade. August 27, 1904. Film Collection, CWM FM 106. Robert L. Parkinson Library and Research Center, Circus World Museum, Baraboo, WI. 6 May 2017.
Bazin, André. *What Is Cinema? Vol. 1.* U of California P, 2005.
Benjamin, Walter. *The Work of Art in the Age of Its Technological Reproducibility, and Other Writings on Media,* edited by Michael W. Jennings, The Belknap Press of Harvard UP, 2008, pp. 19–54.

Carmeli, Yoram S. "Compassion for Animals, Indifference to Humans." *Aesthetics in Performance: Formations of Symbolic Construction and Experience,* edited by Angela Hobart, Berghahn Publishing, 2007.

Chaplin, Charles, director. *The Circus.* A-Film Distribution, 2011.

Davis, Janet M. *The Circus Age: Culture & Society Under the American Big Top.* U of North Carolina P, 2006.

Deleuze, Gilles. *Cinema 1: The Movement Image.* Translated by Hugh Thomlinson. U of Minnesota P, 1997.

DeMille, Cecil B, director. *The Greatest Show on Earth.* Paramount Pictures, 2007.

Dobson, Nichola. *The A to Z of Animation and Cartoons.* Scarecrow, 2007.

Feld, Kenneth. "A Message from Kenneth Feld." *Timeline of Ringling Bros. Circus.* Feld Entertainment, 21 May 2017. https://www.ringling.com/timeline.

Fellini, Federico, director. *La Strada.* Criterion/Janus Collection, 2006.

Gunning, Tom. "Attractions: How They Came into the World." *The Cinema of Attractions Reloaded,* edited by Wanda Strauven, Amsterdam UP, 2006, pp. 31–41.

Heist, Walter G. *Ringling Bros. and Barnum and Bailey Circus at Madison Square Garden.* 1946. Film Collection, CWM FM 621. Robert L. Parkinson Library and Research Center, Circus World Museum, Baraboo, WI. 6 May 2017.

Lefebvre, Henri. *The Production of Space.* Translated by Donald Nicholson-Smith. Blackwell Publishing, 1991.

Murray, Charles T. "On the Road with the Big Show." *Cosmopolitan,* June 1900, pp. 115–127.

Robinson, David. Liner notes. *The Circus.* MK2 Studios, DVD, 2004.

Shrake, Peter. Personal Interview. Robert L. Parkinson Library and Research Center, Circus World Museum, Baraboo, WI. 6 May 2017.

Stoddart, Helen. *Rings of Desire: Circus History and Representation.* Manchester UP, 2000, pp. 80–157.

Van Pool, Paul. *Behind the Scenes with Ringling Brothers and Barnum and Bailey Circus.* 1940. CWM FM 28. Robert L. Parkinson Library and Research Center, Circus World Museum, Baraboo, WI. May 6, 2017.

_____. *Circus Parades and Old Times.* Circa 1928–1939. Film Collection, CWM FM 206. Robert L. Parkinson Library and Research Center, Circus World Museum, Baraboo, WI. 6 May 2017.

Wittmann, Matthew. *Circus and the City: New York, 1793–2010.* Yale UP, 2012, pp. 84–86.

The "Universal Soul" of the American Circus at Mid-Century

David Blanke

Beginning around the middle of the last century, Americans dramatically changed their attitudes toward modern mass culture. At its core, this reassessment shifted the balance between shared or consensual values derived from commercial pastimes and the more personal, oftimes perverse pleasures sought by individual consumers. The rapidly changing historical context only accelerated these reconsiderations. Beginning in 1945 a more mature modern consumerism emerged, one tempered by memories of depression and wartime privation yet also energized by a surging economy and triumphant post-war zeitgeist. This drove a new national dynamic that celebrated personal fulfillment through goods made manifest by a host of new consumer opportunities, particularly the suburban home, television, and the personal passenger automobile. Simultaneously, government and big business—their collusion strengthened by more than a decade of national crisis—promoted a brand of "American Way" capitalism that appropriated these individual consumer desires as the engine to drive greater economic efficiency, a concentration of political power, and an elevation of national interests over those on Main Street. Ironically, this heightened emphasis on centralized control produced a growing sense of anxiety in the country, leading many Americans to question claims that their individual consumer habits truly revealed the strength of their citizenship, which in turn fueled the counter-culture less than a decade later (May 2000; Wall, 2008; Cross, 2000).

These significant shifts in the appraisal of the individual and communal benefits derived from mass culture destabilized many traditional commercial producers. Large integrated firms, such as the Ringling Bros. and Barnum &

Bailey Circus or Hollywood film studios, sought to accentuate their appeal to the general audience by highlighting the shared pleasures of a single national culture. But the circus, once the gateway to rare marvels and curiosities, now struggled to justify their customers' precious time and pique their increasingly diverse interests. Filmmakers, too, produced stories that—through industry self-censorship—largely ignored compelling new questions over the meaning of race, class, age, and gender in post-depression, post-war America. Weekly theater attendance plunged by more than half, from an average of 2.35 visits per household in 1946 to 0.99 visits by 1953. Annual profits for Paramount and MGM, two of the industry's largest integrated studios, fell from $57.1 million to $11.2 million during this same period. Distracted by new families, new homes, and new goods, this "Lost Audience" represented an existential crisis to traditional producers and challenged widely held assumptions about the shared qualities of the mass audience (U.S. Bureau of Census, 1960, 15).

Of course, critics of mass culture had long doubted the authenticity of a consensus derived through the marketplace. Max Horkheimer, Theodor Adorno, Herbert Marcuse, and others at the Institute for Social Research (aka, the Frankfurt School) led the charge. Modern materialism, they argued, remained enthralled to the totalizing effects of industrial capitalism and centralized governmental policies that abetted ideological conformity. While Hollywood or the circus may falter, mass culture critics held that the country's penchant for personally pleasurable yet politically meaningless pastimes had not fundamentally changed but merely moved on to the equally vapid novelties of television, rock-and-roll, and the drive-in strip mall.

But new cultural producers adapted to the changing times by reimagining the balance between consensus and perversity in the modern mass audience. In film, young directors like Billy Wilder, Alfred Hitchcock, and a host of New Wave realists from Europe engaged the minds of millions through more critical and self-reflective attitudes toward the film experience. Method acting, location filming, and grappling with the modern problems of race, gender, sexuality, faith, and even substance abuse found innovative, more realistic ways to probe traditional questions about individual freedom and collective values. Wilder's Noir classic, *Sunset Blvd* (1950), actually celebrates the death of the Hollywood studio system yet retains a faith in the shared values held by its (notably few) sympathetic characters and, by extension, the mass audience. Anxieties that, for some, signaled a threat to the country's historic destiny were, to men like Wilder, new opportunities to probe the indeterminacies of consensus. The masses were *both* active leaders, worthy of intelligent entertainment, *and* passive followers, damned to dance to the tune of industry if they accepted their fate. Wilder's irreverent humor captured this new dynamic when he admitted that "everyone in the audience is an idiot, but taken together they're a genius" (*Billy Wilder Speaks*, 2006).

It was within this riotous cultural realignment that Cecil B. DeMille released *The Greatest Show on Earth*, the most popular circus picture of the 20th century. The film—released in January 1952—offered patrons a big-budget, star-laden spectacle packed within a convoluted morality play involving an imperiled circus, the threat of organized crime, a mercy-killing clown, and a lovelorn elephant trainer. As discussed below, the picture served as something of an autobiography for the circus, for American commercial film, and even for the director himself. The film packed theaters, generated nearly $12 million in profits (more than many *studios* earned that year), and netted the director his lone Academy Award for Best Picture, in 1953. During the award presentation—the first televised live—Master of Ceremonies Bob Hope's quips cut to the heart of his industry's fears over their Lost Audience. Introducing the famed director, Hope observed that "Cecil B. DeMille is indeed Mr. Motion Picture. His films have brought something new to the theaters. They call them customers" (DeMille Archives, Box 498 Folder 5).

Yet in spite of this success—or, indeed, because of it—the film remains clouded in controversy. Few today would credit *The Greatest Show on Earth* as a superior film to John Ford's *The Quiet Man* or Fred Zinnermann's *High Noon* (both bested in the Academy's vote), nor would the dated style of the circus picture—including its saturated Technicolor and Edwardian melodrama—survive the decade. Moreover, DeMille's work was released during the depths of the nation's post-war ideological soul-searching that attacked unions, undermined civil liberties, demanded loyalty oaths, and televised investigations into alleged subversion. The director's well-known battles with closed shop laws and his infamous ouster as leader of the Screen Directors Guild, in 1950, sustained a view that the Academy of Motion Picture Arts and Sciences rewarded DeMille for a hegemonic vision of American Way consensus that was now dragging Classical Hollywood cinema to its doom. Ignoring the simple pleasures derived from both the circus and DeMille's brand of filmmaking (and rejecting any possibility that these choices were linked to shared values in the American public), critics scorned the film's obvious public appeal. *TIME* magazine saw *The Greatest Show on Earth* as merely the "mammoth merger of two masters of malarkey for the masses, P. T. Barnum and Cecil B. de Mille" (Hutton, 2009, 263).

This is an overly simplified, faintly self-congratulatory interpretation of the complex cultural transition overtaking America at mid-century. Arguably, the central appeal of the film remained DeMille's grand visualization of traditional cultural spectacle within the context of modern post-war America. His pointed defense of consensus—of the shared goals of the performers, the shared pleasures of the audience, and the shared threats to their cultural independence—sought to reify notions of a broad agreement amongst the citizenry that McCarthyism and Critical Theory merely caricatured. Moreover, DeMille's self-awareness of these high-stake debates was unmistakable. Following his stinging rebuke from the Directors Guild, two years before the release of *The Greatest Show on Earth*, the venerable director threw himself into pre-production work on location in Sarasota, Florida, where he lived with and documented the modern circus. His autobiographical touches—including a reference to the circus manager's notoriously cluttered office, much like DeMille's own, which by then had become part of his legend—and his documentarian's eye lent the work a style more in line with the emerging *cinéma vérité* than his typical Hollywood hokum. Even more telling—given the backhanded compliments of *TIME* and many others—DeMille embraced the paradox of individual pleasure expressing shared values. Affixed on the wall of the director's own, very real office was a quote by Barnum reading, "the public is a very strange animal, and although a good knowledge of human nature will generally lead a caterer of amusements to hit the people, they are fickle, and oftimes perverse." Through spectacle, affectation, and the diversity offered by three competing rings, DeMille argued that it was exactly these *choices*, made by individual patrons and not the hegemonic positioning of the culture industries, that sustained a broad cultural consensus (DeMille Archives, Box 498, Folder 9).

DeMille's linkage of the circus, consumed pleasure, and national character was both clear and affirming. "The Circus is America," he declared, and "no one can escape its magic." In a promotional essay, titled "The Soul of the Circus," DeMille explained how circus attractions revealed the shared pleasures of the audience, who all came to its performance "eternally a child, filled with a most elemental wonder at the most familiar novelties." Embracing the audience's perverse creativity and desire to be amazed, performers in all forms of mass entertainments "banded together in a common cause, sharing common sorrows and sufferings, enjoying common successes, [but] feeling the independence and liberty which comes from individual effort." To DeMille, this perverse "unity" was "the strength of the circus." It mirrored "the strength of our liberty and the foundation of our way of life" and revealed a broadly shared, persistent, and powerful consensus "as American as the Statue of Liberty." Sustaining these common values, the circus and Hollywood films like *The Greatest Show on Earth* demonstrated "the enormous strength that can lie in cooperation, tolerance and unity" (DeMille Archives, Box 445, Folder 14).

DeMille's self-awareness sprang from a lifetime of experience. The second son of a noted Broadway writer who could not sustain a viable career in theater himself, the 33-year-old DeMille came to Hollywood in 1914 at a distinctively fortunate moment. By then, both the photographic technology and the distribution of feature films had matured to meet a growing desire for longer, more complex stories. Converting his familiar family name and links to the "legitimate stage" to a unique cinematic brand, DeMille built his reputation through hard work, talent, and a deft ability to offer movie-goers a timely mix of hedonism and high principles. Failing as an independent, the director saved his career in 1932 by returning to Paramount Pictures where he re-emerged as "Mr. Hollywood," a venerated spokesman for his industry. While his ideological travails within Hollywood go beyond the scope of this essay, suffice it to say that DeMille saw himself as both a staunch libertarian and booster of the Barnumesque qualities of showmanship that defined Classical Hollywood cinema. He was a shrewd businessman, active in many fields, and generally thought that personal moral failures—like greed and corruption—posed the greatest threat to capitalism. In this sense, and made clear by his conception of the universal "soul" of the circus, his interest in filming *The Greatest Show on Earth* emerged as a natural by-product of these early life's lessons. The story of a band of talented entertainers overcoming corruption and persevering in the face of post-war cultural competition not only spoke to Ringling Brothers, in 1952, but also the commercial film industry and the director himself. While he had intended to do a modern "stream of civilization story" for years, he was stunned to find just how powerfully the circus portrayed the "unifying forces in American life" that sustained his six decades in popular entertainment (DeMille Archives, Box 445, Folder 14).

Notably, while *The Greatest Show on Earth* focused on the consensual themes evident in DeMille's brand of mass culture, initially it was the perverse individual pleasures—the carnival spirit—of the circus that piqued the director's greatest interest. In a private conversation with his long-time assistant director Bill Pine and two trusted screenwriters, Alan LeMay (who later wrote *The Searchers* and *The Unforgiven*) and Jesse Lasky, Jr., and documented by Gladys Rosson, the director's personal secretary and lover, the group toyed with various scenarios for the "circus picture" as they travelled aboard the Santa Fe "Chief," running from Los Angeles to Chicago, on August 26, 1940. "We really worked on it" DeMille later recalled. Fortunately, Rosson took detailed notes and ascribed comments that preserve their relaxed, friendly, and at times farcical conceptualization (DeMille Archives, Box 633, Folder 9).

Whether due to the relief they felt from completing their last picture (*North West Mounted Police*, 1940) or their anxiety over the film's first screening awaiting them in New York, the conversation turned giddy. They discussed two farcical plot lines: the unrequited love of the strong man for the bearded lady, who was married to a circus clown, and the deadly love triangle that developed between them. Appreciating their exchange requires two important bits of foreknowledge. The first was DeMille's habit of casting

Lynne Overman and Akim Tamiroff as humorous character actors: the first as a tall, flinty Yankee, the second as a rotund, emotional yet kind-hearted foreigner (Russian by birth, Tamiroff played a Frenchman in *The Buccaneer* and a Mexican in *Union Pacific*, both sympathetically). Second, beginning with *North West Mounted Police*, DeMille personally recorded the voice-over narration for all of his subsequent films. The director's familiar, warm, and articulate delivery, honed by twelve years on the radio, was typically coupled with extended montage sequences. Their combined performance magnified the grand sweep of his films' visual spectacle (and partially compensated for his failings with dialog). No doubt many of his comments aboard the Chief were delivered with same sound-booth authority that he applied to the words written by Lasky and LeMay in their most recent film, finalized only a few days earlier.

The group cast Overman, the gritty American, as the circus strong man—but one who suffers from hay fever, uncontrollable flights of emotions (he cries and frequently faints), and who is considered something of a "pansy" by the circus crew. Professing his undying love for the bearded lady, the strong man dreams of a quiet suburban life with children (the first, Lasky added, is born fully bearded and named Moses); a life far from the gaping eyes of the perverse circus audience. The bearded lady is beautiful but her whiskers are so thick that it enrages the circus gorilla every time she passes his cage. DeMille, ever the visualist, suggested a slow introductory pan of the woman beginning with her dainty feet (a personal proclivity that, no doubt, earned some sly smiles that evening), to full hips and bust, and finally the neckline and "this enormous bush" of a beard on her face (DeMille Archives, Box 633, Folder 9).

Rosson's notes indicate how the team enjoyed playing with the various humorous possibilities within this traditional narrative. Tamiroff, the clown, learns of his wife's infidelity. He plans to murder the strong man during that evening's performance. DeMille deadpanned that he likes the overall effect of the melodrama—"the sympathy, the tenderness"—and pressed his team, tongue-in-cheek, to describe the characters' motivation.

> DeMille: Why does the girl no longer like Tamiroff?
> Lasky: Because he is too kind.
> DeMille: Yes! Because he gives her everything: he's too kind!

DeMille quickly turned from plot to visual imagery: "Five thousand children a day scream with delight at this man. The duck loves him that he goes around with. He has a duck and a dog and a goat following him around. The only thing in the circus that doesn't love him is his wife. But her story has to be—not the woman in *Pagliacci*, who was no good, but … her story has got to be a 'Polly of the Circus.'"

LeMay: She *hates* circuses, and she never saw anything else in her life.
DeMille: The great world outside is what she wants! It isn't money or anything of that sort…. It's just [his clown make-up], the spots, the silly little mouth he puts on!
Lasky: Every time that duck quacks, it goes through her like a knife.

Knowing the censors would never allow a would-be murderer to escape justice, the team looked for ways to punish the evil clown. DeMille has Tamiroff, despondent that his plot had failed, enter the gorilla cage to commit suicide (as they are once again enraged by the sight of the bearded lady). The clown brings a telephone with him, intending to call his rival to read, melodramatically, from the "last line in *Hearts Are Trumps*: 'You can live for her. I can die for her. Goodbye.'" Unfortunately, the gorilla swipes the phone. It rings. The clown's wife has called, attempting to reconcile with her husband. Hearing only the ape, DeMille adds, she slams the receiver down yelling "By God, if you're drunk when I get there I'll…" and storms off to the cage. In the end the clown survives. The bearded lady arrives clean-shaven and the animal calms. DeMille suggests a second upward pan for the film's finale. When the camera reaches her beautiful face, the strong man faints (DeMille Archives, Box 633, Folder 9).

Certainly a bit of harmless fun useful to pass the time, but their discussion also suggests aspects of DeMille's later construction of *The Greatest Show on Earth* that are too often overlooked. For example, the proposed dialog clearly shows that his team considered its melodramatic plots as little more than convenient contrivances. Like the love triangle that he and dozens of other directors relied upon as their stock-in-trade, the group laughed *at* not *with* the outdated foolishness. The director's reference to *Hearts Are Trumps* is a giveaway; linking the fun aboard the Chief to the hopelessly old-fashioned Victorian melodrama which also happened to be the first play that DeMille had ever acted in professionally. Conversely, the send-up shows just how interested he and his writers remained in visual characterizations—the bearded lady, the sentimental strongman, the duck-loving clown, and the ever-watchful circus patrons.

In spite of his growing interest in the circus as the ideal setting for his adaptation of *Grand Hotel*, in 1940, DeMille found himself blocked from developing the picture by David O. Selznick, who owned the rights to the story of the Ringling Bros. and Barnum & Bailey Circus (RBBBC). But Selznick failed to seal the deal. The famed circus, which like Hollywood had lost a significant portion of its urban audience, struggled with liquidity. After a disastrously expensive tour of Cuba and, in 1944, a deadly tent fire that killed 168 patrons (requiring indemnity payments of $750,000 in 1951), Selznick abandoned the project completely. He sold the film rights to Paramount which announced, in June 1949, DeMille's plan for a circus production.

RBBBC, which could not even pay for new costumes, benefited from both the influx in capital and the prestige offered by their collaboration with a large Hollywood studio. In exchange for ten years of exclusive rights, Paramount paid the circus $25,000 per year, $75,000 in advance of royalties, and 10 percent of the gross once the studio had recouped its expenses. RBBBC demanded only that no mention of the fire be made in the film nor the use of fire in any aspect of the work's dramatic treatment. DeMille's epic portrayal of a train derailment—a device he used in both *The Road to Yesterday* (1925) and *Union Pacific* (1939)—did harken back to a deadly 1929 industrial accident, but this occurred through the Hagenbeck-Wallace Circus and was allowed by RBBBC (Birchard, 2004, 345–347; Louvish, 2007, 395).

DeMille's desire to cast the film within a modern context was key to his conception. He disliked most previous circus pictures and their oppressive nostalgia for a bygone era. To prevent this, DeMille took to the road to document the modern conditions that faced performers, those who produced the shows, and their audience. He lived on site for three weeks during the summer of 1949 in Sarasota, Florida (RBBBC's winter home in 1927), and then again in the spring. Normally preferring to shoot in the controlled confines of the Paramount studios, DeMille captured the bulk of the film on location, in Sarasota, and as RBBBC toured the northeast, from January to May 1951.

Freed from the pressures and routines of Hollywood, DeMille reveled in the physical, open-air environment of the circus. He rejected accommodations at a nearby hotel to stay on site, with Gladys Rosson and his 14-year-old biological grand-daughter Cecilia ("Citsy"), in a modified railroad car. Celebrating his 68th birthday in August 1949, the director displayed the energy of a man half that age. Publicist Phil Koury wrote that DeMille "virtually [became] the circus' fourth ring—a relentless, tireless figure, constantly on the move in the steaming heat of the big top." He rode elephants, performed stunts, and climbed to the top of the trapeze platforms to assay angles and gauge the technical requirements of proper lighting and focus. He exhausted the national press who followed him everywhere. During the twice-daily practice sessions for the performers, Rosson wrote, the director "love[d] roaming around at will, stopping in here and there to chat, or make some pleasantries to a group about to go on." The attraction was mutual, as "he already has a line-up of devotees" among the entertainers, support staff, custodians, and even some animals. No doubt the aging legend's ego played a role in his enthusiasm. The public found DeMille "a bigger attraction than the elephants," circus manager Art Concello reported, and the Sarasota crowds quadrupled whenever they knew "Mr. Hollywood" was in town. The director, Concello concluded, proved to be "the most amazing 'act' playing in the Greatest Show on Earth!" (Koury, 1959, 36; DeMille Archives, Box 633, Folder 9; Box 646, Folder 3; Box 653, Folder 6).

DeMille's handwritten notes—totaling 135 pages—hinted at how his picture would feature these modern settings and avoid the "circus staged" appearance of previous works. In sentence fragments and descriptive adjectives, he chronicled the subtle, meaningful moments of life under the big top that revealed individual yet shared pleasures and which animated his understanding of cultural consensus. These included how an audience reacts to the breezes within the tent on a stormy night ("very good shots"), the assembly-line seriousness of performers changing into and out of their satiny costumes, the slang they used, the movement of the animals as they sensed their performances approaching, and the large groups of people milling about in their "wrappers" (bathrobes) after the work was through. John Jensen contributed numerous sketches to accompany these notes. These highlighted the visual drama provided by the complex mechanical infrastructure of the modern circus: the cages, safety nets, vendor stalls, and the dismantling of the big top which often went unnoticed. Even seemingly trivial events, such as the morning meal where one could "see 2,800 eggs fried at the same time," proved fascinating. "I wanted to get a shot of that so much," he later regretted, but "I haven't room for half of what I have." These impressions served as important master shots in the final film, grounding the melodrama in the modern everyday lives of the audience and performers. The result was a densely visual conception of the story; a part-documentary, part-impressionistic love poem to the perversity of the circus (Louvish, 2007, 398; DeMille Archives Box 633, Folder 7; Box 652, Folder 2; Box 653, Folder 6).

Specific touches, such as the extended montages he included showing the raising of the big top and loading of the train, ground the picture into the mechanized reality of mid-century America, but it was the director's attention to the emotions of individual audience members and performers that truly modernized the film. DeMille's notes recorded the sight of a terrified child, urged by her parents to feed peanuts to an elephant, of a "prosperous and dignified couple" lightheartedly "wearing gaudy red and green felt souvenir Mexican hats," and a procession of mildly irritated parents, eyes fixed on the show, as they marched their kids to the bathroom. "It is a never-ending parade," he marveled. Trapeze artists held casual conversations at the top of the tent yet the "tension and fear" never left "their faces." The various animal-handlers, acrobats, and clowns worked under constant peril but their expressions remained cheerful and confident until the exact moment that they reached the exit, when their weariness again became evident. This balletic tension between the audience and performers fascinated DeMille. For the acts intensified by the ringmaster's seductive narration the crowd behaved almost as a collective unit: laughing, gasping, and issuing nervous asides simultaneously. The individual and the collective were unified through spectacle. They even ate their popcorn and ice cream in unison. DeMille studied them as they concentrated on the aerialists, intrigued by how affective performance "hypnotized" and bonded the crowd. Describing both the audience and the attractions, he concluded the "circus is an exciting, friendly, turbulent, kind but lusty home." Immediately upon returning home from his first tour, he wrote to assistant director Eddie Salven confirming the name he must give to his new epic: "The Greatest Show on Earth" (DeMille Archives, Box 633, Folder 8; Box 634, Folder 5; Box 652, Folder 2; Box 653, Folder 6).

In spite of these powerful links to contemporary life and mass culture, *The Greatest Show on Earth* did not completely avoid its own expressions of cultural nostalgia. Partly, this was due to the generation of workers, performers, and attendees who had grown up in small towns dreaming of life with the circus. Jimmy Stewart, who by 1950 was a bona fide star with Universal, agreed to appear for only a quarter of his normal fee. "I had always loved the circus," Stewart recalled, "and when I heard that DeMille was making a circus film, I sent a wire and asked if I could be in it and play a clown. You see, everyone wanted to do this picture. We all had our dreams about running away and joining the circus." DeMille noted, while is Sarasota, that many of the older film personnel once worked as "a circus performer at some time in [their] life" and that, just as frequently, many circus performers reported their ties to the early film industry. In his first week on tour, DeMille met one circus hand who had worked for him on *The Squaw Man* (1914) and another, Lou Jacobs, for Griffith on *Intolerance* (1916). During their evening relaxation, DeMille and Henry Ringling North found they shared a professional heritage (Cecil's father wrote plays staged by North's father-in-law) and John Ringling North recalled his days as assistant cameraman for Matt Brush at Paramount's Long Island studio. Imbued with this spirit, shared and recalled by many on the set, Stewart romantically concluded how "making this film was a joyous time for everybody, much more than just a movie." With his historical and dialectical mind turning, DeMille conceived of his circus picture as equally a Hollywood picture. While the greatest show on earth might once have been the RBBBC, his film suggested that cinema now claimed this title (Eyman, 2010, 427; DeMille Archives, Box 633, Folder 9; Box 644, Folder 7; Box 653, Folder 6).

This sense of romantic longing—of the circus's indeterminate status as both a thing of the distant past and the material present—appeared most forcefully in the melodramatic narratives of the film. DeMille had long struggled with writing realistic plots and dialog in his films. Generally, this was the product of his complex conceptualizations, indecisiveness, and the panicky control which he demanded over his writers. In *The Greatest Show on Earth*, he mercilessly drove his capable team of screenwriters—Fred Frank, Frank Cavett, and Theodore St. John—to develop a storyline bold enough to feature the powerful images that danced across his mind. The resulting narrative follows four concurrent pathways. The first involves a love triangle between the circus manager, Brad Braden (Charlton Heston), Holly the young aerialist (Betty Hutton), and a seasoned trapeze professional, "The Great Sebastian" (Cornel Wilde). A second follows the unrequited love of an elephant trainer (Lyle Bettger) for his assistant (Gloria Graham), which serves as pretext for the climactic circus train derailment. Third, "Buttons" the clown (Jimmy Stewart) is a former medical doctor on the run from the law for assisting in the suicide of his terminally ill wife, and continually in costume. Finally, and encompassing all three, the circus itself is imperiled by insolvency and threats from an organized criminal element (Lawrence Tierney). To their credit, the writers took full advantage of the marvelous acting talents of their cast and laced the dialog with enough common sense and street smarts to sustain the heavy load. When the plot lines awkwardly crossed—as when Jimmy Stewart's "Buttons" first meets Cornel Wilde's acrobat—the writers share some fun that would not have been out of place aboard the Santa Fe Chief. Pausing to stare at Stewart, who is wearing his full clown face even as the circus traveled between towns, Wilde asks: "Why are you in make-up?" With perfect comedic timing, Stewart replies: "Why are you the Great Sebastian?"

But these moments are rare. While DeMille knew that *The Greatest Show on Earth* offered "a thousand wonderful shots" for every fifteen minutes of film, the overwrought melodrama nearly overwhelms his visual masterpiece. The fact that the mass audience was not put off by these deficiencies speaks to the visual pleasures they derived from DeMille's spectacle (Koury, 1959, 145; Hutton, 2009, 256, 261; Louvish, 2007, 398).

Stripped of its dialog and improbable plot lines, *The Greatest Show on Earth* reveals DeMille's timely curiosity into the nature of modern popular commercial entertainment—what threatens it, sustains it, and links it to the public in such powerful ways. Immediately after arriving on location, DeMille began posing broad and existential questions in his notes, like "what is the evil element in the circus" and "what is it that everyone in the circus fears?" Physical threats like fire, mechanical malfunction, or even the "poisoning of animals" came to mind, but he "could not put his finger on" the dialectic that gave the circus its *popular* intensity. He posed these questions to Henry and John Ringling North, who owned the circus. They cited prosaic matters like scheduling delays and marketing problems, bad weather, and competing entertainment formats such as the radio and television (they graciously did not cite motion pictures). These material realities found their way into *The Greatest Show on Earth*'s finished script and DeMille clearly drew parallels to the threats facing commercial cinema in 1950. The legal prohibition of block-booking, the collapse of the star system, and other formal controls devised to ensure that rapid, high-quality production coincided with changing consumer tastes to threaten the very existence of Classical Hollywood. In describing the circus as a "fighting machine, a thing constantly struggling" against death and decay, he was just as clearly describing his own industry at mid-century. DeMille's voice-over narration, which he drafted himself, fixated on the "massive machine whose very life depends on discipline, motion, and speed." A "fierce, primitive force that smashes" against, yet also triumphs over "impossible odds." To view the circus was to view Hollywood (Louvish, 2007, 396–398; DeMille Archives, Box 644, Folder 7; Box 653, Folder 6).

DeMille's depiction of Brad, the circus manager, suggests an even more personal link to this association. Sharing a short fuse, a cluttered office, a rough handling of direct subordinates, and an intensely competitive drive to complete the tasks put before them, both Brad and DeMille existed as classic, Barnumesque "showmen." This link, added to DeMille's pleasurable experiences while on location, demonstrates—or reveals—how *The Greatest Show on Earth* triggered the director's "instinctive identification with this central ethos of *all* the performing arts." Betty Hutton recalled, while filming in the studio, DeMille suddenly slumping in his chair. Unnoticed by the busy crew, he politely whispered, "Betty, I'm having a heart attack, but please don't let them know." She got him a shot of brandy and he resumed work. "The man was from the old school," she marveled, "he was driven in his movie work, and rarely, if ever, took a day off." Hearing of his subsequent brief hospitalization, John Ringling North sent a sympathy card. DeMille waved off this concern by taking a line directly from Brad's lips. "Nothing stops the circus," DeMille wrote, "and I've got sawdust in my veins too" (Hutton, 2009, 261; Louvish, 2007, 398; DeMille Archives, Box 644, Folder 6).

In spite of significant legal, production, and personal setbacks—indeed, the director later claimed *The Greatest Show on Earth* was "the toughest production" he had ever attempted—the finished film produced spectacular results. The public adored the movie. Preview audiences displayed the same visual "hypnotism" and synchronized behaviors in the theater that DeMille observed under the tent. They laughed, gasped, ooh-ed and aah-ed as if a part of the soundtrack. Following the November 7, 1951, public screening at the Centre Theatre in Salt Lake City, DeMille spent the bulk of his remaining time correcting minor technical issues—in detail focus, sound editing, and color corrections—before premiering the film at the Radio City Music Hall to standing-room crowds on January 10, 1952. That year alone, the film grossed nearly $16 million and netted Paramount a profit of $6.6 million (and DeMille $3.3 million) (Louvish, 2007, 395, 396, 402; Birchard, 2004, 341, 347; DeMille Archives, Box 646, Folder 9).

Understanding *why* the film worked so well proved harder to determine. Betty Hutton thought, like most critics, "that his movies were basically corny" and that the mass audience ultimately was drawn to his work because he featured these simple sentiments. Sharing her thoughts with DeMille, Hutton "knew he wasn't enjoying much of what I had to say." Phil Koury tilled the same soil. "DeMille's drama," he maintained, "was not meant for [critics] … It did what it was supposed to do; it sold pictures on a mass basis." But while belittling the commercial mass audience may be a time-honored critical tradition, it misses the ongoing dialectic, voiced by Billy Wilder, between cultural idiocy and genius. What drove the dynamic, then and today, remains the familiar pleasures derived by fans through the visual performance of spectacle. Moreover, these shared pleasures must be viewed within the shifting context of the times. The anxieties of the circus at mid-century were the same as those of Hollywood and, by extension, those of the broader American public. In exposing these common anxieties—through the fascinating visual pleasures of the modern circus—DeMille correctly described the cultural "Soul of the Circus." Given his detailed pre-production work and its successful transference to the film, post-war Americans had ample reasons to cheer for expressions of "cooperation, tolerance and unity" (Hutton, 2009, 260. Koury, 1959, 193).

Ultimately, as screenwriter Jesse Lasky, Jr., noted, DeMille's effort to champion cultural consensus worked because it was powered by the perversity of personal pleasure. While it remained "easy to snicker and toss off psychiatry-couched phrases about DeMille's movies being garish, oversimple, [or] outrageously ornate," Lasky concluded, their immense popularity "succeeded in fulfilling the purpose of their elaborate preparation: they entertained. And that may not be a bad epitaph for dead movie makers" (DeMille Archives, Box 445, Folder 14; Lasky, 1973, 157).

The recent end to Ringling Bros. and Barnum & Bailey's management of their famous spectacle—whose last performance was on May 21, 2017—suggests that the same eulogy could be applied to the appeal of mid-century mass culture. While the circus survives, new and improved, producers like DeMille would struggle today to justify a single universal soul to describe its audience.

Works Cited

Billy Wilder Speaks. Directed by Volker Schlöndorff. Kino International, 2006.
Birchard, Robert S. *Cecil B. DeMille's Hollywood.* The UP of Kentucky, 2004.
Cecil B. DeMille Archives. Harold B. Lee Library. Brigham Young U, Provo, Utah.
Eyman, Scott. *Empire of Dreams: the Epic Life of Cecil B. DeMille.* Simon & Schuster, 2010.
The Greatest Show on Earth. Directed by Cecil B. DeMille. Paramount Pictures, 1952.
Hutton, Betty, with Carlo Bruno, and Michael Mayer. *Backstage You Can Have: My Own Story.* The Betty Hutton Estate, 2009.
Koury, Phil A. *Yes, Mr. DeMille.* G.P. Putnam's Sons, 1959.
Lasky, Jesse L., Jr. *Whatever Happened to Hollywood?* Funk & Wagnalls, 1973.
Louvish, Simon. *Cecil B. DeMille: A Life in Art.* St. Martin's, 2007.
May, Lary. *The Big Tomorrow: Hollywood and the Politics of the American Way.* U of Chicago P, 2010.

Orrison, Katherine. *Lionheart in Hollywood: The Autobiography of Henry Wilcoxon*. Scarecrow Press, 1991.

The Road to Yesterday. Directed by Cecil B. DeMille. Cinema Corporation of America, 1925.

Union Pacific. Directed by Cecil B. DeMille. Paramount Pictures, 1939.

U.S. Bureau of Census. *Historical Statistics of the United States, Colonial Times to 1957* Government Printing Office, 1960.

Wall, Wendy. *Inventing the "American Way": The Politics of Consensus from the New Deal to the Civil Rights Movement*. Oxford UP, 2008.

Spectrality and Spectatorship

Heterotopic Doubling in Cinematic Circuses

Whitney S. May

In 1951, Cecil B. DeMille and John Ringling North collaborated on what remains the most elaborate circus-on-film project in American cinematic history. Paramount's blockbuster hit *The Greatest Show on Earth* blended Hollywood actors with the 1,400-person crew of The Ringling Bros. and Barnum & Bailey's '51 season. The drama of its storyline was punctuated by real, dazzling circus acts, and its luscious, Golden Globe-winning cinematography paired visual, actor-driven narrative with documentary-style glimpses behind the tent-raising and -breaking of a typical circus show. By the time it debuted in 1952, the film offered a comprehensive, panoramic view into a spectacularly executed intersection of circus and film, all in glorious Technicolor. It was most certainly, as the *New York Times* hailed it that year, a "lusty triumph of circus showmanship and movie skill" (Crowther).

A concentrated example of this union of entertainment industries lies in the film's final scene, a split edit from its closing Circus Day Parade to a medium close-up of a barker exuberantly inviting viewers to return to the circus because "You can shake the sawdust off your feet, but you can't shake it out of your heart." This moment articulates a theme not only significant to the film's storyline, but also intrinsic to circus as an art form: that is, the circus is just as much an interior experience as an exterior one. In entering the Big Top, the line implies, we invite the spirit of the circus into ourselves, where it leaves its mark.

The circus elicits this remarkable comingling of internal and external sensory experiences by nature of its contradictory character, which provides a space wherein reality irrupts ineluctably into fantasy. When the circus comes to town, after all, familiar landscapes become spectacular ones. Animals become humanized and humans animalized. Bodies are contorted and distorted, their limitations explored—and often rejected altogether—by feats of seemingly inconceivable daring and cathartic triumph. Identity evanesces into something performative, fluid, and as transient as a speedy prop switch between gags. These elements and more become disorientingly destabilized in the circus ring at the epicenter of their erosion, thus carving out a unique space for critical inquiry where previous understandings are held in suspense. In essence, the circus is a place frenetically preoccupied with interrogating understood borders, because it accommodates a gathering of inwardly directed, phenomenal collapses where boundaries lose their fixity. Within the charged *entre deux* space that remains of this displacement, circus-going subjects are granted singular terrain on which to encounter, and make sense of, themselves and, by extension, their positions within the real world.

In his influential work on the role of place in cultural interrogation, French philosopher Michel Foucault designates locations that facilitate an inversion of the real and unreal as "heterotopias," which are "something like counter-sites, a kind of effectively enacted utopia in which the real sites, all the other real sites that can be found within the culture, are simultaneously represented, contested, and inverted" (24). Foucault's attention to the topic is uncharacteristically brief, focusing primarily on the cemetery as a space for examination of, principally, mortality, religious expression, and class division. Although Foucault only fleetingly approaches something akin to the circus, offering fairgrounds as "marvelous, empty sites on the outskirts of cities that teem once or twice a year with stands, displays, heteroclite objects, wrestlers, snakewomen, fortune-tellers, and so forth" (26), I propose that the circus, in all its exquisite horror and repulsive intrigue, is an ideal case study for consideration as a heterotopia because of its position at the center of so many competing ideological valences. For the purposes of this essay, I focus on artistic representations of the circus, where this reflective effect is necessarily translated and visually crystallized. Specifically, circuses on film codify the epistemological leverages of heterotopic space into concrete visual symbols of enclosures, mirrors, and uncanny doubles. Therefore, it is by analyzing the cinematic circus and its accouterments that we can best consider the circus's function as a unique, hypercritical space by which to orient ourselves within the sociopolitical fabric of our culture.

~

In *Circus! From Rome to Ringling*, Marian Murray describes the circus as a site where "Brilliance runs side by side with dinginess; comedy with horror; the meretricious with the genuine; the mediocre with the sublime" (25). Her assessment is an astute one because it recognizes that the circus's unparalleled sublimity hinges on both its topographic and ideological positions at the juncture of so many opposing forces, where previously understood borders are dissolved and rendered perceptibly neutral. What's more, that centric placement is also itself fundamentally itinerant. Indeed, unlike the theatre, perhaps its closest approximation, the circus's sublimity is enhanced by its constant mobility. "Sublimity" is as much a spatial designation in this case as it is an ontological one, in that "sublime" and "liminal" share the same Latin root, *limen*, or "threshold." At its most fundamental, geographical level, the circus is always poised over a threshold, only ever "here" in an abstract and temporary sense, or otherwise in constant motion. By dint of its inherent transience, the circus, particularly the always-nomadic American circus, is in a constant state of both arrival and departure. Whether by wagon, truck, or train, when the circus comes to town, a vacant field or an empty lot expediently transforms, as if by magic, into an itinerant city of canvas wherein familiar geography fades surreally into the extraordinary. Here, the real and fantastic chafe against one another, so that the circus site remains just recognizable enough to feel inviting, yet alien enough to evoke anxiety. Dylan Trigg would consider this spatial friction a "disturbed sense of orientation and distance," wherein "the world loses its familiar constancy, and now assumes the quality of being partly unreal" (*Topophobia* xx). Never quite real or unreal, but always uniquely both, the Big Top's peripatetic nature compels subjects within it to question reality and fantasy, and more pressingly, their physical and psychic positions between these extremes. Mirroring the dissolution of the barriers between reality and fantasy at the circus, the space between a subject and its environment in this place-driven interplay becomes charged with a sort of spatial anxiety that Trigg refers to as "topophobia."

Herk Harvey's low-budget cult classic film *Carnival of Souls* (1962) models this consistent fixation on the circus's liminal position as the driving force of its psychological power. Specifically, it makes heavy use of fence imagery in order to communicate the circus's distinctive means of dissolving barriers and allowing a unique space for subjective interaction. After being involved in a traumatic car crash that kills her two friends, Mary Henry (Candace Hilligloss) relocates to a quiet town to serve as its church's new organist. Concerned about her reclusive behavior and hoping to draw her out of her shell, the church's minister (Art Ellison) takes her to look at the desolate remains of an abandoned carnival nearby. Mary, fascinated, asks him if they can go inside, and without waiting for his answer, prepares to scale the fence surrounding the place. The appalled minister stops her, explaining that it isn't safe inside which is why there is a barrier around it. Mary concedes, though thoughtfully considers a gap in the fence, remarking that "It would be very easy to step around it." Despite the danger and without fully comprehending her own motivations, Mary becomes obsessed with transcending the barrier between herself and the circus, an imperative dramatized by the circus's placement at the forefront of her recurring nightmares throughout the remainder of the film. She cannot realize that finally managing to cross the boundary and enter the circus will carry profound consequences for, if not her life, then certainly her understanding of herself.[1]

The circus's primary means of actively confronting and dissolving barriers lies in many of its performances. The desire to experience danger has always been one of the more immediate and marketable draws of the circus, where the acts are nothing if not spectacular usurpations of understood threats to the human body. Of the circus, Helen Stoddart articulates in *Rings of Desire: Circus History and Representation* that "Physical risk-taking has always been at its heart: the recognition that to explore the limitations of the human body is to walk the line between triumphant exhilaration and, on the other side of this limit, pain, injury, or death" (4). At the circus, and more centrally in the circus ring(s), human resilience can be measured in increments of peril, where bodies defy immediate threats like fire and animal savagery, or eschew gravity or other forms of physical restriction. Representatively, this contributes to its power as a space between extremes for exploring and reconfiguring broader constraints on the body and the placement of that body in relation to its environment. Moreover, this suspension of certainty leads to a chaotic disarray of understood codes that enhances the circus's characterization as "a creature of fact and fantasy, of experienced age and perpetual youth," where "beauty of form, line and color, blended into swift and intricate movement, is contrasted with bizarre grotesqueries" (Murray 25). As the locus of the many competing antipodes at the heart of its acts, positioned therefore on so many thresholds, the circus offers a space wherein the boundaries between these extremes are their most porous, and invite—or demand—the crossing of all of them at once. The circus remains the focus of intense curiosity because it is a place invigorated by contradictory impulses. Poised at the fence in *Carnival of Souls*, Mary perhaps articulates this best when, after the minister asks what attraction the carnival could hold for her, she replies: "I'm not sure. I'm a reasonable person, I don't know. Maybe I want to satisfy myself that the place is nothing more than it appears to be."

By virtue of its liminal intersections, the circus is, at its most fundamental level, a place that is more than it appears to be, a place that resists placement. However, in order to consider the breadth of the circus's reflective power as a heterotopia, we must also take into account its inherent suspension of time. Circus scholar Janet Davis observes that "Inside the crowded tents, time also seemed in abeyance as spectators tried to comprehend three rings, two stages, and an outer hippodrome track of constant, relentless activity" (52). Once inside the Big Top, time loses its restrictive properties for subjects already spatially alienated from the outside world. With the apparent erasure of the world and time outside the tent, subjects are more immediately engaged with the fantastic displays of the circus repertoire, which is itself a spectacular inversion of temporal parameters that lends itself to wider cultural interpretation. Take, for example, Davis's location of the modern circus's representational prowess in its competing temporal influences, where "The circus's simultaneous contradictory impulses of nostalgic, normative representation and subversion of established social hierarchies made it an appropriate emblem of an age of transition" (228). The circus, certainly as it is most often represented on film, is a site where antiquity coexists with modernity. Magic and technology are invoked in tandem, so that immediate senses of time ("slices" of time, as Foucault would designate them) lead up to broader and more disorienting chronological suspension.

Just as the circus's seemingly endless spatial positions direct critical attention inward, so too does its collapse of temporal ones. As a result, the circus-going subject becomes ontologically disconnected from spatiotemporal constancy outside its experience under the Big Top, and therefore loses its image of a body in possession of itself. The result of this spatiotemporal dissolution is an outright fracture of identity that indelibly haunts the Big Top, already a place at the center of so much preternatural dynamism. It is no surprise, therefore, that the wildly competing energies of the circus would invoke uncanny doubles, since the subjective need for reorientation compels a subject to encounter and make sense of itself within the world in order to resolve its subjective conflict. To return to *Carnival of Souls* as a dramatic example, Mary's understanding of herself, and the subjective implosion that triggers the film's climax, happens after she meets her doppelgänger in the carnival. Once she observes the double of herself dancing with the other souls trapped in the circus, which here functions as a limbo or *entre deux* space between life and death, she questions and, to her horror, finally realizes, her own unfortunate position between these extremes.

Herein lies the key to the circus's subjective power. In compelling the subject to consider and try to orient itself within both its environment and its disrupted ontological framework, the circus challenges the subject's sense of itself as a unified body. Jacques Lacan reflects on this dynamic in his work on the mirror stage, wherein a fixation arises on the image of a reintegrated body which can only be seen in mirrors or mirror-images. The subject becomes both drawn to and inverted in the mirror, recognizing the object of its regard as an approximation of itself that both attracts and haunts it by way of the reflection's separateness. In the case of a heterotopia, this inversion is distinctive to the mirror-place. The circus, in particular, facilitates this reversal by invoking a specific double in order to execute its business of exploring psychic and bodily limitations. This figure at once repulses and invites each subject regarding it, often by explicitly mimicking that subject and sometimes even by openly confronting it. It is a caricature of humanity, a reflection distorted in a fun-house mirror that emerges as a specter bent on deliberately collapsing the subjective barriers between itself and the spectators that regard it. It has been adapted, standardized, and coopted; its cinematic representations have served to reconfigure it to symbolically and literally nightmarish proportions. It is that figure so dear to the circus's sawdusty heart: the clown.

~

A 1931 edition of the *Boston Masonic Mirror* lists, among its court sessions, the hilariously titled case *Commonwealth vs. Mr. Harrington, Downie, Master Clowns, Clown Stokes, Mr. Bacon, and Sergeant Andrews*. In this case, following a performance in Sunbury, Pennsylvania in 1829, six members of a circus company were individually charged with witchcraft. The bill accusing them claimed that they possessed

> power of witchcraft, conjuration, enchantment, and sorcery and being moreover
> persons of evil and depraved dispositions, and as magical characters having private
> conferences with the *spirit of darkness*, did … expose to the view of diverse and
> many people of this Commonwealth various feats, acts, deeds, exhibitions, and
> performances of magic and witchcraft [Ellmaker 273, emphasis in original].

That the clown could inspire such passionate and collective feelings of paranoia regarding the supernatural is unsurprising, given the uncanny nature of the figure's roots. Murray situates the clown's earliest incarnations with Greek mimes, which communicated familiar stories by way of exaggerated gesture. In this sense, narrative was personified in an acting form, and possessed bodily autonomy. This medium gained both popularity and reach with the expansion of the Holy Roman Empire, because it could translate easily across various regions with different dialects. Translatability, or rather *mobility*, remains a fixture of the clown's history. Murray details an Italian play with prototypical clowns written in 1558 that featured villagers as its central characters. "Gradually," she writes, a "whole family of [character] types appeared, with each representing the supposed characteristics of the inhabitants of a given city" (72). These would go on to inspire harlequins, Punches, Pierrots, and various other clown characters that linger to this day. So it goes that even before they entered the circus tent, clowns have always been characteristically linked, by virtue of their theatrical mirroring, to the *places* they occupy.

Explicit, culturally contingent mimicry would endure in the clown's performative history throughout the ages. Indeed, after his examination of clown performances and semiotics, Paul Boissac deduces that "tradition, for clowns, is not a set of ready-made tricks but a set of rules that operates on the constitutive rules of the contextual culture" (169). A necessary component of clown performances, he concludes, lies in targeted, culturally specific signals designed to link a clown to their audience via the specific city in which any given performance occurs. To illustrate this theory, Boissac recounts a running circus gag that he witnessed repeatedly, and that bears considerable, abiding resemblance to the villager-impersonating gags of the clown's Italian ancestors:

> The clown proper rushes through the ring, loaded with luggage. He is stopped by the white-faced clown, who asks where he is going. The answer is, "To the airport." Then he is asked where he is flying to. The verbal response is the name of a small suburb of the city in which the performance is taking place. At the same time the clown points in the opposite direction. Every time the clown arrived in a new city, he found out which suburb was looked down upon by the people there and its direction with respect to the circus ring. In this simple example, the relationships between escapism and exoticism and between means and goals were reversed. Furthermore, the clown's pointing in the opposite direction is very consistent, despite its verbal response, since it indicates that all his behavior is a mirror image, displaying a sort of inverse symmetry [169].

This gag is a superb dramatization of the clown's inherent ability to reflect a given culture by carefully recognizing and infiltrating it. As a mirror likeness, the clown attracts its audience by presenting it with an image of a reconfigured body, and further, by inverting that image. It at once regards, and is regarded by, the audience it encounters, unsettling the delineations between audience and performer, subject and object, by way of an otherworldly association that recalls the uncanny.

The clown is a visibly spectral creature imbued with a unique capacity, necessarily like the circus it haunts, to dissolve clear barriers by occupying the space between them. Likening the clown to clay for its malleability, anthropologist Don Handelman locates the figure's cultural influence in its ability to transcend accepted boundaries: "This power changes the shape and meaning of cosmos: if boundaries are altered, then so is the relationship between those parts that these borders order. Clown types are out-of-place on either side of a border, and in-place in neither" (247). Like the circus, the clown's liminal nature rejects placement. Because it cannot be definitively anchored on either side of any barrier, the clown appears in spaces where barriers are suspended; it is therefore a *symbol* of that porous, heterotopic space. The clown is, to be sure, "an ambulatory manifestation of boundariness" (Handelman 247). It is a haunting apparition of the circus's boundarylessness as a liminal locus of inwardly directed binary conflicts. In fact, its very visage evokes the most conspicuous binary set between which it freely travels: life and death.

Although there are many different clown veneers, the most pervasive configuration since the installment of the Ringling Bros. and Barnum & Bailey Clown College is the *auguste* clown, which appears unequivocally corpse-like in its makeup. In addition to its typical exaggerated misshapenness, with its pale face, customarily blood-red lips, and heavily shadowed eyes, the clown easily characterizes a macabre reanimation of a cadaver. Indeed, though routinely shot from cannons, drowned, set ablaze, crushed, and otherwise brutalized, the clown is a figure that refuses to remain, when it should by all accounts be unquestionably, dead. Able to withstand such forces by curtailing their implied bodily limitations, and in fact able to openly deride them, the clown becomes a sort of neither-living-nor-dead creature whose powers of alterity allow it to torment those who encounter it. Noël Carroll, investigating the connections between horror and humor, emphasizes the clown's liminal power thus:

> Not only does the clown, like a horrific monster, indulge in morally transgressive behavior—butting people about and taking sexual liberties—but like the dark doppelgängers of horrific fiction, the clown-monster is a double, a categorically interstitial figure that celebrates antitheses or "ab-norms" [155].

Unfettered by the restrictions that limit the human body, the clown becomes a negative double of humanity. It provides Lacan's mirror-image of a unified body, a focal point for the psychic need to reconfigure the certainty that is lost when a subject transitions from safe to uncertain space—in this case, when it trades familiar geography for the surreal circus. As an almost-but-not-quite human figure, the clown allows a subject to reorient itself within its physical and psychological environment when that subject's sense of self has been ontologically disturbed by an incursion of fantasy on reality.

Crucially, the clown's spectral power exempts it from human sympathy. Freud's model of the uncanny stipulates that a subject is intensely motivated to relegate its doppelgänger to the periphery of that which is human in an effort to safeguard what remains of its own sense of self. In this case, in order to prevent the clown-Other from infiltrating the human-Self, the subject that views it does so at an affectively safe distance. Philosopher Henri Bergson stresses the importance of "absence of being" or "anesthesia of the heart" on the part of an audience as they regard a comic performance like the clown's dangerous slapstick (4, 5). We recognize clowns as human-*like*, but dissociate them from ourselves enough that we are able to laugh at their gags. This is why, for example, when the industrious, World War II–era clown Paul Jung's famous steamroller act included a machine that routinely flattened any clown that got in the way of its massive (foam) wheel, audiences were able to laugh uproariously over the apparently flattened (oilcloth) figures left in its wake (Culhane 254). Thus, not only does the circus localize a reconfiguration of social paradigms, but the clown, as a double invoked to continue this process, encourages revisions of human empathy and cruelty.

Another memorable—and distressing—example of this doubled absence of empathy lies in one of the earliest cinematic representations of the circus on film, Charlie Chaplin's 1928 silent *The Circus*. In this case, Chaplin's famous Little Tramp character darts into a circus ring as he flees unjust persecution by the police. His attempts to escape the officers chasing him and, more broadly, to survive the systemic abuse so often heaped upon the iconic character, are misunderstood by the audience as a clown's performance, and his plight is met with seemingly callous laughter. This is an interestingly self-critical interpretation of the clown's inhumanness, in that it demonstrates that our negative double the clown, and the circus ring it vivifies, have the ability to catalyze our own inimical impulses. That which we regard as Other signals our darker inclinations, animating them as an otherworldly avatar that mobilizes those impulses within the socially acceptable framework of performance. Function, it would seem, invites form. This is a theme that would coalesce throughout the 20th century. Its crystallization occurs alongside significant spatial adjustments to the circus, as well as the vibrant, limitless potential of cinema.

~

When Barnum and Bailey's Circus implemented two additional rings into the traditional one-ring circus layout in 1881, P.T. Barnum and James Anthony Bailey may have suspected that the decision would alter the contours of the circus forever after. What they cannot have anticipated is the extent to which this decision would particularly revise and solidify the clown in our popular imagination. The second and third rings significantly increased the distance between the performers and their audiences, prompting practical theatrical adjustments to the formulas of their acts. Most distinctly, the talking clown fell out of fashion when its speech could no longer be heard over the din of two other active rings. The clown now communicated through hyperbolic visual devices and grossly exaggerated facial expressions. In its silence, the *fin de siècle* clown became a more disturbing figure, now even more akin to a mirror image, so that the newly extended distance between the clown and its audience was as much psychologically isolating as it was spatially alienating. Still, the clown endured as a figure of attraction and intrigue for circus audiences.

The change to the circus space also solidified the clown's position as a sort of mirror image of the culture that produces it. Davis emphasizes the modern leanings of the new circus layout as follows:

> The visually oriented three-ring circus flourished in tandem with multiple visual forms at the turn of the century: department stores filled with mirrors and reflective glassy surfaces, early motion picture actualities seen at saloons, railway stations, circuses, and world's fairs, and splashy new newspaper formats with big photo-filled sports pages; the three-ring circus was symbolic of an emergent "hieroglyphic civilization"[2] [24].

In fact, the silent clown's aggrandized, vaudevillian antics were ideal material for the burgeoning world of cinema. Indeed, one of the very first silent films even featured a clown.[3] From this instance on, for better or for worse, neither the clown nor the circus have ever been far from the silver screen.

Due to their similar preoccupations with entertainment and spectacle, the circus and the cinema have long maintained a turbulent association. Davis notes that, fairly quickly, "movies, radio, and (from the 1940s) television provided audiences with compelling and immediate images that displaced the circus as an important source of information about the world" (229). The intimate nature of film prompted circus administrators to attempt mediating the distance the three-ring layout had initiated, a technical project that would prove detrimental to it later. Stoddart adds that while innovations in lighting bridged the gap between performers and spectators, "this proved no match for film close-up in terms of establishing a sense of intimacy, close proximity and familiarity with the object of the gaze whose eyes and facial expression in general offer signs of interiority—of emotion and personality" (*Rings* 59). As the three-ring layout stretched the exterior and interior distance between spectacle and spectator, film offered a tempting coziness between them. Even in terms of spectacle, the bailiwick of the circus, film seemed to be gaining ground, particularly with the advent of color. Stoddart examines this relationship elsewhere in "The Circus in Early Cinema: Gravity, Narrative, and Machines":

> Whereas the circus, as a live popular art form, could only enact these confrontations with gravity in real terms as human skills (the accuracy of the knife-thrower, the balance of the high wire walker or trapeze artist, and so on), the cinema bypasses human physical skill to present the technological spectacle of the machinery of cinema as the awe-inducing spectacle or effect [14].

By the middle of the century, the damaging effects of the silver and small screens, as well as staggering reparations for the Hartford Circus Fire of 1944, had reduced the paragon of American circuses to near bankruptcy. When Ringling Bros. and Barnum & Bailey Circus limped into its 1955 season (notably, only one year before its final Big Top performance), it was $1 million in debt, and only being kept afloat by $1.3 million in royalties from the film *The Greatest Show on Earth*. Many feared that the circus as an institution had reached its end when Ringling Bros. and Barnum & Bailey Circus finished its 1956 season in Pittsburgh; *Life*, for example, featured the headline "BIG TOP BOWS OUT FOREVER," while the *New York Times* lamented "The Big Top Folds Its Tents for Last Time" (qtd. in Culhane 273–74). The circus as an industry appeared to be dying. The stage was set for the most sensational overhaul of the circus layout since the addition of its second and third rings in 1881. And, ever connected to the circus as a place, the clown as we understand and interpret it would once again be informed by a reallocation of space; this time, its function as a cultural mirror would throw into startling relief the priorities of American commodification in excess in the later 20th century.

~

In 1967, Irvin Feld acquired The Greatest Show on Earth from the Ringling family. A literal snake-oil salesman turned circus tycoon, Feld eagerly embraced consumerism, locating in the packaging and mass-production of the circus experience a potential for profound profit. Soon after purchasing Ringling Bros. and Barnum & Bailey Circus, he planned Ringling retail outlets and opened Circus World, a theme park in Florida, in 1974. Feld possessed a fondness for large arenas, and in a significant move, abandoned the historically nomadic, Big Top circus format for one revised to accommodate permanent venues. However, anchoring the once-peripatetic nature of the circus to fixed venues undeniably diminished the geographic magic of the circus experience, and solidified the spatial designations that had previously thrived in their fluidity.

Feld also reallocated space for the exorbitantly priced snack stands now standard in the industry, as well as circus-themed merchandise shops where patrons could procure souvenirs to commemorate their trip—for a hefty premium, of course. David Lewis Hammarstrom particularly laments in *Fall of the Big Top: The Vanishing American Circus* that "the circus [program] itself, which sometimes would cost you more than the cheapest seat in the house, was so bulky... that—consumer alert—you might need a mini-cart to wheel it off" (58). Feld's overall project in these adjustments is a reflection of the corporate spirit endemic to his time, wherein experience could be reified and mass-produced for profit. Even as Feld's changes made their way into the fabric of circus staging, Marxist political theorist Fredric Jameson documented his observations about the experiential consequences of the capitalistic climate in 1979. In a culture fixated on commodification, Jameson writes, "by its transformation into a commodity a thing, of whatever type, has been reduced to a means for its own consumption. It no longer has any qualitative value in itself, but only insofar as it can be 'used'" (131). In this sense, Feld's revisions to the circus enervated its spirit by compressing its symbols into commodities for mass-consumption.

The clown, the symbol of the circus's power to dissolve barriers and, indeed, the very "soul of the circus," was the most noteworthy casualty of Feld's commercial enterprise (Coxe 213). Recognizing the returns on investment of marketing to children, Feld revised the entire circus atmosphere to appeal to youngsters. He modified the clown to be more approachable, dismissing the grotesque creatures from circus days previous, and popularizing the friendly faced iterations still at play today. Hammarstrom lambasts this decision, remarking that "Mr. Feld let the shady brigade all go to make way for a brighter, giddier procession of silly, sanitized faces guaranteed not to frighten the meekest poppet" (59). In need of an immediate supply of this new, affable version of clown, Feld even founded his well-publicized Ringling Bros. and Barnum & Bailey Clown College, which began churning out clowns in the "Ringling Style" in 1968, and ran all the way through 1997. Of this assembly-line practice, Ernest Albrecht quips in *The Contemporary Circus: Art of the Spectacular* that "Since the Ringling management seemed to prefer a particular type of clown face, the criticism was that the school was more interested in cloning than in clowning" (200). By attempting to decrease the distance between spectator and specter, the clown, once a figure loaded with the preternatural, inscrutable energy of the circus, had been stripped of its meaning and relegated to a mass-produced commodity. In line with Jameson's lamentations, the clown had been reduced to a means for its own consumption. Warped by the circus industry into a relic of consumerism, the clown would re-emerge in a different medium as a nightmare of its former configuration: the "scary clown" genre of film had arrived.

∼

In his cultural critique of the "scary clown" icon, Benjamin Radford credits the Chiodo brothers' cult classic *Killer Klowns from Outer Space* (1988) with introducing evil clowns into popular culture.[4] Although much of the film's staying power hinges on its genre-establishing indulgences of hyperbolic clown imagery, it's one of the film's more perfunctory moments that captures the enduring sense of the clown in the contemporary, popular imagination. As its central, teenaged couple flees after exploring a crash-landed, circus-themed spaceship, they find themselves pursued by the ship's crew, a mob of horrifyingly distorted, alien "klowns" wielding guns that fire the treats sold at the expensive snack stands Irvin Feld introduced to the circus layout. Debbie (Suzanne Snyder) shouts "Popcorn? Why popcorn?" as the couple dodges a volley of the stuff. Mike (Grant Cramer) responds: "Because they're clowns, that's why!" The clown, in this newly minted genre, was intrinsically the exaggerated sum of the corporatized circus's accouterments, the result of commodification made menacing. What's more, as Feld sanitized the clown in the circus to endear it to children, it's no coincidence that on film, the clown became a frightening figure that preyed on them.

When it comes to this prevalent figure, the clown's circus roots have been aggrandized and reconfigured by the immediacy of film's power to shape popular culture. With the Chiodo brothers, Stephen King's *It*[5] (published in 1986 and popularized by its television miniseries adaptation in 1990), and Rob Zombie's *House of 1,000 Corpses* (2003) to name but a few, the clown's circus roots have seen a sensational update. However, while the clown's pop-culture presence has experienced a clear reconfiguration, these changes only exaggerate qualities already endemic to the clown as a negative image of humanity, the interaction with which compels legitimate subjective and, more broadly, cultural critique.

A more recent entry into the "scary clown" film genre, Jon Watts's under-rated 2014 horror *Clown* offers an exquisite example of this potential for such commentary. The film follows Kent McCoy (Andy Powers), a loving father who dons a mysterious clown costume he finds in the attic of a house he's selling (almost never a good idea) when the clown he has hired for his son's (Christian Distefano) birthday party cannot attend. Already portrayed as a devoted parent, McCoy feels added pressure to provide a clown for the party because his son loves the figure so much that the event is clown-themed. In the interest of the child's happiness, he puts on the costume, which insidiously seals itself to his own skin. Over the course of the film, the "evil spirit" of the clown slowly possesses McCoy, subsuming his own identity and filling him with its own desire to ritualistically murder and eat children.

Several aspects of this film make it a perfect case study of the clown in popular culture. First, the clown entity that haunts the costume is, as we learn, linked to the ancient "Clöyne," a preternatural creature that predates the expurgated ("Ringling Style" of) clown McCoy believes he is accessing when he encounters the costume. McCoy's invitation of the clown identity into his own sense of self is motivated by his desire to entertain his child; this is a more genuine version of Feld's commercial focus on children. McCoy becomes the clown via the props of the character: the colorful suit, red nose, and rainbow wig act as isolated parts that reconfigure his whole in the same way that Ringling's Clown College reconstructed the clown figure for mass culture. Furthermore, the clown-sprit that has possessed McCoy revises his initial, well-meaning desire to delight children, inverting it into a murderous and cannibalistic fixation on them. Where these desires lead him, with a cri-tique of consumerism in mind, is no surprise: McCoy eventually kills and eats two children at a Chuck E. Cheese, a location where marketing to chil-dren and consumption implicitly merge into consumerism. While various other "scary clowns" haunt the contemporary imagination, Watts's *Clown* offers a perfect model for examining the clown's function as a reflection of the, in this case, corporate culture that produces it.

After Feld's sanitization of the figure, the "scary clown" genre of film serves as an indictment of mass production and its nightmarish impact on a subject's sense of self. In the culture that creates Bozo the Clown and Ronald McDonald to peddle mass-produced wares to children, the "scary clown" emerges to critique blatant consumerism by characterizing its monstrous potential. The commodification of the circus experience and its symbols, and the horror that emerges thereof, reveals the circus's significance as a mediating force for the popular imagination; further, the "scary clown" in popular culture reflects the physical and psychic positions of the subject in its very real world. It allows for the consideration of a subject's—and culture's—limits, be they ideological, psychological, or even political.[6] Via the "scary clown," we explore what remains when those limits are transgressed. If, as Hammarstrom indicates, Feld's revisions to the circus space "fairly broke down the invisible barrier which had previously separated spectator from performer," with the result that "the [circus] of Feld was hyperactively reachable" (58), then it is through our cinema, and more specifically through the "scary clown" genre, that the clown reaches back.

$\sim$

Bouissac considers the circus "a kind of mirror in which culture is reflected, condensed and at the same time transcended," adding that "perhaps the circus seems to stand outside the culture only because it is at its very center" (9). As a heterotopia at the center of so many understood ideologies and thus in line with Foucault's thinking, the circus acts as a reflective space for not only self-regard, but also for broader cultural evaluation. It exists as an *entre deux* space where bodily and psychological limits are rendered inoperative. The experiential inversion of reality and fantasy unique to the circus engenders similar incursions of subject and object, self and Other. In experiencing the circus and its ability to negate these delineations, circus-going subjects experience a need to reorient themselves more firmly in their senses of self. This is both a spatial and ontological task given the irruption of external and internal experience, and elicits a fixation on the image of the body as a reconfigured whole that haunts the subject confronted with it. This explains the clown's function at the circus as a sort of doppelgänger through which the circus-going subject may reorient itself.

In *The Thing: A Phenomenology of Horror*, Trigg elucidates that "Confronted with a doppelgänger, we tend to react, not with the narcissism suggested by encountering our mirror image, but with horror at the implication that our subjectivity has been duplicated and therefore deformed" (98). While the clown has existed in relative harmony with us for centuries, physical adjustments to its distance from the audience (first lengthening that distance with the three-ring format, then diminishing it via the clown's mass-produced hyper-accessibility) has had a profound impact on the related ontological space between specter and spectator at the circus. Curtailing the clown's reflective power by commodifying it and the circus it inhabits has resulted in the horror Trigg implies. The effects of corporatization and mass production have warped the figure into a nightmare of capitalism bent on consuming the children that motivated its mass-marketed sanitization in the first place.

Following Lacan's theory, the true horror of the uncanny lies not nec-essarily in what we regard in the mirror, but ultimately, what regards *us* in return: "the final revelation of *you are this—You are this, which is so far from you, which is the ultimate formlessness*" (154–155, emphasis in original). Iden-tity is far more pliable than we care to acknowledge, and far more susceptible to distortion. Heterotopic spaces offer us unique and terrifying mirrors through which to encounter ourselves, and in ourselves, that perilous truth. In his assessment of the charged associations between subject, object, and place with regards to literature, Robert T. Tally, Jr., writes that "the dynamic spatiotemporal relations among subject, situation, representation, and inter-pretation invite critical approaches to literature that are sensitive to the uncer-tain, often shifting, but always pertinent ways that place haunts the mind (22)." In the case of the circus, representations and interpretations of place render subject and object available to one another by invoking a doubled Other through which to reorient the self. The circus and the clown it conjures haunt our cultural consciousness by reminding us that no matter how certain we are in our own identities and the environmental, ontological, and cultural positions they occupy, we will nevertheless remain "*the ultimate formlessness.*" Via the circus, especially when it is mediated through film, we invite that knowledge into ourselves, where it lingers like a shadow on the periphery of our awareness. And, you know what they say: "You can shake the sawdust off your feet, but you can't shake it out of your heart."

NOTES

1. It is perhaps worth noting that Wes Craven's loosely adapted 1998 remake of the film also problematizes the surrounding fence, albeit considerably less artfully. While its heroine (Bobbie Phillips) tries to escape a gang of the dead souls trapped within the carnival and led by the film's antagonistic clown (Larry Miller), her path out of the circus is blocked by a fence. She blinks, and in an instant appears on the other side, only to turn and find the clown and company behind her once again, now outside the enclosure and free to pursue our pro-tagonist into her real world.

2. For more on the "hieroglyphic civilization," see Warren Susman's *Culture as History: The Transformation of American Society in the Twentieth Century.*

3. This was Edison Manufacturing Co.'s 1900 short *The Clown and the Alchemist.*

4. Interestingly, in an interview with Radford, Edward Chiodo recalls that the inspira-tion for his dislike of clowns comes from a childhood encounter with one at Ringling Brothers at Madison Square Garden. In Ringling fashion, the clown had frightened the young Chiodo by intruding into his space and "doing all this big slapstick stuff right in [his] face" (qtd. in Radford 56). This documents a concrete instance of Ringling's adjustments to the clown figure precipitating the "scary clown" genre of film.

5. Although *It* was released as a television miniseries, and certainly it garnered different attention in the immediate proximity of its release than the other films this chapter considers, *It* has always been distributed as if it were a film. That is, although its length as a television series required that it initially be split into two VHS tapes in its original 1991 packaging, both parts have always been distributed together. Since its DVD release in 2002 spliced together both parts and edited them to fit a widescreen format, younger audiences will only ever have experienced the series as a film. Indeed, at the time of this writing, the 2017 remake of *It* is in production as a feature film.

6. While a more detailed discussion would fall outside the scope of this chapter on cinema, it is worth noting that at the time of this writing, the upcoming seventh season of FX's hit television series *American Horror Story*, which is set to focus on the 2016 United States presidential election, has made heavy use of the "scary clown" figure in its advertising.

WORKS CITED

Albrecht, Ernest J. *The Contemporary Circus: Art of the Spectacular*. Scarecrow, 2006.

Bergson, Henri. *Laughter: An Essay on the Meaning of the Comic*. Translated by Cloudesely Shovell Henry Brereton, Arc Manor, 2008.

Bouissac, Paul. *Circus and Culture: A Semiotic Approach*. Indiana UP, 1976.

Carnival of Souls. Directed by Herk Harvey. Lion International Corp., 1962.

Carroll, Noël. "Horror and Humor." *The Journal of Aesthetics and Art Criticism*, vol. 57, no. 2, 1999, pp. 145–160.

Chaplin, Charlie. *The Circus*. United Artists, 1928. *Kanopy*, txstate.kanopystreaming.com/video/circus.

Clown. Directed by Jon Watts, Dimension Films, 2014.

Coxe, Antony Hippisley. *A Seat at the Circus*. 2d ed. Archon Books, 1980.

Crowther, Bosley. "De Mille Puts 'Greatest Show on Earth' on Film for All to See—Premiere at Music Hall." *New York Times*, 11 Jan. 1952, www.nytimes.com/movie/review?res=9C06E2DB153BE23BBC4952DFB7668389649EDE.

Culhane, John. *The American Circus: An Illustrated History*. Henry Holt and Company, 1990.

Davis, Janet M. *The Circus Age: Culture & Society Under the American Big Top*. U of North Carolina P, 2002.

Ellmaker, Amos. "Commonwealth vs. Mr. Harrington, Downie, Master Clowns, Clown Stokes, Mr. Bacon, and Sergeant Andrews." *Boston Masonic Mirror*, edited by Charles W. Moore and Edwin Sevey, vol. 3, no. 35, 23 Feb. 1832, p. 274.

Foucault, Michel. "Of Other Spaces." *Diacritics*, Translated by Jay Miskowiec, vol. 16, no. 1, 1986, pp. 22–27.

The Greatest Show on Earth. Directed by Cecil B. DeMille, Paramount Pictures, 1952.

Hammarstrom, David Lewis. *Fall of the Big Top: The Vanishing American Circus*. McFarland, 2008.

Handelman, Don. *Models and Mirrors: Towards an Anthropology of Public Events*. Berghahn Books, 1998.

Jameson, Fredric. "Reification and Utopia in Mass Culture." *Social Text*, no. 1, 1979, pp. 130–148.

Killer Klowns from Outer Space. Chiodo, Stephen, Charles Chiodo, and Edward Chiodo. Trans World Entertainment, 1998.

Lacan, Jacques. *The Seminar of Jacques Lacan: Book II: the Ego in Freud's Theory and in the Technique of Psychoanalysis, 1954–1955*, edited by Jacques-Alain Miller. Translated by Sylvana Tomaselli, Cambridge UP, 1988.

Murray, Marian. *Circus! from Rome to Ringling*. Greenwood, 1973.

Radford, Benjamin. *Bad Clowns*. U of New Mexico P, 2016.

Stoddart, Helen. "The Circus and Early Cinema: Gravity, Narrative, and Machines." *Studies in Popular Culture*, vol. 38, no. 1, 2015, pp. 1–17.

_____. *Rings of Desire: Circus History and Representation*. Manchester UP, 2000.

Tally, Robert T., Jr. *Topophrenia: Place, Narrative, and the Spatial Imagination*. Indiana UP, 2019.

Trigg, Dylan. *The Thing: A Phenomenology of Horror*. Zero Books, 2014.

_____. *Topophobia: A Phenomenology of Anxiety*. Bloomsbury Academic, 2017.

The Normal Abnormal

The Case of Cirque du Freak: The Vampire's Assistant

Lisann Anders

Circuses are commonly considered a space of entertainment and amusement, and associated with a show of acrobatics and animals. However, in the past they were also a space where deformity and otherness were displayed in the tradition of freak shows, in which people who were marginalized by society were forced to make a living through their peripheral position, i.e., by means of displaying themselves as objects of horror and fascination (cf. Brottmann and Brottman; Furguson). In the 19th and early 20th centuries, these shows were quite popular—audiences were attracted to the unfamiliar in the familiar.

With the invention of photography in the 19th century, freaks[1] could, however, not only be seen or gawked at in a circus setting (or in carnival), but also be mediated and distributed like objects through photographs. This voyeuristic aspect the camera offered was later translated into the medium of film, in which marginalized groups have always played a role of interest. Susan Sontag observes with regard to the Freak Show still running in the 1960s at Coney Island that these performers, "are evicted from their restricted territories [...] increasingly come to infiltrate consciousness as the subject matter of art, acquiring a certain diffuse legitimacy and a metaphoric proximity which creates all the more distance" (35). It is therefore not surprising that film picked up on freak shows and the circus, respectively, where the dichotomy between closeness and distance is most apparent.

Circus films can roughly be put into two categories: romances (comedy or drama) and horror. The latter is particularly fascinating since it continues the tradition of freak shows by adding a pinch of violence and supernatural.

Movies such as *The Unknown* (1928), *Freaks* (1932), *Circus of Horrors* (1960), *Psycho-Circus* (1966), *Vampire Circus* (1972), or *Cirque du Freak: The Vampire's Assistant* (2009) focus on this dark side. These films demonstrate that not only has the freak show experienced a revival, as Leslie Fiedler puts it, in which "human curiosities [...] passed inevitably from the platform and the pit to the screen, flesh becoming shadow" (16), but it has never been completely absent; it has simply changed its stage.

The circus space can often be read as a space of transgression, in which boundaries blur (cf. Foucault),[2] and is thus depicted as a heterotopic space[3] that makes it possible for the individual to choose his or her destiny due to the freedom this setting offers. It allows actions outside the limitations of social boundaries. In this regard, heterotopias are spaces that are physically real but simultaneously unreal due to their constructed nature. Paul Weitz's film *Cirque du Freak: The Vampire's Assistant* (2009), which is based on Darren Shan's novel series *Cirque du Freak*, also known as *The Saga of Darren Shan*, depicts an excellent example of the circus as a heterotopic space. In the film, the protagonist Darren Shan (Chris Massoglia) starts out as a normal teenager and changes into a "supernatural" freak in the form of a half-vampire; while vampires cannot be true freaks (because they are not human), within the context of this film they function as such. Here, Foucault's concept of space is especially useful when defining the circus, which frames the action of the movie, as a "crisis heterotopia," a space separated from society in which individual developments take place such as, for example, coming of age.

In contrast, a "heterotopia of deviation" encompasses institutions where individuals are placed whose behavior is outside the norm (cf. Foucault 24–25). Even though the film portrays performing artists as differently bodied, the members of the freak show *choose* to be part of this unusual theatrical group in order to make a living, not because they are legally or institutionally bound to it.

Thus, the line between these two forms of heterotopia is not clear-cut in the film. The circus is presented as an active space of individual development, i.e., a crisis heterotopia, but simultaneously, it comprises traits of a heterotopia of deviation due to its marginalization at the fringes of society. Being a freak, in the context of the film, can be either an involuntary state or a conscious decision, and can be confining and liberating simultaneously. To be more precise, outsiders in the film *Cirque du Freak: The Vampire's Assistant* are confined to the circus space by society, but at the same time they can liberate themselves by means of that space, and thus gain a voice. In fact, the group of freaks gives a voice to individual outsiders and functions as a safety net and surrogate family to teenagers as well as adults. The circus unifies the individual voices to an integral whole by means of the performers' carnivalesque performance, which pronounces their otherness. Whereas for bystanders these freaks disturb the social norms, in the circus space the abnormal *is* the norm.[4]

In the following, I will explore the search for identity in the realms of the circus as well as the freedom and restraints that come with such a setting, by means of Paul Weitz's film adaptation of the first novel of *The Saga of Darren Shan.*[5] The primary focus will be put on the teenage protagonist of *Cirque du Freak*, Darren Shan, who goes on a journey of liberation, identification, and growing up within the frame of the circus.

Darren, a sixteen-year-old teenager, lives a picture-perfect life in a well-off family environment. He is the ideal son—handsome, popular, good grades at school—if it were not for his friendship with Steve Leonard (Josh Hutcherson), a rebel, truant and generally bad influence. What connects the two boys is their longing for freedom. Steve wants to escape his home situation with an alcoholic mother and a rather bleak future ahead, whereas Darren would like to break out of his restrictive future others have planned for him. The prospect of "college, job, family" (00:06:36) does not appeal to him; in contrast, he seems to be intimidated by the idea of being narrowed down, limited or even imprisoned by his family's expectations and society's structural norms. This is emphasized by the camera movement, which zooms in on Darren and encloses him, followed by a repeated montage of his future life, showing him as a college graduate, in an office job, and as a dad (00:06:36). As his surroundings visually close in on him, his thoughts are dominated by the words of doom in the form of a voiceover, followed by an intercut in which Darren imagines himself speaking these words to his own son. The voiceover, which repeats his father's words and imitates his intonation, makes Darren realize that he has no say in his own life; he lacks a voice of his own.

Steve eventually convinces Darren to go against the directives of adults and when the two boys come across a flyer for a freak show, both disregard the enjoinders from their teacher not to visit the circus in which the show exists. In effect, with their decision to attend not just the circus but the marginalized freak show, they rebel against parental as well as institutional authority and constraints.

This is illustrated by means of several binary oppositions which the boys transgress in order to be free. The circus show takes place at night, thus setting the circus space and the profession of a circus artist apart from ordinary day jobs. Night also implies dreams and the fantastic, for which the freak show in the movie is an excellent example since this circus does not display freaks in the sense of "ordinary" human deformities as was often the case in 19th and 20th century freak shows, but instead stars supernatural, fictional freaks. The supernatural element is introduced by adding uncanny elements to body parts in the Freudian sense of the term. For example, Alexander Ribs' (Orlando Jones) organs are visible, which evokes a classic feeling of uncanniness as something that usually remains hidden comes to the surface and is thus estranged. Ribs is not the only supernatural freak whose uncanniness is evoked by unnatural characteristics of the body. The classic freak show attraction of the bearded lady in the form of Madame Truska (Salma Hayek) gets a supernatural twist through a magically growing beard, Corma Limbs (Jane Krakowski) can make her limbs grow back after she cuts them off, and Rhamus Twobellies (Frankie Faison) not only has two bellies, as his name suggests, but he can also build a bike in them after swallowing some iron bars and heating them in his bellies with a blow torch. In addition, this circus of fantastic freaks also includes hybrids between animal and human, represented primarily in the teenage members of the circus family such as Rebecca (Jessica Carlson), who looks normal at first glance but has a monkey tail, or Evra the Snake Boy (Patrick Fugit), who has snake skin.[6] Finally, vampires complete this collection of uncanny beings, whose freakish and frightening otherness lies in their supernatural deviation from the norm.

Leslie Fiedler explains the nature of the freak as a creation of projected fantasy by pointing out that:

> The true freak [...] stirs both supernatural terror and natural sympathy, since, unlike fabulous monsters, he is one of us, the human child of human parents, however altered by forces we do not quite understand into something mythic and mysterious, as no mere cripple ever is. [...] Only the true freak challenges the conventional boundaries between male and female, sexed and sexless, animal and human, large and small, self and other, and consequently between reality and illusion, experience and fantasy, fact and myth [24].

Similarly, the performers in the *Cirque du Freak* evoke this supernatural terror through their bodily qualities, though they are not true freaks as Fiedler theorizes. Adding to their multi-layered qualities, they might be categorized as fabulous monsters as well, mysterious and mythic. In *Cirque du Freak*, their supernatural aspects are made explicit and aestheticized. Although there are several characters who are repulsed by the bodily otherness of the freaks, it also becomes clear that freaks, especially fantastical, supernatural, fictional freaks are in fact desirable and beautiful rather than horrific.

The vampire is probably the best known and darkest of these ambiguous, hybrid freak figures since he not only challenges the boundaries more than other freaks, by being an undead creature, but he is also often portrayed as an object of desire, i.e., an object who desires and who is desired. Moreover, he is oftentimes imagined as a monster with seductive qualities. The term "monster" is important in the context of the film's fictional freak show since it often refers to "creations of artistic fantasy like Dracula, Mr. Hyde, the Wolf Man, King Kong, and the nameless metahuman of Mary Shelly's *Frankenstein*" (Fiedler 22). Consequently, the monster is a fictional creation that embodies both human traits and supernatural features and is often associated with darkness and night. Likewise, the vampire is associated with night, he represents the unknown and is in an in-between state, caught between life and death.

Analogously, the circus is also associated with night and functions as an "anti-space," a space at the boundary, out of the norm, a space that appears to be unreal and that "presupposes anti-behavior" (Lotman 140–141). Furthermore, night generally ensures that freaks can remain hidden from societal norms and thus that the freak's voice remains generally unheard. However, in the circus space their silence is broken; this space offers them a platform to perform, to be seen *and* heard, and creates illusions within which identity is performed. In this space, the circus artists perform their freakishness and create the illusion of being the ultimate other, empowering themselves as individuals and as a group against the prejudices of the norm.

This is made a subject of discussion when at one point a mob of what are considered to be "normal" people, including Darren and Steve's teacher, interrupts the freak show at the town's theater with the claim that the theater is closed and that the freaks should leave. The teacher tries to hide his disgust behind a mask of charity, i.e., that freaks should not be exploited for public amusement and mockery (00:19:19). The freaks react with sarcasm toward this false benevolence, as Alexander Ribs dramatically demonstrates, saying, "Thank you. Thank you so much for looking out for us. So you gonna let us move in with you, give us jobs?" (00:19:31), before he opens his shirt in a performative fashion to show his deformed body and evoke disgust in the protesters. Not only through the utterance of an old woman, "We don't want you filthy people here" (00:19:21), but also by means of the shocked and disgusted reaction to Ribs' appearance, it becomes evident that society regards the freaks as abject.[7] The freaks, meanwhile, due to the theatrical surroundings and the presence of each other, have the ability to present their point of view and, simultaneously, hold up a critical mirror to the social norm.

Elizabeth Grosz notes that "freak" "is a term whose use may function as an act of defiance, a political gesture of self-determination [...]: it makes clear that there are very real and concrete political effects for those thus labeled, and a clear political reaction is implied by those who use it as a mode of self-definition" (56). She goes on explaining that freaks "are those human beings who exist outside and in defiance of the structure of binary oppositions that govern our basic concept and modes of self-definition. [...] They imperil the very definitions we rely on to classify humans, identities, and sexes—our most fundamental categories of self-definition and boundaries dividing self from otherness" (Grosz 57).

Without the Other, the norm does not exist. They are in fact interdependent, as Peter Stallybrass and Allon White elucidate in *The Politics and Poetics of Transgression*: "[...] the 'top' attempts to reject and eliminate the 'bottom' for reasons of prestige and status, only to discover, [...] a psychological dependence upon precisely those Others which are being rigorously opposed and excluded at the social level. It is for that reason that what is *socially* peripheral is so frequently *symbolically* central [...]" (Stallybrass & White, 5; original emphasis). Moreover, they pick up on Mikhail Bakhtin's notion of the carnivalesque, which focuses on the grotesque body (cf. Stallybrass & White 7).

The bodies within the Cirque du Freak thus resemble the grotesque body in carnival, which enables transgression and can be seen as a site of resistance against the oppressing forces of the "high," or the normal, by means of provocation and exaggeration. Carnival reveals and demystifies underlying hierarchical structures and gives the "low," or the abnormal, a critical voice for the duration of carnival while the high can emulate the low through the grotesque, which is expressed by means of costumes and masks (cf. Stallybrass and White). Referring back to Bakhtin, Brottman and Brottman consolidate the presentation of the bodily (de)formations and the freak show by explaining, "the grotesque begins where exaggeration reaches fantastic dimensions" (105). They further outline that even though Bakhtin focuses primarily on the tradition of carnival, he also includes the circus in his description of grotesque festivities (cf. Brottman and Brottman 104). However, whereas in carnival the norm and the Other are turned upside down, meaning that during the festivities the "low other" is in power and can mock the socially accepted "high," this does not necessarily hold true for the circus—or, if it does, it is quite limited.

In the circus space of *Cirque du Freak*, the norm and the Other are not necessarily reversed since the circus offers a performance, a display of the Other, in which the audience still remains in the role of the authoritative norm and does not intend to imitate the Other. The norm and the Other only share the same space during the time of the performance; the Other is given a voice for the time of the performance but the power hierarchy is not inverted, since the norm is not actively affected in their position of power.

Nevertheless, even within the circus space the freak is experienced as a threat to social norms and binary oppositions, not "an object of simple admiration or pity, but [is] a being who is considered simultaneously and compulsively fascinating and repulsive, enticing and sickening" (Grosz 56). The supernatural performances of the Cirque freaks are fascinating, while their bodies are considered repugnant by society within the scope of the film. In fact, the film focuses on the grotesque by making it fantastic in an exaggerated way, i.e., by making it fictional, which transgresses the binaries of natural and supernatural as well as of repulsive and desirable. As such, the vampire operates as a (fantastic) freak in the parlance of this film. This ambiguity of the freak in general and the vampire in particular gives voice to the fictional, freakish circus artist here because the peripheral, heterotopic space of the stage empowers him (or her).[8] It is within this fictional work that fictional freaks get a voice to allegorically stand in for any marginalized group which tries to gain a voice through community.

While this does not always hold true for the teenagers in the film,[9] in general, the (adult) other is heard and seen here by means of his or her performance, gaining power from the very fact that he *is* the Other, which he is fully aware of; this self-awareness is gained through the circus community which elaborates the Other's voice as a sort of union of freaks.

Initially, when Darren first encounters freaks in the theater space, he does not see their normality, or their longing for a peaceful life, because he is blinded by the act of performance. He considers the circus as the abnormal in order to identify and define himself as the norm, even after he has been turned into a half vampire and has become an assistant to the mysterious vampire, Larten Crepsley (John C. Reilly), one of the performers of the circus. In a later conversation with Evra, Darren emphasizes this position:

EVRA: So how are you effed up?
DARREN: Effed up?
EVRA: Freaked up? How, what, what kind of freak are you?
DARREN: Oh, I'm, I'm not a freak. I'm normal.
EVRA: You're normal?
DARREN: No, I mean I'm half vampire but I'm completely normal.
EVRA: You're half vampire. But you're normal. I like that (00:54:46).

Darren is reluctant to self-identify as a freak as he cannot see how this state can be (politically) liberating. Instead, he considers himself in a spectator role, i.e., as one who is fascinated by "the limits of our own identities as they are witnessed from the outside" (Grosz 65). His hesitation to embrace his other self can be explained by means of the role of the audience in freak shows and their reaction since the "viewer's horror lies in the recognition that this monstrous being is at the heart of his or her own identity, for it is all that must be ejected or abjected from self-image or make the bounded, category-obeying self possible" (Grosz 65). Darren tries to maintain his humanness by rejecting his inner freak even to the extent of refusing to drink human blood, despite Crepsley's attempts to teach him how to do so without harming the victim.[10]

It can be argued that he regards his freak side as a mirror image that "threatens to draw [him] into its spell of spectral doubling, annihilating the self that wants to see itself reflected" (Grosz 65). This hybridity of the self by means of the idea of mirroring is especially interesting in terms of vampirism since vampires do not have a (literal) mirror image. Darren is afraid of losing himself, his identity as a human being, in the void of his hybrid state where he is merely the image, not the subject self anymore. As suggested by Lacan, this would mean that Darren is afraid of entering a pre-mirror stage in which he disconnects with society, loses his language, and forgets his own self (cf. Lacan). He is afraid of losing his voice as a human being. This fear, however, also has another layer to it, namely the fear of castration. This concept is linked to Freud's notion of the uncanny, which is, as mentioned before, often associated with freak shows and vampires but finds its point of reference in the adolescent anxieties of castration and the double. Darren's fear of being de-humanized and thus deprived of his voice can be compared to the fear of losing body parts; in Freud's theory, it is primarily the loss of sexual organs that is discussed. Furthermore, Freud outlines that the uncanny finds itself in the concept of the double, which presents a conflict between two person-alities in which one (side) has to be repressed in order to make the other side function according to the rules and norms of society (cf. Freud). Darren represses his freakish self and is thus scared when it comes to the surface by means of bloodlust and superpowers, such as fingernails that are as sharp as daggers or saliva with healing powers. Therefore, he tries to define himself as being *not* Other because he sees the other in himself as a threat.

While gradually accepting his role as the counterpart to the norm and gaining a voice as a freak in his own right is one aspect of Darren's path to self-discovery, the coming of age aspect plays an equally important part. All the teenagers of the film, especially Darren and Steve, are trying to own a place within the world of adults. Therefore, on a second level, they are treated as Other even inside the circus due to their hybrid, liminal state, caught between childhood and adulthood. Interestingly enough, adolescents are often compared to freaks and monsters in psychoanalytical approaches:

> But the myth of monsters is twice-born in the psyche. Originating in the deep fears of childhood, it is reinforced in earliest adolescence by the young adult's awareness of his own sex and that of others. The young male finds that even after his whole body has ceased to grow and his scale vis-à-vis the rest of the world seems fixed once and for all, his penis disconcertingly continues to rise and fall, swell and shrink—at times an imperious giant, at other a timid dwarf [Fiedler 31].

It has to be noted that Fiedler's psychoanalytic approach to the monster myth as well as Freud's analysis of the fear of castration is problematic in terms of female characters, as they are completely neglected in these definitions. How-ever, what can be taken away from Fiedler, as well as Freud, if they are general-ized a little further and seen as theoretical approaches, is the feeling of estrangement from one's own body in puberty. This can then be applied to the way Darren fears and rejects the new bodily features his vampirism encompasses. This bodily "monstrosity" in the form of bodily transformation makes the teenagers in the film double-freaks, so to speak. They are freaks *and* adolescents, they are different from humans and they are neither children nor adults—and importantly, they are different even from the adults living in the circus.

Darren and Steve's transmogrification, or transgression, into vampires— hybrid beings often portrayed as figures of seduction in literature and popular culture as noted above—is reflective of their coming of age. Their state of being neither entirely one nor the other, neither child nor adult yet also already both, is already apparent upon their arrival at the theater freak show when they are at risk of being barred entry. Advised by Mr. Tall[11] (Ken Watanabe) to lie about their ages, they do so and are granted access. In this small scene, the boys' in-between state becomes evident. They are rebelling against parental authority but they still need the help of an adult to find their way. Still, their arrival at the Cirque du Freak can already be considered an attempt at liberation and growing up.

The freak show appears to Darren and Steve as the ultimate space of freedom in which neither social rules—freak shows are illegal after all—nor bodily norms apply. However, they cannot embrace the freedom of the circus space, yet since they are not part of the circus family. They are merely observers; they are the "high" norm that is fascinated by the "low" other. In Steve's case, this fascination surpasses spectatorship; he longs to be part of this group of freaks in the form of a vampire. For him, ultimate freedom is not only the circus space but also, and primarily, immortality; he wants to exceed a life full of constraints by dying and thus transcending and preempting both life and death. When, after the show, Crepsley refuses to turn him into a vampire under the pretext that Steve is still a child, this emphasizes the problematic position of the adolescent. After Steve insists, Crepsley tests his blood, proclaims it evil and sends Steve away (00:25:49). What Crepsley does not anticipate, though, is the danger an angry and lonely teenager poses; by telling Steve he is evil, he *makes* him evil. Steve transforms into a vengeful character, engulfed in an abyss of rage, grief, and frustration, who takes his anger out on everybody who has done him wrong. This plays into the hands of Mr. Tiny[12] (Michael Cerveris), who discerns Steve's despair and takes advantage of the situation, tricking Steve into believing that Darren has betrayed him as a friend. Moreover, Tiny plays him like puppet in his plan to use Steve as a trigger for war among the undead. As the embodiment of fate, Des(mond) Tiny shapes Steve's identity and makes him a vampaneze, planning to utilize him as a trigger for war among the undead.[13]

Likewise, Darren is also manipulated. Crepsley does not just turn him into a vampire but in fact makes Steve's life contingent on Darren saying yes to being turned. Darren's decision is not only for his friend but it is also another act of rebellion against his parents' wishes; if he refused, he would return to the life they have planned for him. Darren needs to prove that he is adult enough to make his own decisions. Ironically, in his longing for freedom from parental control, he turns blind to Crepsley's manipulation (00:35:57). Like Steve, Darren is tricked into his path of life, into his destiny. This again substantiates both Darren and Steve's positions as adolescent characters who do not want to be constrained by any authority but who are, at the same time, directed by adults. Nevertheless, they are led into a space of freedom from parents and into a more adult context. For them, the transformation into abnormal figures means a step toward freedom.

However, even though Steve might consider himself free, he stays more confined than Darren since he is part of Mr. Tiny's chaos plan. He is meant to be evil; hence, he is evil. Darren, however, has a choice between good and bad, he can write his own destiny—a decision only the circus space allows since it is neutral and therefore not influenced by Mr. Tiny, nor is it as prefabricated, predictable, and stable as Darren's parental home. The circus is constantly changing and moving and thus encourages the growth and development of identity in either direction. But even within the circus, Darren has to prove himself worthy if he wants to stay and become a part of the circus family. That means he first has to gain a voice of his own before being able to gain a voice as a circus member. He has the choice between turning his back on the circus and joining Steve in his evil cause or he can decide to be good and stay as a member of the circus community.

Hence, even within the periphery there are obstacles to overcome on the way to a voice and ultimate freedom. Darren can be free from social norms and parental control, as Evra points out, "Well, there are no parents here" (00:55:40), yet surrogate parental authority still exists in the form of Mr. Tall and Crepsley. The important difference from the other father figures in the film, i.e., Mr. Tiny and Darren's dad, is that the circus fathers do not want to plan the lives of the teenagers in general nor of Darren in particular. Instead, they guide and encourage him to find his own path. The film thus suggests that it is the circus setting which helps one gain his own voice and, in so doing, create an identity that is not projected by authoritative entities but constructed by one's own decisions. In essence, the focus of the film shifts from Darren's journey from the norm to the freaky other, to his inner journey of finding and accepting his true identity.

This journey is marked by choices and challenges, and in order to find his true identity he needs to learn to create illusions (such as appearing dead) just as the illusion the circus creates for society (that of people who seem to be other) is necessary for the circus as a space of performance. Rachel Adams picks up on the notion of an active freak, who gains a voice through being a freak:

> Freak shows are guided by the assumption that *freak* is an essence, the basis for a comforting fiction that there is a permanent, qualitative difference between deviance and normality, projected spatially in the distance between spectator and the body on

stage. To characterize *freak* as a performance restores agency to the actors in the sideshows, who participate, albeit not always voluntarily, in a dramatic fantasy that the division between freak and normal is obvious, visible, and quantifiable [6].

By performing the identity of a freak, Darren is able to know and understand the real. Thus, the film suggests that being a freak is not a state of being but a choice. In addition, his performance is not limited to the circus space but can also be seen on a meta-level in the form of the film's play with spaces. Darren has to face his fears of losing his identity on a theater stage, thus *performing* his transformation into a freak.

In contrast, Steve chooses not to be a freak, not wanting to be part of the equal community of others, even though he deviates from the norm, too. Therefore, whereas for Darren the circus represents a space of freedom, for Steve it would be a confining environment (cf. 01:24.05). He wants to have a voice, yes, but not a democratic one. His ideal voice would be dictatorial and thus associated with the terror an anarchical speaker entails, who considers any set of rules confining.

This is contrasted with the neutral, peace-seeking voice of a circus community, whose members embrace certain rules within the circus space in order to live an orderly ordinary life. Darren chooses to be good and law-abiding, not for the sake of the community but for his own sake. He wants to be a good person. While Steve's motivational drive is hate, Darren's drive is love; he does not want to hurt people but save them. However, though Darren has compassion and empathy for others, he finds it difficult to love himself. It is only when he accepts his vampirism, his otherness, that he is accepted by the circus community—he chooses to become other, he chooses his destiny, he chooses to love. His acceptance, shown in the communal vote in favor of Darren as a member of the Cirque du Freak, marks the moment he moves from the strange, liminal state of adolescence to being an adult. He has realized, as Rebecca explains, that "being human is not about *what* you are. It's about *who* you are" (01:28:40). It is only when Darren accepts his true identity that he can be truly free from others' expectations and from his own past. And it is only when he accepts the freak within himself that he can be normal in the abnormal.

NOTES

1. The term "freak" is used here to delineate those people who, in the past, would have been referred to as such, those whose physical appearance or talents made them outsiders and often outcasts.

2. In Charlie Chaplin's *The Circus* (1928), the protagonist finds refuge in a circus while being prosecuted by the police, indicating that the space of the circus is a place of shelter from social constraints. Even though Chaplin's film does not include freaks, it shows the circus space as a haven outside the framework of what is considered normal.

3. Michel Foucault defines heterotopic space as "something like counter-sites, a kind

of effectively enacted utopia in which the real sites, all the other real sites that can be found within the culture, are simultaneously represented, contested, and inverted" (24).

4. The film also ties in nicely with the tradition of cult films in contrast to mainstream movies due to its special transitions and the very topic of the film itself, since freak show movies are still not considered mainstream. Thus, as David Church elaborates, although "viewing freakish imagery may ostensibly abject the borders between self/other and normal/abnormal, those blurred boundaries are re-solidified by the overarching reception of cult films themselves as otherly and abnormal" (11).

5. The saga by author Darren O'Shaughnessy, who writes under the pen name Darren Shan, consists of twelve novels, which are divided into four trilogies. *Vampire Blood* depicts the first trilogy with *Cirque du Freak: A Living Nightmare* as the first book and *The Vampire's Assistant: The Nightmare Continues* as the sequel. Both novels were used for Weitz's film adaptation.

6. That it is the teenagers who are depicted as hybrid characters is particularly interesting due to their ambiguous state of being between childhood and adulthood. Rebecca and Evra cannot be discussed in detail here but the analogy to the vampire, which will be discussed in Darren's character analysis, can also be applied to the human-animal hybridity and would be interesting to consider for further research on this topic. Moreover, Rebecca and Evra have always been freaks and do not undergo a transformation, which is another reason they are left out here. Rebecca plays an important role for Darren's personal development, though. In the course of the movie, she not only becomes a close friend but also his love interest.

7. Julia Kristeva's theory of the abject is not discussed here but the societal marginalization of the freak and her concept would be quite compatible for taking the discussion further.

8. Though Foucault's notion of heterotopia is grounded in real space, the Cirque du Freak can be considered a heterotopic space within the fictional space of the film itself.

9. Evra, the snake boy, tries to make himself heard on stage through music but is not able to do so because his snake eats the microphone. The struggle of teenagers gaining a voice will be touched upon later, in the discussion of Darren's search for identity.

10. In *Cirque du Freak*, vampires do not kill for blood but only sedate people with their breath.

11. Mr. Tall is the leader of the Cirque du Freak.

12. We do not get to know much about Desmond Tiny in the film. He is there from the very beginning of the movie and makes sure that Darren and Steve receive the flyer of the freak show. At first, he seems to be a spectator but he soon takes on the role as a manipulative force. He holds some kind of magical powers (he can bring the dead back to life by transforming them into little creatures, known as the 'Little People') and he tries to actively provoke chaos and war. His motives are not revealed in the movie but he seems to find pleasure in the manipulation of people and the sight of destruction.

13. The "Vampaneze" are aggressive, violent vampires who kill not only for sustenance but for pleasure.

Works Cited

Adams, Rachel. *Sideshow U.S.A.: Freaks and the American Cultural Imagination*. U of Chicago P, 2001.

Brottman, Mikita, and David Brottman. "Return of the Freakshow: Carnival (De)Formations in Contemporary Culture." *Studies in Popular Culture*, vol. 18, no. 2, 1996, pp. 89–107.

Carmeli, Yoram S. "Text, Traces, and the Reification of Totality: The Case of Popular Circus Literature." *New Literary History*, vol. 25, no. 1, 1994, pp. 175–205.

Church, David. "Freakery, Cult Films, and the Problem of Ambivalence." *Journal of Film and Video* vol. 63, no. 1, 2011, pp. 3–17.

Cirque du Freak: The Vampire's Assistant. Directed by Paul Weitz, performances by Chris Massoglia, Josh Hutcherson, John C. Reilly, Salma Hayek. Universal Pictures, 2009.

Ferguson, Christine. "'Gooble-Gabble, One of Us': Grotesque Rhetoric and the Victorian Freak Show." *Victorian Review*, vol. 23, no. 2, 1997, pp. 244–250.

Fiedler, Leslie. *Freaks: Myths and Images of the Secret Self.* Simon & Schuster, 1978.

Foucault, Michel. "Of Other Spaces." *Diacritics* vol. 16, no.1, 1986, pp. 22–27.

Freud, Sigmund. "The Uncanny." 1919. Translated by David McLintock. Penguin, 2003.

Grosz, Elizabeth. "Intolerable Ambiguity: Freaks at/as the Limit." Edited By Rosemarie G. Thompson. Freakery. *Cultural Spectacles of the Extraordinary Body,* New York UP, 1996, pp. 55–66.

Kristeva, Julia. "Approaching Abjection." [From *Powers of Horrors,* 1980], edited by Kelly Oliver. *The Portable Kristeva,* Columbia UP, 1997. pp. 229–247.

Lacan, Jacques. "The Mirror Stage as Formative of the Function of the I as Revealed in Psychoanalytic Experience." [Delivered at the 16th International Congress of Psychoanalysis, Zurich, July 17, 1949.] *Écrits.* Translated by Alan Sheridan. W.W. Norton, 1977. pp. 1–7.

Lotman, Yuri M. *Universe of the Mind: A Semiotic Theory of Culture.* Tauris, 2001.

Okolie, Andrew C. "Introduction to the Special Issue—Identity: Now You Don't See It; Now You Do." *Identity* vol. 3, no. 1, 2009, pp. 1–7.

Shan, Darren. *The Saga of Darren Shan: Vampire Blood Trilogy.* HarperCollins, 2000.

Sontag, Susan. "America, Seen Through Photographs, Darkly." *On Photography.* Rosetta Books, 2005.

Stallybrass, Peter, and Allon White. *The Politics and Poetics of Transgression.* Cornell UP, 1986.

Horror Movies, Horror Bodies

Blurring the Freak Body in Cinema

JESSICA L. WILLIAMS

Drawing on film theory in general, and on Carol Clover and Linda Williams' feminist readings of horror in particular, this essay thinks through Tod Browning's *Freaks*, a horror staple about the lives of freak show and circus performers, and the central catalyst in cinema's appropriation of the disabled body, often portrayed as a "freakish" body, in horror. My exploration of the film lays the groundwork for the later discussion of *The Funhouse*, a Tobe Hooper film which confronts forms of otherness in notable ways. Ultimately, my readings of these films illustrate how the horror in horror movies happens when normal bodies come into direct contact with "freak" bodies.

I choose to call the presentation of human oddities for money, and the people who are presented, by the names "freak show" and "freaks," respectively and respectfully. To some, it may be jarring to hear a person with disabilities or anomalies referred to as a freak, or their performances a freak show. To clarify, the term "disabled" throughout this essay refers to a cultural perception of disability. In other words, while it may be true that certain people with physical limitations may not consider themselves disabled, the large majority of general society would. So "person with disabilities," "disability," or "anomaly," all refer to physical deviations from what is socialized as a "normal" and "healthy" body. The use of the term "freak" to describe such bodies seems appropriate in the sense that I am using the language of the freak show, a language in which the term freak is not derogatory. Freak, as used here, does not refer to the entire population of people with disabilities, but rather those who have publicly displayed their bodies (or have had their bodies put on display) for purposes of entertainment, art, or profit.

Disabled bodies—both human and of the monster variety—are often portrayed as monstrous bodies in horror film, posing either a physical or social threat, and conflating binaries in ways that are always ambiguous and problematic. Further, the human body in these films becomes monstrous— and becomes disabled—when it comes into contact with the monstrous/disabled body, which plays into the fear of disability as something to which no one is immune, and feminizes disability.

Even though film moves the freak body away from the viewer in space and time, it moves the normal body much closer to the freak body—they are often in direct contact—on screen. Because film spectatorship allows multiple identifications for the viewer, horror opens up the possibility of both demonizing and identifying with the freak. Ultimately, these explorations will serve as support for my argument that horror's viewer-object relationship makes its treatment of freaks more complex than we see on the surface, by blurring the lines between normal and freakish bodies.

What We Fear in Freaks

Freaks has been written about in most freak and circus scholarship since the 1970s, but while others have focused on the ostensible fact of disabled bodies, my discussion primarily focuses on the freak-norm[1] relationship and the ambiguous representations of disability in *Freaks*. My ultimate concern lies in the ways freakish bodies are mediated by cinema, a concern that hinges on the very relationships between normal and freakish bodies within the film.

Since its resurrection as a cult favorite in the 1960s, *Freaks* has become a landmark text in the modern study of sideshow. In fact, it has become, as Rachel Adams states, "the foundational text through which authors and artists in the twentieth century came to understand the freak show" (63). While Adams may be overstating the point, she is correct in implying that the film has had a dramatic impact on freak show scholarship. This is problematic because, despite the fact that it often feels like a documentary, *Freaks* is a fictional story about freakish bodies; yet, this fact has not stopped it from becoming "a point of reference for all subsequent representations of [freak show] culture" (63).

Loosely adapted from Tod Robbins' short story, "Spurs," *Freaks* presents a dual narrative that is part pseudo-documentary and part narrative. The beginning of the film feels like a documentary in that it takes us inside the world of a traveling carnival and provides audiences with a new level of access. The beginning of the film is comprised of short vignettes of the various carnival and sideshow performers. Browning famously cast real freak show performers including, among others, the famous Siamese twins Daisy and Violet Hilton; Johnny Eck, the half-boy; Prince Randian, the human torso; and Josephine-Joseph, the half-man/half-woman. More significant to the plot is the dwarf couple Hans and Frieda, played by siblings Harry and Daisy Earles, around whom the narrative tension centers. Two norm couples fill out the cast: Cleopatra, the Amazonian trapeze artist and her lover Hercules, the ultra-masculine strongman; and Venus and Phroso, a circus performer and a clown.

Freaks failed, in part, because it confronted people with the presence of freakish bodies, but this is not the only element that stopped people from embracing the film. Audiences were turned off by two key elements. The first is that *Freaks* shattered illusions about people with disabilities in showing them doing things that nondisabled audiences also did—eating, socializing, giving birth—a spectacle not unlike what would have been seen, or at least suggested, at the freak show. Especially unsettling for viewers is the suggestion of sexuality and gender ambiguity in the film. Robin Larsen & Beth Haller's "The Case of *Freaks*" provides an excellent overview of the public reception and rejection of *Freaks*, and what this rejection means about our society's relationship to differently abled bodies. Their discussion of disability and sexuality is especially interesting. The article stresses the physical differences between the sexually involved characters, Hans and Cleopatra in particular: "Hans stresses his 'abnormal' sexual desire" when he tells Cleopatra that "most big people [laugh at him because] they don't realize that [he is] a man with the same feelings they have" (166). Perhaps subtle by today's standards, such a line would have been seen as quite suggestive in the '30s. After all, the implication is that Hans is not too small to have intercourse with Cleopatra, an innuendo that leaves viewers wondering about the logistics of such a contrasting physical match. Many of the film's other sexual suggestions leave viewers wondering things like "How do Siamese twins make love?" (166–67) and "What is under Joseph/Josephine's costume?" Larsen and Haller feel that such suggestions made audiences "uncomfortable rather than titillating them" (170). However, I would argue that it made them uncomfortable specifically *because* it titillated them. It is clear that audiences were made uncomfortable by the suggestion of abnormal bodies as sexual bodies. The film covers over this discomfort with the "appropriate" sexual pairings; we end up with at the end of *Freaks*, namely Hans and Frieda—both freaks—and Phroso and Venus—both norms.

The second and more significant reason for *Freaks'* failure, in terms of this study, is that *Freaks* collapsed the distance between norm and freak that had been established by the actual freak show. While it was always careful to stress the differences between viewer and object, *Freaks* directly confronts the relationship between the two. Such confrontation unsettled the average viewer who was able, possibly for the first time, to experience self-reflection as part of the "freak show." Unfortunately for MGM and *Freaks*, such self-reflection quickly led to fear and insecurity because it allowed the viewer to see themselves reflected in the anchoring "normal" protagonists, as well as in the film's freaks, and thus realize that they could become disabled themselves, not just blurring the line between viewer and object, but crossing it completely.

The audience is ambivalent about which characters they are supposed to identify with on the screen. Hans, a logical choice because he is victimized by Cleopatra, is never really a sympathetic character because of the way he treats Frieda (who may be the most truly innocent, sympathetic, and normal character in the film). Viewers cannot sympathize with a man who treats the woman who loves him so poorly. The starring characters in *Freaks* are humanized in the fact that not one of them is all good or all bad (even Frieda has some negative characteristics; she is a pushover who's willing to take abuse from Hans). Further complicating issues of viewer identification is that the narrative perspective continually shifts throughout the film. The viewer is instructed by these narrative shifts to occupy a space of dual identification. Audiences are initially drawn to the normal bodies on screen, but quickly transfer our identification to the freaks when they are victimized by Cleopatra. By providing the audience few normal bodies with which to identify, the film assumes the audience's identification with and then rejection of Cleopatra. She is, like the audience, a norm in a world of freaks. Thus, Cleopatra becomes a stand-in for the audience in mirroring their fears within the film. She is horrified when the freaks tell her she is one of them, and of course she does become a disabled freak at the end of the film.

If Cleopatra is a stand-in for the able-bodied viewer, then her closeness with the freaks is frightening and her fate is all too real a possibility. As Tobin Siebers explains,

> Only 15 percent of people with disabilities are born with their impairments. Most people become disabled over the course of their life. This truth has been accepted only with difficulty by mainstream society; it prefers to think of people with disabilities as a small population, a stable population [...] Most people do not want to consider that life's passage will lead them from ability to disability. The prospect is too frightening, the disabled body, too disturbing [59].

To be disabled means to enter unwillingly into a new subject position, one wrought with social challenges that will, at least in part, redefine a person's identity. Thus Cleopatra is doomed to experience some of society's greatest fears: the fear of losing control, of losing the body, of becoming unattractive, and of becoming an outcast. The disabling of an able-bodied person in *Freaks* makes disability palpable and brings it closer to home for the viewer.

Freaks, and audience reactions to it, reinforced the cultural link between morality and disability. This paradigm takes the form of two extremes: the disabled person is thought of as either morally superior or morally corrupt. *Freaks*, with its violent ending—turning a norm woman into a freak—reinforces the latter, making visible the negative cultural assumption that a bad outside is equivalent to a bad inside. We have historically been presented with the idea that freakish bodies only belong to those who are violent, degenerate, or stupid. In *Freaks* this is portrayed by the freaks' attack on the norms—they choose to enact revenge in a violent and evil way and, as a result, audiences would assume that they are morally corrupt. But this concept is especially reinforced by Cleopatra's freakification: it is difficult not to feel that she deserves everything she gets at the film's end. Hence, she is made a freak because she is so immoral.

The ultimate horror in *Freaks* is not simply in putting freak bodies on screen. That the film was rejected, panned by both audiences and critics, suggests something more than manufactured horror—it presents real life possibilities that were simply too real for audiences. Thus the film enters into the horror genre through the blurring between normal and freakish bodies. *Freaks* is a frame story; it begins and ends with a sideshow barker talking up the "living, breathing monstrosities" in his freak show. Not sixty seconds into the film, the barker tells the audience that "but for the accidents of birth, you might be even as they are. They did not ask to be brought into the world, but into the world they came." The barker quickly ushers the crowd over to a lowered pit exhibit into which audiences cannot see. The reactions of the film's crowd as they peer down into the exhibit—a woman screaming, people turning their heads away, expressions of disgust—tell the viewer that the freak exhibit is indeed a horrible sight. The barker then tells the crowd the story of how Cleopatra was once a beautiful trapeze artist who was considered "the peacock of the air." This story is, of course, the film's central storyline which I have already discussed. At the film's close, the viewer returns to this frame and here the barker finally allows us to look upon Cleopatra, now as a deformed chicken woman.

This frame serves various purposes. Although the film enters the world of the freak, the frame shrouds the film in normality and assures the viewer that they are entering the freak show through the normative gaze. As if we, too, were at a freak show, our interest is piqued by the opening frame and by the end of *Freaks* we cannot wait to see what is waiting for us in the exhibit. Viewers are left with a shocking image that simultaneously makes the film horrifying and ridiculous. We are frightened when we see what has become of Cleopatra, and her freakification is the film's final and most assertive way of telling the viewer that disability is something that can happen to anyone at any time, particularly if that person has acted in immoral ways. In exploiting Hans and therefore the freak body, Cleopatra sentences herself to a fate in which her body becomes a freakish spectacle. With her freakification, *Freaks* holds a mirror up to its viewers and forces them to question their own relationship to the freak body. In a sense, her freakification becomes our own. However, at the same time, her nearly cartoonish embodied form at the end keeps the fear of our own freakification at a distance. While we can all become disabled, becoming a chicken/human hybrid is obviously not a realistic depiction of disability. *Freaks* threatens us with the loss of our own normal bodies while at the same time reassures us that we are not living in the same reality as the film.

Why Horror?

Freaks was never a mainstream success even after its rerelease, and its cult status, while significant in its own right, makes it a poor example to gauge society's preoccupations at the time of its renewal. To be clear, its rejection when it was first released certainly *does* speak to society's cultural attitudes at the time, as it was released by a major studio who envisioned the film as a commercial Hollywood horror movie that could rival the recent successes of Universal's "new horror cycle" (Larsen and Haller 165). In other words, *Freaks* was envisioned and promoted as a mainstream film, and it was the average American audience who rejected it. It was not, however, the average American audience who embraced it upon its rerelease in 1962, but rather film aficionados and horror enthusiasts.

Thus, a better point of examination is the rise of horror films that, working in the tradition of *Freaks*, brought the freak body back to the big screen, questioned what it means to be a freak, and commented on the freak-norm relationship. Unlike *Freaks*, however, these films do this in a way that suggests that the viewer is unwilling or unable to view the freakish body in an overt way. The disabled body is not a central focus *as* a disabled body in most horror the way it is in *Freaks*. In other words, the disabled or freaked body is used as a tool to evoke fear or pity, but is rarely discussed and is not treated as a disability. As Robert Bogdan notes, "In horror films the association of evil with disability is [...] ubiquitous. Horror film 'monsters' are scarred, deformed, disproportionally built, hunched over, exceptionally large, exceptionally small, deaf, speech impaired, visually impaired, mentally ill, or mentally subnormal" (vii). The freak body tends, in most horror films, to appear as either victim or monster and is not always physically disabled in clearly recognizable ways, but is more often mutilated, deformed, and/or sexually dysfunctional.

Through horror, cinema is able to be more disclosing than the freak show because of the contact it allows us with the freak body, but also more removed in its examinations of that body. The camera allows us to see the freak body in seemingly unrestricted ways. Of course the viewer is seeing what the camera chooses to show and is thus not *really* unrestricted, although it certainly feels that way at times. Audiences are privy to the intimate moments of the freak body in ways not permitted by the freak show; my later discussions, especially that of *The Funhouse*, will illustrate this. On the other hand, the camera is positioned as the normal gaze; thus we are never viewing the freak body through the eyes of the freak. Viewers only gain access to the freak body because we are doing so through a normative lens.

Human Monsters and the Feminization of Disability

The word "monster" was once a term used to refer to fetuses and human beings with deformities or physical disabilities. As Fiedler notes, "'Monster' is as old as English itself, and remained the preferred name for Freaks [*sic*][2] from the time of Chaucer to that of Shakespeare and beyond" (20). Now deemed an offensive term for human oddities, "monster" is most often associated with horror films and comic books. These monsters were the reason for Universal Studios' great success in the horror genre in the first half of the 20th century. The term "Universal Monsters" refers to the long list of monster movies released by Universal from the early '20s through 1960 including *Dracula, Frankenstein, The Mummy*, and *The Phantom of the Opera*. The films' monsters were not human oddities but entities such as werewolves, zombies, vampires, creatures, and other *things*.

Noel Carroll states that the monster in horror is incontestably threatening and dangerous, though not necessarily physically so. A monster that "kills and maims is enough" to satisfy this criteria; however, the monster may also pose a psychological, social, or moral threat to a society. For instance, it can destroy a person's identity or the moral order of a society, or advance an alternative society. Monsters can also trigger "enduring infantile fears, such as those of being eaten or dismembered, or sexual fears, concerning rape and incest" (42). Carroll adds that monsters are also defined by their impurity, which is often seen in what he calls their "fusion." This is simply another way of saying that monsters shatter binaries, as do freaks, such as "inside/outside, living/dead, insect/human, flesh/machine, and so on" (42–43). As the remainder of this essay will illustrate, disabled bodies—both human and of the monster variety—are portrayed as monstrous bodies in horror.

Leslie Fiedler warns readers that they must not confuse these movie monsters with his "Freaks" or "Curiosities." As he says, "the freaky young do not [conflate the two]. Even stoned out of their minds at the latest horror show of some campus film series, or alone in their rooms watching the Fright Night feature on TV, they are aware that monsters are not 'real' as Freaks are" (23). Though he does not say so, Fiedler is in fact highlighting the fact that by putting abnormal bodies on the screen in the form of monsters, a connection is being made between monsters and freaks. In other words, by warning us not to confuse the two, Fielder assumes that one could, that there is something monstrous about both the movie monster and the freak. Monsters, in his example, take the place of freaks, standing in as a neutralized version of a scary reality.

Horror allows us to confront otherness through the monster. A short passage from Katherine Dunn's novel *Geek Love* highlights this. Dunn's novel features a carny couple, Aloysius "Al" Binewski and his wife "Crystal" Lil, who use drugs and radiation during Crystal Lil's pregnancies in order to breed human oddities who they feel are superior to norms. Their children are: Arturo, who has flippers instead of hands and feet; Olympia, an albino, hunchbacked dwarf who is considered the most normal of the siblings; Iphy and Elly, Siamese twin girls; and finally Chick, who is physically normal but has the gift of mind control. In one scene, Arturo talks to his sister, Olympia, about why he likes to read horror stories. He says that the stories do not scare him because the monsters in the stories—"written by norms to scare norms"—are just like him. He tells his sister, "[w]e are the things that come to the norms in nightmares [....] These books [...] don't scare me because they're about me" (46). Arturo shows great insight here, paralleling the reactions he has caused in people with those of the victims in the horror stories he reads. He sees a monster in himself because others see a monster in him. Fiedler, however, sees a difference between freak and monster, and adamantly argues that, unlike the monster, the "true Freak" (such as Arturo)

[s]tirs both supernatural terror and natural sympathy, since, unlike the fabulous monsters, he is one of us, the human child of human parents, however altered by forces we do not quite understand into something mythic and mysterious, as no mere cripple ever is. Passing either on the street, we may be simultaneously tempted to avert our eyes and to stare; but in the latter case we feel no threat to those desperately maintained boundaries on which any definition of sanity ultimately depends. Only the true Freak challenges the boundaries between male and female, sexed and sexless, animal and human, large and small, self and other, and consequently between reality and illusion, experience and fantasy, fact and myth [24].

Fiedler denies that the monster in the pages of a book or on a screen can evoke the same fears and sympathies as a "true freak" can. This becomes complicated, however, when the monster on the screen is "one of us, the human child of human parents" as is, for example, Norman Bates, who I will use as a quick example of the rise of the human monster in horror.

Norman is, of course, not merely a human monster. Norman is a hand-some (physically nondisabled, thin, and white), sympathetic, *likeable* char-acter who happens to do monstrous things. The product of a dysfunctional home life, Norman is as much sympathetic victim as he is monster. We root for him, wanting him to break free of his mother, and this fact does not change when we find out that Norman has assumed his mother's identity after murdering her. We are horrified at this fact, but we do not cease to see Norman as a human being. Even though Norman does become a physical horror in his cross-dressing, the one brief scene in which he appears in drag does not undo his physical normality. *Psycho* highlights horror's shift of focus from a supernatural monster to a human one. With this shift, horror forges an association between the monstrous body and monstrous acts.

Psycho stages the fearful encounter at the border of abnormal and nor-mal. This is true even in Norman's relationship to his mother's body; he becomes monstrous when his body and that of his mother's come into contact. While *Psycho* gives us some insight into the human monster and the femi-nization of the freak body, it does not offer the opportunity for a reading of real disability because Norman's body is not actually a disabled body. There are many horror movies that do, however, present disability in a more forth-right way.

One such film is Tobe Hooper's *The Funhouse* which highlights the con-nection between horror and the carnival, which one might call an extension of the circus. The opening credits of *The Funhouse* are interspersed with images of animatronic carnival figures: children, clowns, a fat lady, an old woman wielding a butcher's knife, and an executioner, among others. The movie begins in a bedroom where the viewer sees—through the eyes of the killer—many dark and sinister objects. As the killer stalks around the room, we see a cage filled with mice, giant flies and spiders strewn about the room, and various scary masks and torture devices hanging from the walls. There is memorabilia from carnivals and monster and slasher films everywhere. Clearly, audiences are meant to believe that we are in the lair of a killer. An arm reaches out and grabs a large, rusty knife from the wall and then he slips a mask over his face. Our view is now limited, as we can only see what the killer sees out of the mask's two eye holes.[3] He stalks down the hallway where we know a teenage girl, Amy, has just stepped into the shower. A mock *Psy-cho*-style shower scene follows, from the killer's point of view, in which Amy is "stabbed" by her younger brother's rubber knife. The viewer is quickly taken out of the horror and reassured that this is little kid stuff; there is noth-ing to be afraid of. Hooper, with such a dramatic opening, immediately and directly forges a connection for the viewer between the human monsters in films such as *Psycho* (the white male wielding a knife) and the monsters in films like *Frankenstein* (the memorabilia in the bedroom) with the carnivalesque freak show (the carnival figures that appear over the opening credits).[4]

The rest of the movie takes place at a traveling carnival which Amy visits (against her better judgment) that night on a date with Buzz, her new boyfriend, Liz, her best friend, and Richie, Liz's goofy boyfriend. While at the carnival, the couples visit a freak show but human freaks are not exhibited—only freakish animals are on display (it is the 1980s after all—we can't exhibit freaks in freak shows, only in horror movies. Of course because this *is* a horror movie, we will confront the freak body in a different way). When Amy pulls her hand back from Daisy Mae, the two-headed cow, Richie teases her, "It's not gonna rub off on ya," reminding us that the able-bodied are often subconsciously afraid of contact with abnormal bodies because they fear becoming disabled themselves. It is Richie, in fact, who is the most fascinated by the freaky animals, dragging the others into the must-see "feature attraction" of pickled punks.[5] It is also Richie who puts the group in mortal danger, and he is punished for his transgressions as well as his interest in all things freaky; he is the first to die. Amy also seems to have a strange connection to the carnival, although she does not necessarily seem to enjoy it as Richie does. There are three odd moments in the film where Amy is drawn to meet the gaze of three carnival workers in prolonged stares: the freak show barker, the funhouse operator, and the girlie show barker (all played by the same actor, Kevin Conway). These moments of connection via the gaze, which abruptly interrupt the film's action, serve to reinforce the difference between Amy's normalcy and the freakishness of the carnival.

The horror does not take place until the carnival shuts down for the night. Hooper makes it a point to show the lights slowly going out, the crowd dispersing, and the rides stopping. The camera pans over the carnival grounds and reveals that the only people left are the carnies. Not all are freaks, of course; in fact, we only see one or two typical freak show bodies but, because all of the able-bodied, non-carnival workers are leaving, we get the sense that we are very clearly somewhere we are not supposed to be. The viewer does not belong here any more than Amy and her friends do. As the camera returns to the dark funhouse, where the group has decided to camp out for the night, the viewer knows that they will be punished for trespassing into the world of the carnival.

It is here that Amy and her friends discover that Gunther, the son of the funhouse's barker, Conrad, lives in the basement below the ride. We know very little about Gunther, just that he helps his father operate the ride, he always wears a Frankenstein's monster mask, and he never speaks. We have seen Gunther a few times before this, though in seemingly insignificant shots. After they leave the girlie show, for instance, Gunther walks past them and the guys make fun of him while Amy comments on how strange he is. Buzz jokes that it "looks like old Frankenstein has to get his jollies also." This scene foreshadows what the group later witnesses in the funhouse.

During the night, the group hears voices coming from below them. Peering through the floorboards, they watch Gunther as he engages Madame Zena, the fortune teller, as a prostitute. While it is unusual for the freakish body to be displayed as a sexually active body, Gunther certainly fits the profile of the sexually dysfunctional body. The two do not actually have sex; Madame Zena gives him a hand-job and while he does ejaculate, he does so prematurely (all while wearing his *Frankenstein* mask). It is unclear whether this is what he paid her for or whether it was meant as a prelude to intercourse. Regardless, Gunther responds with embarrassment and anger over his premature ejaculation, demanding that Zena return the hundred dollars he paid her. When she refuses, he chokes her to death and then removes his mask. The rest of the plot centers around Gunther and Conrad discovering that the teens witnessed the murder. The characters are killed off one by one: Conrad kills Richie, Gunther kills Liz, Buzz kills Conrad, Gunther kills Buzz, Gunther chases Amy and then accidentally kills himself. Amy is the only survivor—another final girl.[6]

It is interesting that the viewer doesn't see Gunther without his Frankenstein mask until after he fails as a sexual partner and is thus emasculated. Immediately thereafter, he reasserts his masculinity by killing Zena, and the viewer is horrified. When the mask is removed, we realize that the movie monster (in this case, Frankenstein's monster) is harmless in comparison to the true horror of the deformed body. Gunther is truly hideous. His facial deformities are difficult to describe, but Hooper has said in interviews that he has a "cleft head" (Hooper). His red eyes are set quite far apart, and he has a severe cleft palate that seems to travel up his entire face. His mouth is large, has fangs, and is dripping with copious amounts of drool. The viewer cannot help but be horrified at the sight of him. Within the context of the film, Fiedler's earlier point that movie monsters cannot be confused with real freaks seems accurate. The monster mask literally hides a much scarier reality. Of course, in choosing a monster mask, Hooper connects the movie monster with the monstrous body and, like *Freaks*, reinforces the connection between freakish bodies and morally corrupt deeds. This also reasserts, once again, that at the center of horror is not the monster, but the viewer's fear of contact with the monstrous body.

Ultimately, the film makes a comment on the helplessness of the freak body. The freak animals, for example, are on display and can do nothing about it. Upon viewing a cow with a cleft palate (clearly foreshadowing Gunther's freakishness) and the two-headed cow in the freak show, Amy comments on how sad the animals look. We are, of course, meant to make a connection between these animals and Gunther who, wild and without speech, seems very much an animal himself. Though they are frightening, we are meant to pity both the animals and Gunther. Hooper urges us to realize that, like Hans in *Freaks*, they may be different, but they have feelings. During the scene between Gunther and Zena, we cannot help but feel sorry for him, especially after he kills her and realizes what he's done. He beats himself and hides in the corner while Conrad yells at him and talks him into killing the kids upstairs. It is clear that Gunther only "takes care of the problem" reluctantly, after being sweet-talked by Conrad who reassures Gunther that he will take care of him and that the sound of Gunther's "voice" doesn't scare him. That we are to pity Gunther is made even more apparent when he kills Liz. As he approaches her, Liz offers sex in exchange for her life, telling him, "I can make you feel good." Gunther seems willing to accept her affection; he hugs her and strokes her hair, clearly starved for any kind of human connection. He only ends up killing her because she stabs him, rejecting his affection.

Tobe Hooper's monstrous freaks in *The Funhouse* are self-hating, powerless, animalistic, and/or sexually dysfunctional. While the viewer does experience a certain amount of pity for characters like Gunther, such feelings are secondary to disgust or fear. Even in *Freaks*, the viewer is ambivalent because the freaks are as guilty as Cleopatra. These examples illustrate that the freakish bodies we see in horror are not merely scary to look at. They are scary as well in our connection with them—they can touch and be touched, they can be human and engage in the same everyday activities that we can, and even when they do horrible things they are still capable of feeling sadness, empathy, and loneliness. Viewers can see that the monster might almost be normal, and can picture themselves being almost monstrous, i.e., we are reminded of the blurry distinction between normal and freak bodies, which is in itself horrific.

Bringing Back Freaks

Freaks brought the freak show from the carnival to the movies, a transference that has had a significant effect on cinema, notably in the genres of horror and disability melodrama. *Freaks* was not a direct representation of the freak show, but a cinematic interpretation that allowed a different kind of access to the freakish body. In seating audiences in a theater, *Freaks*, and the horror films that followed, succeeded in simultaneously bringing freaks and norms closer together on screen, while distancing freaks and norms in the space of spectatorship. The medium of film rejects the freak show format and, because the freaks cannot look back, the freak-norm relationship is challenged, though it is not eradicated. Rather, these films attempt to work out the problematic relationship between different bodies, allowing audiences a physical distance in the theater that is essential to facilitating self-reflection in viewing the freakish body on a screen.

I do not mean to suggest that the freakish body can only be confronted in a darkened theater. However, the medium of film can and has served as a conduit for viewers to work through their reactions to freakish bodies. *Freaks* has been the most successful film in provoking ambivalent yet thoughtful responses to the portrayal of the freak in film and, further, the ethics in looking at the freak. With its suggested sexuality, theatrical representations of freakish bodies, and reluctance to show audiences any more than necessary, the carnival freak show offered a highly mediated, spectacularized interpretation of otherness. *Freaks* offers a highly mediated, carnivalesque spectacle as well. However, unlike its successors, *Freaks* generally does not fall prey to damaging paradigms of disability such as the supercrip, or pity paradigms, and when viewers do feel inspired by or pity for the characters with disabilities, it is because actions and circumstances have warranted such responses, not because they are disabled. While *Freaks* is not perfect in resisting such paradigms, it is largely more successful than similar films. Almost all of the scholarship on *Freaks* reads the film adversely, but in doing so many are buying into injurious tropes about people with disabilities.

For example, many have criticized the "stiff, self-conscious performances" of the film's cast. The "wooden delivery" of their lines leaves much to be desired and may keep audiences from becoming immersed in the film. The drama, described as "contrived," is also panned. Rachel Adams calls the plot a "thin story of love and vengeance that makes a flimsy pretext" for gathering the group of freaks together on film (67). It is an unusual case, indeed, that most members of the cast were not actors used to speaking but freaks who were used to being stared at. While the fact that they are often stiff and awkward keeps us aware that we are watching a film, and thus keeps us aware of our own presence in the theater and thus our own bodies, this allows for self-reflection. Further, the admittedly awkward introductions serve a larger, more important purpose; these early scenes allow us to get used to looking at difference and thus act as an invitation into their lives.

Freaks was progressive in its view of people with disabilities as healthy, sexual beings. The film, while forcing the viewer to consider the erotic possibilities of freakish sexual pairings, nevertheless also forces us to realize that freakish bodies are not broken or incapable of human love and affection. An example is found in the scene in which the Bearded Lady gives birth to the Walking Skeleton's child. Another character leans over and asks her, "What is it?" When most people ask a new mother "what is it?" we expect the answer to either be "a boy" or "a girl." The joke here is that the phrase is a tongue-in-cheek nod to a famous freak show advertisement that anyone familiar with the history of the freak show would recognize. One of P.T. Barnum's most famous freak performers, a man with microcephaly (commonly known as a pinhead), was famously billed as "Zip, the What Is It?" The scene plays out like an inside joke of the freak show. That it is also a comic moment that pokes fun at the fear of procreation by freaks, speaks to *Freaks'* attempt to neutralize and normalize the freakish body. It also treats freak sexuality as not simply something subversive or shocking, but something lighthearted and ordinary.

The box office failure of *Freaks* made honest representations of disability a difficult tradition to carry on, and the films that succeed do so as alternative representations to those in *Freaks*. Everything that *Freaks* was panned for has been shifted in post–'60s horror. If *Freaks* is not the freak show but an interpretation of it, then the horror movies which I have discussed are not the freak show either, nor are they working quite in the tradition of *Freaks*. Rather, they work in an odd anti-tradition, keeping away from the boldness and "indecency" of *Freaks* and finding alternative ways to present freakishness that, while less honest and more prey to damaging cultural perceptions of disability, still embrace the spirit of *Freaks* and the freak show itself. With the normalizing gaze, the fear of contact with the freak, the sexual narratives surrounding the freak body, and the sympathetic characterizations of the monstrous, horror defines the freak body in relation to normal activity while asserting that we still see and think about the freak body as abnormal. And in films that feature such bodies, we are confronted with our own fears about disability—a fear that is exploited and drawn out via the confrontation between "normal" and "monstrous" bodies.

NOTES

1. "Norm," short for "normal," is a term I will use interchangeably with "able-bodied" throughout. I like the harshness of the term "norm," especially when paired with the brusque term "freak."

2. Fiedler capitalizes the word "freak" throughout his study. I will not note this preference with [*sic*] repeatedly.

3. This is, of course, "borrowed" from Halloween.

4. Diane Negra's article, "Coveting the Feminine: Victor Frankenstein, Norman Bates, and Buffalo Bill," puts Frankenstein and Bates in direct conversation, as seen in her title. Negra provides an excellent Freudian reading of the ambiguous gender identities represented in the three texts.

5. The term is used to refer to human fetuses preserved in formaldehyde, displayed in jars in sideshows.

6. The term "final girl," coined by Carol Clover, refers to the trope in horror films of the last remaining girl at the end of the film who is left to confront, thwart, or even defeat the killer.

WORKS CITED

Accordino, Michael, Robert L. Hewes and Jeanmarie Crimoli. "Public Perceptions of People with Disabilities." *Psychology of Disability*, edited by Joseph F. Stano, Aspen Professional Services, 2009.

Adams, Rachel. *Sideshow U.S.A.* U of Chicago P, 2001.

Bogdan, Robert. *Freak Show: Presenting Human Oddities for Amusement and Profit.* U of Chicago P, 1988.

Carroll, Noel. *The Philosophy of Horror.* Routledge, 1990.

Clover, Carol J. *Men, Women, and Chainsaws.* Princeton UP, 1992.

Dunn, Katherine. *Geek Love.* Vintage, 1989.

Fiedler, Leslie. *Freaks: Myths and Images of the Secret Self.* Anchor, 1978.

Freaks. Dircted by Tod Browning. Metro-Godlwyn-Mayer, 1932.

The Funhouse. Directed by Tobe Hooper. Universal Pictures, 1981.

Hooper, Tobe. "The Funhouse Retrospective: An Interview with Tobe Hooper." *Shock Till You Drop.* Ryan Turek. 22 June 2010.

Larsen, R., and B. Haller. "The Case of Freaks." *Journal of Popular Film and Television,* vol. 29, no. 4, Winter 2002, pp. 164–172.

Negra, Diane. "Coveting the Feminine: Victor Frankenstein, Norman Bates, and Buffalo Bill." *Literature Film Quarterly,* April 1996, pp. 193–200.

Psycho. Directed by Alfred Hitchcock. Shamley Productions, 1960.

Siebers, Tobin. *Disability Theory.* U of Michigan P, 2011.

The Spectacle of Sensation in British Film

Circus of Horrors, Berserk! and Vampire Circus

FERNANDO GABRIEL PAGNONI BERNS

Introduction: A Night at the (Horror) Circus

As audiences worldwide know, circuses are all about exotic animals, glitter, clowns, big tops, acrobats, and laughs. And, of course, murders. Bloody murders. Scantily clad girls bathed in blood. That is, if the circuses in horror films are to be believed.

Circus and horror films are good companions; both are vehicles of popular entertainment, filled with sensationalism and, most important, shock value as crucial parts of their aesthetics (Stoddart 93). Sawing a woman in half, throwing knives at a beautiful lady, and the exhibition of uncanny freaks inspiring awe and fear in equal parts, are just a few examples of the articulation between horror and fascination that both the circus and the horror film provide. Thus, it is easy to see why so many circus-related horror films exist. More striking, however, is the fact that the four made in the 1960s and first years of the 1970s were British productions. *Circus of Horrors* (Sidney Hayers, 1960), *Circus of Fear*[1] (Werner Jacobs, John Llewellyn Moxey, 1966), *Berserk!* (Jim O'Connolly, 1967), and *Vampire Circus* (Robert Young, 1972) share the circus as setting and a horror plot. Furthermore, all of them (especially *Circus of Horror* and *Berserk!*) share a narrative that privileges the interconnection of horror situations (sensationalism) with images lifted from real circuses, such as wild lions or elephants walking through groups of scantily clad young women (also sensationalism). For one ticket, audiences were enthralled by two different forms of titillation, both related to spectacle and the gaze. As John Jervis makes clear, the spectacular and the sensational are barely distinguishable in the pervasive power of mass media (Jervis 6).

Following Guy Debord and his classic *The Society of the Spectacle*, we note that spectacle consists of the transformation of life into pure image. Pure spectacle herein is, for example, an eternal present without a past (the scars from World War II turned external beauty through plastic surgery in *Circus of Horrors*), and repetition (*Circus of Fear* lifts entire scenes from Hayers' film), while everything is turned into commodity, especially the female body (*Circus of Horror* and *Berserk!*), and audiences are slowly vampirized (*Vampire Circus*).

The problem resides not in the need for such images but rather in the society that needs such forms of spectacle. The British 1960s saw a "first steady, then accelerating growth in both the cultural and leisure market" (Laing 29). Free cinema emphasized the tensions between realism (documental images lifted from real circus) and fiction (the horror plot), while commoditization slowly swallowed daily life. The films herein analyzed, blending real circus and horror, got Britain back to its roots of Victorian sensationalism while displaying interesting examples of the society of spectacle. Still, I argue, the horror elements such as an undying past, vampiric female sexuality, and the blurring of categories of normality/abnormality situate these films, filled with shock value, as perverse critiques of visual commoditization.

Spectacle and Sensationalism in Britain's Cultural Roots

Four examples of horror films with a circus as their main setting hardly can be described as a "flourishing" phenomenon. Still, while the UK has four horror/circus films to offer in the 1960s and early 1970s, other countries had none, so they would appear to represent a certain sort of "British" flavor. In this sense, both sensationalism and circus lie at the roots of industrial modernity, as people tried to reconcile the rapidly changing social scenario with new forms of representation and narrative. Through modernity, the British culture industry employed the adjective "sensational" to market new changes in popular culture and aesthetic taste that privileged "basis" sensations (Gabriele 1). This new form of narrative was sustained by the desire "to mediate the fragmentation of modernity into a manageable cogent unity" (Gabriele 2), giving a sense of unitary order to disparate realities. The new spectacles, filled with shock, dread, and magic as they were, tried to produce a stable world from the "dizzying multiplicity of industrial modernity" (*ibid.*). Spectacle was an instance that drew attention to technology itself, the taming of nature, and the commodification of the marvelous into a coherent narrative while, at the same time, being an "infinite dispersion or distraction" (Jervis 133) in which disparate events were internalized through the body as sensations (Shock! Thrills! Wonder! Awe!) and thus, turned spectacle (Jervis 38).

Sensationalism refers inextricably to Britain's roots: sensationalism and the Victorian age came together. In turn, sensationalism recognizes roots in the Gothic fiction of the past; in its extreme and eccentric scenarios, sensationalism "draws on the excess, extravagance and monstrosity of a Gothic register" (Moran 12). The films here analyzed basically return to the Victorian sensibility of thrilling displays of violence, awesome sights, and upside-down morals, now in Technicolor.

The concept of "sensationalism" lies at the basis of literary texts producing physical sensations in their readers, who follow the texts' macabre adventures to experience the anguish and dread felt by the characters. Not only did the plots of sensation fiction involve characters facing thrilling situations, they had "designs on the reader's body as well, appealing directly to the senses and stimulating, according to various reviewers, such physiological reactions as creeping flesh, shocked nerves, teeth on edge, elevated blood pressure, and even sexual arousal" (Hughes 260).

Following Hughes, sensationalism in the Victorian age regularly cited the daily newspaper and the news of actual crimes as the source for their plots. The hybrid between realism (actual crimes) and fiction is recuperated in the horror films here analyzed, which stage fake thrilling images (murders) interspersed with scenes lifted from real circuses, thus competing with the entertainment provided by the big tops. As Hughes indicates, there was a substantial class dimension in the "sensation" phenomenon. The most readily available source of sensationalism was the flourishing penny press (the Penny Dreadful), that world of literally unbound serials aimed at the lower and working classes (267) looking for cheap shocks.

Horror films have also been seen as entertainment aimed at the working class, considered guilty of being made only for the satisfaction of the low instincts of the masses. Some countries treated the genre with more respect than others, but it was generally considered an unfortunate market. Especially in the UK, the horror film was considered as a sub-product aimed at sick, subnormal people. "A crude sort of entertainment for a crude sort of audience," a "crude, sensational exploitation merely aim[ed] at giving the bluntest of cheap thrills," as the reviews recollected by Julian Petley, which appeared in newspapers through the 1950s to the 1970s, argued (34). The history of British censorship reveals the pejorative gaze that the horror film genre has had to endure through its history, from the first examples of Gothic melodramas by Tod Slaughter, to the "video nasties" scare in the 1980s.

Circuses, on the other hand, while not *produced* exclusively for the lower classes—in that they were quite expensive for the poorest (Ward 83)—appealed more to the "audiences of the lowest kind" (Burwick 174) than the bourgeois in their never-ending parade of thrilling scenes. Further, both the circus and the sensation novel "were highly commercialized forms of mass entertainment" and as such, "regarded as devalued forms of art" (Stoddart 97) at least until people such as P.T. Barnum gave respectability to this form of entertainment in the U.S. As Janet Davis argues, residual parts of the carnival grotesque survived in the circus. In their performances, "circus artists sometimes drove a wedge between respectable entertainment and transgressive thrill" (Assael 11), provoking responses such as fear or shock.

The circus in the Victorian age promoted its sensations using, among other devices, sex: "thousands of lithographs saturated the site of each future show, portraying barely dressed women in a range of bodily attitudes" (Davis 83), promising scantily clad acrobats and bareback riders, images which run parallel to the sensational heroine of the Penny Dreadful, more sexualized than their counterparts in earlier fiction and melodrama. In brief, there was a culture of shock in 19th century Britain and the circus was part of it.

Victorian culture and the circus were complementary, following Brenda Assael who chronicles the ways in which the sensibilities of the Victorian Age and the world of the circus complement each other. For example, an important turn in the social history of curiosity took place in the Victorian Age, when "a desire to know aroused a fascination with exotics brought from the far reaches of the colonial world and beyond" (62), producing a new way of seeing. Curiosity was no longer considered "vulgar" but a tool for enlightenment and power over those under the scrutinizing gaze. Touched by the gaze of the audience, the disparate performances in a circus's night were an information bank of representation, exhibiting everything that could or should be represented. Within the circus, "feats traditionally portrayed on canvas were transformed into live representations of national heroes and the battles they fought" [such as the Napoleonic Wars], offering important readings on the forging of British national identity (46) while contributing to the culture of remembrance and hero worship (47). Equestrian dramas such as *The Battle of Waterloo* or *St. George and the Dragon* reunited huge crowds (Ward 76). Lastly, just like sensational fiction, the circus displayed a temporal topsy-turvy view of Victorian society (85), where women, cross-dressers and children could be on top of the power hierarchy while traditional morals, thanks in part to the clowns, were downplayed.

The Victorian circus "disturbed the seemingly safe staged distance between self and Other because it was interactive" (Davis 27). All that the circus asks from the spectator is complete involvement; entertainers talked back to audiences, teased them, and fooled them. The circus also invited audiences to see a spectacularization of the Other—sexualized women and men in tight leotards, freaks, immigrants, savage animals, etc., were turned into spectacle. All these different geographies, sexualities, bodies, and species, aped each other, blurring any distinction between them while turning them all into objects to-be-looked-at. In brief, the sensation fiction of the Victorian age and the thrills provided by the circus are reunited in the horror film, specifically, in the British horror/circus film.

Especially relevant to our interests is Tom Gunning's "cinema of attractions," defined in contrast to the narrative film that later became dominant in U.S. film production. The period of the "cinema of attractions" (roughly, from 1896 to 1903, at the core of modernity) was characterized by exhibition strategies emphasizing the act of display rather than depending on internal coherence and storytelling progression. It is best exemplified by the presence, within the film, of live performers such as magicians (for example, in Georges Méliès's cinema). In this kind of cinema, the theatrical visual spectacle was the more important aspect of the film. It exploited the elements of "shock, surprise and trauma" (70) rather than linearity. It was, in brief, a cine-sensation rather than the story film we all know today. To the cinema of attractions, the circus was seen as the ideal setting for overturning clear narratives (Fenner 209). Thus, there are affinities "between circus and cinema in film's early era, both spectacles sharing an interest in shocking the bourgeois public and displaying bodily feats" (Ledesma 141). Sensation was what every spectacle in the late Victorian period sought in its spectators, and all three—the cinema of attractions, the circus, and the sensation novel—are related in this capacity to thrill. The horror/circus film is, then, heir to these related traditions.

The denomination "horror/circus film" is appropriate if we keep in mind that these films fill much of their length with circus-y spectacle emptied of any narrative importance. Instead, as exemplified in particular in *Circus of Horrors* or *Berserk!*, they contain the narrative coherence of sensation fiction: uniting disparate events into a unit. This idea is developed by French theorist Guy Debord and his comrades into the concept of a "society of spectacle" in the Situationist International.[2]

For Debord, spectacle "unifies and explains a great diversity of apparent phenomena" (10). Debord's conception, first developed in the 1960s, "describes a media and consumer society organized around the production and consumption of images, commodities, and staged events" (Kellner 2). For Debord, the mass media are just a limited (albeit important) aspect of spectacle. What is important is the fact that the determination of events is "replaced by a passive contemplation of images which have, moreover, been chosen by other people" (Jappe 6). Debord dedicated no mention of the circus phenomenon in his *The Society of the Spectacle*. However, it is possible to find clear links between the circus and the society of the spectacle. To Debord, not only is spectacle a metaphor of modernity, but capitalist society itself is spectacle. The cosmopolitan popular culture, so strong in the post World War II period, reveals the function of spectacle and the consolidation of cultural commodities as people, past and present events, ideas, and ethics are transformed into images and sold as such. Spectacle is seen as the "circuses" in "bread and circuses"[3] for the masses, the site of escapism *par excellence*. Spectacle is "a massive internal extension of the capitalist market—the invasion and restructuring of whole areas of free time, private life, leisure and personal expression" in which the individual becomes "an increasingly passive consumer of fetishized products" (Storey 58).

Debord published his text in the 1960s amid social and cultural upheavals. In it, he suggested that the world can no longer be grasped directly, but only mediatized. Spectacle "is not primarily concerned with a looking at images but rather with the construction of conditions that individuate, immobilize, and separate subjects" (Crary 74), an idea that resonated strongly in the "swinging London" times, in which a sense of identity was given by fashion, bachelor lifestyle, glam, Mod subculture, and other cultural commodities linked inevitably to the market. As Robert McAuley argues, during the 1960s, it seemed Debord's ideas about a "society of the spectacle" were "beginning to define modern British culture" (21). Ultimately, the post-war UK was a country and era of consumer revolution and technological change supported by higher incomes and the increase of "spectacularization" of daily life. "Within a competitive commercialized leisure market in which money was exchanged for visual gratification," the "vibrancy of a consumer culture governed by an unrefined and insatiable appetite for spectacle" (Assael 109) was enthroned.

The circus was one of the roots of the culture of mass consumption in the history of the UK, so it is not by chance that this form of spectacle is recuperated in a society obsessed with shocking images and spectacles. People wanted new, exciting forms of entertainment, and cinema itself was losing audiences to television, an important impact on consumer culture. By the end of the 1960s, "television had replaced newspapers as most people's main source of news and had cut deeply into the popularity of other media and forms of entertainment" such as cinema (Obelkevich 146).

Within this scenario, the circus was "reborn" in film, a way to concentrate two forms of spectacles in decline—film and the circus—into one, both sharing the issue of sensationalism, the latter especially exacerbated in horror cinema. However, rather than the participatory nature of a real circus, this new cinema of attractions invited viewers to complete commodification and fetishism: scenes lifted from real circus were badly sutured into narrative, often despite the fact that many of the scenes were not horror-related but cute. In this sense, *Vampire Circus*, with its vampiric performers slowly bleeding out the viewers, can be understood as an ironic twist to the circus/horror films.

In the next section, my purpose is to demonstrate how *Circus of Horrors*, *Berserk!*, and *Vampire Circus* recuperate the sensationalist roots of the Victorian age and the cinema of attractions, now framed within a "society of spectacle."

Disjointed Narratives and Spectatorship in Horror/Circus Films

In the 1960s, British horror was not entirely in good shape. The Gothic horror, produced by Hammer Film Productions, is highly regarded now but the studio's real Golden Age was the late 1950s after the opening of *The Curse of Frankenstein* (Terence Fisher, 1957) and the early 1960s. Hammer Film Productions survived well into the 1970s, but it never achieved figures equal to those produced in the second half of the 1950s. Through the 1960s, Hammer produced more flops than hits as the studios become a "sinking ship" (Meikle 174). Further, Hammer faced direct competition when other studios and new production companies such as Tigon or Amicus started to churn out their own cheaper horrors. America, on the other hand, was mostly uninterested in producing horror anymore (until George Romero's *Night of the Living Dead* in 1968 and the savage decade of the 1970s), with just a handful of glossy horror films during the decade (for example Alfred Hitchcock's *The Birds* in 1963 and Roman Polanski's *Rosemary's Baby* in 1968). So while horror was still a profitable genre in the 1960s, it was far from being in the best of shape. Thus, it is not by chance that cheap horror films were made with circus scenes sutured into the narrative; in the creation of spectacle, the combination of horror and cute poodles jumping through paper rings was genius. Though the plots are dissimilar, both *Circus of Horrors* and *Berserk!* present a narrative that blends together, under the umbrella of spectacle, horror, blood, semi-naked women, pop songs[4] and cute poodles.

Hayer's *Circus of Horrors* begins in 1947 England, when British Doctor Rossiter (Anton Diffring) has to make a rushed escape to France when one of his patients, Evelyn Morley (Colette Wilde) has grisly problems with her surgery. Once in France, he operates on Nicole (Yvonne Monlaur), a circus owner's daughter deformed by bombs from the war. Later, after letting the owner (Donald Pleasence) die at the hands of a bear, he becomes the owner of the circus and, under the name Dr. Schuler, continues transforming disfigured women into the beautiful stars of his show, the process he began with Nicole. Scotland Yard and a reporter become interested when women (all of them sharing a criminal past) who want out of the circus begin dying in bizarre accidents, and they suspect that the good doctor is responsible.

The film begins with a shot of a semi-naked woman with a severely disfigured face. The brief scene works as a synthesis that prefigures the film as a whole, as the beautiful, scantily clad body with the horrible face unites sex with horror. Later, as Rossiter looks for a place to hide in France he finds Nicole, a teenager whose face is scarred after a series of bombings during the Second World War. Rossiter is fascinated with the girl and the idea of turning her into a beautiful "thing."

After her surgery, the film jumps from the 1940s which is depicted as a sad age, the war still lingering in society, to the 1960s, and the circus flourishes and becomes rich under Rossiter's leadership. In essence, the film jumps from an era of trauma to one of spectacle. This shift parallels the interventions practiced by the doctor on disfigured women as he transforms them and makes them beautiful; the traumatic reality of the past is wiped away by the act of transforming physical traces of the bombings, and trauma of the past, into beauty and spectacle.

In this process, it seems, traumatic events cannot be represented as anything but spectacle, as an artificial, sanitized surface that impedes any historical reconstruction; the past has been turned circus-y. As Adam Lowenstein argues, "when traumatic experience becomes equated solely with the "unrepresentable," then the respect for victims/survivors transforms, paradoxically, into a silencing of both experience and representation" (5). The painful French (and by extension, British) past is transformed, thanks to plastic surgery, into spectacle, and thus, silenced: what Simone de Beauvoir called, in 1961 (a year after the opening of the film), "a sort of tetanus of the imagination" (qtd. in Lowenstein 48).

The Schuler circus specializes in the display of tableau vivant staging of historical/fictitious women such as Sappho or Helen of Troy, acted by the formerly disfigured women. They are there only as beauties to be looked at, so the impossibility of a recuperation of a real past is twofold: thanks to the logic of the industry of spectacle, the historical past is turned into a frozen, uncritical image of beauty where strong women are de-powered when turned into objects to be looked at rather than figures with agency; secondly, these historical figures are represented by women whose personal scars have been healed not through strenuous psychological labor or internal healing but rather, plastic surgery. Nicole, after her operation, is worried about not recognizing herself, her subjectivity now irrecoverable. Melina (Yvonne Romain), a woman running away from the law and another of Rossiter's creations, is turned into a sensual spectacle of beauty (Helen of Troy) which prompts her to repeat insistently "I don't feel pain any more"; she is healed from a traumatic past by removing scars from her face. However, Rossiter's attempt to

A tableaux vivant depicting the past as an empty, depoliticized spectacle of beauty in *Circus of Horrors*. Magda (Vanda Hudson) at the center.

erase physical evidence of the recent past is not necessarily benign; in fact, by a process of plastic surgery and grafting, Rossiter could be seen as attempting to erase the evidence of the country's recent history. History is crucial for Debord, as he sees the basis of spectacle as the annihilation of historical knowledge, in concrete, the destruction of the most recent past. Through Rossiter's tableau vivant, the past itself has become a commodity to be passively contemplated.

In fact, Rossiter wants the circus because it is the perfect façade to hide behind, a smoke screen hiding horrors and criminals running from their pasts. Rossiter keeps his girls in line by keeping personal files on their sordid history. One of his most beautiful "creations" is a murderous prostitute he had met in a grim bar years before; another murdered the man who had disfigured her face with acid. This narrative resembles the reality of criminals of war escaping across the globe and hiding their dark past behind false identities.[5]

Circus of Horrors is padded with scenes filmed in the Billy Smart Circus. Between the murders orchestrated by Rossiter to eliminate the women who stand in his way or try to abandon him, viewers can enjoy acts extracted from a *real* circus. Even though audiences were not actually at the circus, it is a good simulacra: these scenes depict not actors "playing" as circus performers, but real circus performers performing real, sensational acts, thus taking the film closer to documentary. *Circus of Horrors'* narrative of attractions progresses from a prostitute killing a man in a dark alley to a semi-naked glittering female acrobat realizing extraordinary aerial feats, to a comic act performed by clowns, an equestrian scene, a parade of elephants, the taming of roaring lions, and a man dressed as an Indian throwing knives to another beautiful semi-naked woman who ends up dead after Rossiter orchestrates her "accident." Following the logic of both contemporary sensationalism and the society of spectacle, the narrative gives a sense of "totalitarian cohesion" (Debord 36), collecting together disparate contents: the spectacle of circus and the spectacle of murder, narrative film, a cinema of attractions, and the documentary. "Fragmented views of reality regroup themselves into a new unity as a separate pseudoworld that can only be looked at" (Debord 8).

Like *Circus of Horrors*, *Berserk!* gives some sense of unity to scenes of clowns, acrobatics (also lifted from the Billy Smart Circus), and grisly murders. Joan Crawford portrays Monica Rivers, the owner and ring-master of the "The Great Rivers Circus." Monica is a tough-as-nails woman hell-bent on running her circus even if a murderer is killing her employees one by one in bizarre fashion. For example, one tight-rope walker is hanged by his own tight-rope after it snaps during a live performance. Like in *Circus of Horrors*, the narrative chains together scenes of circus performances (equilibrists, the taming of lions, etc.) but, unlike Hayers' film, *Berserk!* presents full length sequences disconnected from the grisly main narrative, thus, a real callback to the cinema of attractions of early filmmaking. Thus, a parade of elephants led by a pretty woman fills five minutes of screen time, as does the act "Phyllis Allan and her intelligent poodles." These lengthy sequences interrupt the main narration and action, a breaking of the general mood especially noticeable in *Berserk!*, a horror film that revels in displaying puppies walking upright. To further destroy any sense of internal logic, there is a lengthy musical number ("It Might Be Me") performed by the circus crew (the strong man, the dwarf, the bearded lady, and the skeleton man) which not only interrupts the proper flow of the narrative, but also tears down the fourth wall. During the singing scene, all four performers sing standing in a row. However, in each solo, the singer leading the song moves closer to the camera until framed into a close shot, and sings his or her part looking straight to the camera's eye, thus to the real viewers seeing *Berserk!* in theaters. This sequence addresses the fact that the film is conscious about its ambivalent nature as spectacle of horror and of circus, providing, without subterfuge, an extra-diegetic moment—a spectacle within the spectacle, as in Méliès' films— in which the characters recognize the presence of a camera.

The circus sequences of both *Circus of Horrors* and *Berserk!* work as autonomous set pieces within the main narrative. With the exception of the scenes where a murder takes place, these "fun" scenes do not propel the narration in any way. They are a form of spectacle—the circus—within another form of spectacle—film. Their purpose is twofold: they help pad the films to a logical running time and they enhance the experience of spectacle. The thrill of a spectacular murder, such as a woman sawn in half in a literal way in *Berserk!*, is just another sensational experience connected to the laughs provided by clowns or the emotion provided by acrobats. Rather than privilege an internal logic, both films foreground the sensation narrative, thus connecting straight to the Victorian era and the sensation novel.

It could be argued that the separate scenes are highly fetishized; each is so spectacular—the semi-naked women, the bloody murders, the circus itself—that viewers, going from shock to shock, simply forget that the main narrative is under severe decomposition. The plot gets increasingly weaker, supplanted by autonomous scenes of attractions and sensation which come to replace coherence. The end of *Berserk!*, for example, defies logic. The killer turns out to be Monica's daughter, Angela (Judy Geeson), who only joins the circus when the film is past its middle point and the first murders have already taken place. Further, there is no clear explanation of Angela's motives to kill and, in the head-scratching climax, she is punished not by the actions of a character within the film but by a lightning bolt that conveniently strikes her after she reveals herself as the killer.

The outcome of the spectacle is narrative decomposition. Nothing truly coherent can be sustained any longer, and the simple exercise of critical thought becomes impossible, for any judgment is interrupted by a sensational scene and sentimental imperatives. Both films, rather than follow the logic of narrative cinema, follow the logic of circus: there is no discernible common thread but rather a series of spectacularized scenes weakly connected one to the other.

Both Dr. Rossiter and Monica Rivers work as ring-masters presenting to audiences the spectacles of horror. Both try to capitalize on the murders, cashing in on the general public and their morbid fascination with death by ensuring that the "show must go on," even when the Schuler Circus is called "the tragic circus" by the press; of course, box office receipts were better after the murders began, a situation that paralleled the morbid worldview of Victorian fiction. Not unrelatedly, both Rivers and Rossiter call the people "morbid" in their fascination for spectacle of death.

Further multiplying the spectacle, people being thrilled became spectacle in itself. Audiences watching *Circus of Horrors* or *Berserk!*, in turn, will watch audiences watching a circus onscreen. Seated in cinema theaters, people watch people watching, as both films present within their diegetic narrative various shots of audiences filmed during real performances of the Billy Smart Circus. Like a mirror, audiences will see audiences, increasing the sense of spectacle, in close shots of people enjoying a spectacle, and passiveness in audiences watching audiences. Common people have become the spectacle in the society of spectacle. There is no participation; theatergoers simply

In *Circus of Horrors* (1960), a documentary image lifted from a real circus turns anonymous circus-goers into spectacle themselves.

watch others cheering and clapping. The spectator in either case has no control over what he or she is seeing, and scenes of people clapping are inserted as a way to rob spectators of their own role: that of reacting. As Debord states, spectacle is a commodity ruling over all lived experience, a "never-ending monologue of self-praise" (15).

Circus of Horrors was sold to audiences in the 1960s as filmed in "Specta-Color," a made-up name that foregrounds the gaze of the viewers in the film's promotion. Clearly, those promoting the film privileged the act of seeing (spectacle) rather than narrative coherence. At once shocking (murders, aerial feats) and familiar (images belonging to British cultural sensational imaginary), the films reflected what Smelik calls a "performance of the real" in which the real appears at its most staged (67). The narratives blurred the boundaries between reality and performance. The films troubled traditional frames of witnessing; they involved an entanglement of the two modalities of consciousness—perception and imagination—through which distinguishing between fact and fiction becomes a difficult task (Magnusson and Zalloua 8–9). In relation to the gaze, *Circus of Horrors* was part of the "Sadean trilogy" of the Anglo-Amalgamated studio (the other two being Arthur Crabtree's *Horrors of the Black Museum* and the now classic Michael Powell's film *Peeping Tom*, 1960). The trilogy shared an obsession "with voyeurism, fetishized images of female disfigurement and sadistic, Caligari-like patriarchal figures" (Heffernan 128). Thus, *Circus of Horrors* was not alone in the obsessive attention to the gaze practiced through horror films in the 1960s.

Horror cinema circa 1970s was caught up in an artistic dilemma: innovation of style, story, or form became necessary due to expectations intrinsic to the new British cinema of the era, which was quickly leaving behind the highly artificial, staged melodramas of old to embrace the realism taking America by assault. Increasingly throughout the 1960s and 1970s, the conventions of horror aesthetics embraced "emotional realism" (Lowenstein 55). The documentary-like sequences lifted from real circuses, the circus attractions, and sensation horror put into tension the British desire to embrace a more raw form of cinema in the 1970s. Traditional horror, realism, and sensational spectacle were in uneasy collaboration.

The last of the "classic" horror/circus films, Robert Young's *Vampire Circus*, opens in the 1970s, a decade rife with contradictions of its own, charged with the decline of the countercultural movements and ethos, "the youthful optimism of the 1960s degenerated into the sociopolitical rigidity and complacency of the 1980s" (Forster and Harper 2). However, it was also a time of experimentation, optimism, and increase in the visibility of Civil Rights. In brief, "a time of immense complexity in almost every sphere" (Forster and Harper 3).

Vampire Circus concerns a village under siege by a mysterious lethal plague connected with a dark episode in the small community's past concerning an evil vampire Count who once terrorized them. The township is now cut off from the outside world, and while they apprehensively await some outside medical help, a traveling circus arrives. The villagers welcome it as a way to escape their current somber predicament, but the circus is, in fact, a form of revenge for past crimes. The community that eagerly visits the circus to forget their worries in the arena of spectacle, slowly vampirizes and turns victims of their own passivity. As with *Circus of Horrors*, the main characters of *Vampire Circus* are running away from their sordid pasts, and thus are eager to embrace the politics of bread and circuses. The film's long prologue begins with the village's people storming the castle inhabited by the Count Mitterhaus (Robert Tayman) and his bride Anna (Domini Blythe), who have been feasting on the blood of the village's children. The villagers have decided to take justice into their own hands and rid the world of the vampire even through afraid of the Count's power. After killing Mitterhaus, the villagers "rescue" Anna. The wife of one of the villagers, Anna is not a vampire but a woman who has chosen to stay as the Count's consort; she is undressed and flogged almost to death before she can escape from her captors—the village's men.

The punishment seems to be unleashed upon her due her adulteress role rather than her involvement in the murders. As a sexually active woman who prefers her lover over her husband, "she is there because she wants to" as a villager gravely says to Anna's husband. The masculinity of the village is at stake here. Anna's punishment is inseparable from the "politically charged iconography of torture that invites the connection of private affect with public history" (Lowenstein 48). The situation resembles "the *tonte*, those incidents where French women suspected of having slept with the enemy during the Occupation were subjected to humiliating public head shavings" (Lowenstein 51), i.e., the exculpation of national past crimes and guilt via the female body. Through the lengthy prologue, it is explicitly stated that the Count has been kidnapping and killing girls for months. With their silence, the villagers have been the vampires' partners in crime; the village was more preoccupied with keeping the status quo than solving the mystery of disappearing children. At the climax of the prologue, only the Count and Anna are punished for the crimes; Mitterhaus is impaled and the woman escapes.

After the prologue, the film follows a "The Mask of the Red Death" scheme in which the upper class, those protected within the thick walls of their castles, insist on momentarily forgetting all about the plague haunting the country which, they begin to suspect, may be related to the communal murder of Mitterhaus fifteen years before—in effect staying in the "bread and circuses" mentality. Any traumatic public event is, then, momentarily subsumed into the politics of spectacle, a dead end terminating only in sensation.

Vampire Circus contains the common parade of clowns, dwarfs, equilibrists, gypsies, a strong man, and wild animals. The circus also displays the spectacles of a man taming a she-snake, and Emil (Anthony Corlan), a man with the power to transform himself into a panther. Many villagers come to see the sensations and thrills that the circus has to offer and, even when some of the performances are truly frightening (people transforming into beasts), the villagers are more than happy to cast aside their worries for a night or two. Unlike both *Circus of Horrors* and *Berserk!*, Young's film does not contain scenes filmed in a real circus, for a number of reasons. As a period film (circa 1800), *Vampire Circus* presents difficulties in inserting sequences filmed in contemporary circuses. The *mise-en-scène*, a precarious circus in the middle of nowhere, without a tent, furthers the impossibility of matching images of real circuses with the fable of *Vampire Circus*. It is possible to point, however, to another reason: Robert Young's film critiques the politics of *empty spectacle*. The villagers' doom is not the vampires per se, but the villagers' absolute incapacity to stop attending the circus every night, despite being aware from the beginning that something is askew. Even when the town's burgermeister (Thorley Walters) is attacked by vampires in the Hall of Mirrors, the villagers, including those guilty of killing Count Mitterhaus so long ago, continue attending the circus. And despite the growing number of victims, people seem incapable of staying away. They are mesmerized by the spectacle and genuinely surprised to learn that the circus has been in town an entire week before they decide to take logical measures to counterattack.

It is not by chance that the common device used by the vampires to kill their victims is the House of Mirrors, an attraction formulated specifically around gaze. At first, the guests see deformed versions of themselves. The vampires attack only at the last mirror, one that returns a normal image. Within this particular attraction, the villagers gaze at themselves, and as such cannot escape their pasts. There is no more spectacle; just a common reflection. At the film's climax, the survivors burn the circus to ashes, ending not just the film but also an era marked by the decline of melodramatic horror and the brief but interesting corpus of horror/circus films.

Conclusion

This small corpus was an integral part of an era characterized by interlaced struggles over the national legacy of World War II, Britain's traumatic "people's war," at a time when the UK had to "fight as one united nation devoid of class antagonisms" (Lowenstein 58). The process of "spectacularization" and that of "bread and circuses" helped to create the sensation of swinging London, filled with hedonistic tendencies. In this regard, both *Circus of Horrors* and *Berserk!* created a spectacle of the swinging London era in Debord's sense: a powerful media image that reproduced the image of passive spectators participating in visual spectacle, directed by the consumer industry.

The circus/horror films recuperated the logic of the sensational novel of the Victorian age. As the mindset of modernism invited a new type of fiction that unified disparate aspects of the rapidly changing landscape of the nation, the 1960s, an era contradictorily dominated by audio-visual experimentation and audio-visual commoditization, presented spectacle as the utopia into which to escape. If Debord never established a concrete beginning of the society of spectacle, it can be inferred that he marked the 1920s as the starting point. However, the 1960s can be pointed to as the decade par excellence that marks the beginning of the link between image spectacle, the market, and rapid obsolesce of the media (the exploitation of the 3-D system beginning in the 1950s). For some, the 1960s saw the birth of postmodernism thanks to its playful experimentation and the crisis of the visual and its meanings. As Sebastian Groes argues through his book *British Fictions of the Sixties: The Making of the Swinging Decade*, the 1960s was not so much the starting point of the crisis of the visual, but the era marked its intensification and acceleration: fictional representation and the real become one, and experience was increasingly filtered through media.

It is within this scenario that horror and circus narratives blended together to recuperate some of the sensational fiction of the Victorian age and the aesthetics of the cinema of attractions of earlier filmmaking. Rather than a coherent story, *Circus of Horrors* and *Berserk!* offer the (il)logic of the circus: disparate scenes turned events, weakly united through the logic of spectacle. These garish shockers exploited the mixed emotions audiences felt when watching circus performances: the possibility, in fact the prospect, of something going terribly wrong is horrifying, yet exciting.

Through *Vampire Circus*, spectators fall into the trap of spectacle, as spectatorship reveals itself as deadly. Unlike *Circus of Horrors* and *Berserk!*, the victims of *Vampire Circus* are *the viewers* of the show. Only in running away from spectacle could they comprehend their situation and understand that the horror (the circus) comes from their own past. Survival depended on the rejection of passive spectatorship.

By the 1960s, Debord stipulates one of his main theses: "the more the spectator contemplates, the less he lives" (18). *Vampire Circus*, closing the corpus of horror/circus films of the 1960s, warns us as it demonstrates the truth of this dark possibility.

Notes

1. More a crime/mystery film than horror, I leave it aside in my analysis. However, it is indisputable that it forms part of the corpus of British "chillers" with a circus setting.

2. An international organization of social revolutionaries, avant-garde artists, intellectuals, and political theorists. Prominent in Europe 1957–1972.

3. Originating in Rome in the 1st century, the phrase refers to the idea that the masses can be kept happy by food and faster entertainment, regardless of their circumstances or future prospects.

4. "Look for a Star," sung by Gary Mills, haunts *Circus of Horrors* at various times. The song became highly popular and was a hit on both sides of the Atlantic. The records were sold with the poster of the film printed on the record label.

5. In *Berserker*, Monica Rivers (Joan Crawford) compares the circus with war: "people will fall, but the show must go on," further connecting the life under the big top with the waterfront. Also, like in *Circus of Horrors*, people fleeing from their past come to the River Circus to hide away from prying eyes.

Works Cited

Burwick, Frederick. *Playing to the Crowd: London Popular Theatre, 1780–1830*. Palgrave Macmillan, 2011.

Crary, Jonathan. *Suspensions of Perception: Attention, Spectacle, and Modern Culture*. MIT P, 2001.

Davis, Janet. *The Circus Age: Culture & Society Under the American Big Top*. U of North Carolina P, 2002.

Debord, Guy. *The Society of Spectacle*. Hobgoblin, 2002.

Fenner, Angelica. *Race Under Reconstruction in German Cinema: Robert Stemmle's Toxi*. U of Toronto P, 2011.

Gabriele, Alberto. "Introduction: Sensationalism and the Genealogy of Modernity: Transnational Currents, Intermedial Trajectories—A Global Nineteenth-Century Approach." *Sensationalism and the Genealogy of Modernity: A Global Nineteenth-Century*, edited by Alberto Gabriele, Palgrave Macmillan, 2017, pp. 1–26.

Garret, Roberta. "Gender, Sex, and the Family." *British Cultural Identities*, 2nd ed., edited by Mike Storry and Peter Childs, Routledge, 2002, pp. 111–138.

Gunning, Tom. "The Cinema of Attraction: Early Film, Its Spectator and the Avant-Garde," *Wide Angle*, vol. 8, nos. 3–4, 1986, pp. 63–70.

Heffernan, Kevin. *Ghouls, Gimmicks, and Gold: Horror Films and the American Movie Business, 1953–1968*. Duke UP, 2004.

Hughes, Winifred. "The Sensation Novel." *A Companion to the Victorian Novel*, edited by Patrick Brantlinger and William B. Thesing, Blackwell Publishing, 2002, pp. 260–278.

Jervis, John. *Sensational Subjects: The Dramatization of Experience in the Modern World*. Bloomsbury, 2015.

Kellner, Douglas. *Media Spectacle*. Routledge, 2003.

Laing, Stuart. "The Politics of Culture: Institutional Change in the 1970s," in Bart Moore-Gilbert (ed.), *The Arts in the 1970s: Cultural Closure?* Routledge, 2013, pp. 29–56.

Ledesma, Eduardo. *Radical Poetry: Aesthetics, Politics, Technology, and the Ibero-American Avant-Gardes, 1900–2015*. SUNY P, 2016.

Lowenstein, Adam. *Shock Representation: Historical Trauma, National Cinema, and the Modern Horror Film*. Columbia UP, 2005.

Magnusson, Bruce, and Zahi Zalloua. "Introduction: From Events to Spectacles." *Spectacle*, edited by Bruce Magnusson and Zahi Zalloua, U of Washington P, 2016, pp. 3–17.

McAuley, Robert. *Out of Sight: Crime, Youth and Exclusion in Modern Britain*. Routledge, 2007.

Meikle, Denis. *A History of Horrors: The Rise and Fall of the House of Hammer*. Scarecrow, 2009.

Moran, Maureen. *Catholic Sensationalism and Victorian Literature*. Liverpool UP, 2007.

Obelkevich, James. "Consumption." *Understanding Post-War British Society*, edited by James Obelkevich and Peter Catterall, Routledge, 1994, pp. 141–154.

Petley, Julian. "'A Crude Sort of Entertainment for a Crude Sort of Audience': The British Critics and Horror Cinema." *British Horror Cinema*, edited by Steve Chibnall and Julian Petley, Routledge, 2002, pp. 23–41.

Schatz, Thomas. *Boom and Bust: American Cinema in the 1940s*. U of California P, 1997.

Smelik, Anneke. "Mediating Memories: The Ethics of Post-9/11 Spectatorship." *Spectacle*, edited by Bruce Magnusson and Zahi Zalloua, U of Washington P, 2016, pp. 65–87.

Stoddart, Helen. *Rings of Desire: Circus History and Representation*. Manchester UP, 2000.

Storey, Mark. *Rural Fictions, Urban Realities: A Geography of Gilded Age American Literature*. Oxford UP, 2013.

Ward, Steve. *Beneath the Big Top: A Social History of the Circus in Britain*. Pen & Sword History, 2014.

After the Glitter Fades

Analyzing Ingmar Bergman's Cinematic Representation of Circus Life

Kylo-Patrick R. Hart

Anyone who is familiar with the career and lived experiences of Swedish director Ingmar Bergman already knows that he did not have the easiest of childhoods. For example, in his autobiography *The Magic Lantern*, Bergman writes about his upbringing as one filled with regular use of the silent treatment and humiliating punishments by his parents (*Magic* 7–8). He describes the early years of his life as being ones regularly "tormented by desire, fear, anguish and a guilty conscience" (Bergman, *Magic* 146). He constantly felt the pressures associated with growing up in a strict religious family as the son of a Lutheran minister, whom he has characterized as being irritable and depressive, at least in part because his father's actions and family life were regularly the subjects of discussion and criticism from members of the congregation (Bergman, *Magic* 9, 134); such realities led his familial patriarch to worry continuously about being inadequate and motivated the outward appearance of "an irreproachable picture of good family unity [that] was inwardly [one of] misery and exhausting conflicts" (Bergman, *Magic* 134). He never got along particularly well with either his older brother or younger sister, and he regarded both his father and mother as "suffocating and incomprehensible" (Bergman, *Magic* 57) human beings. He recalls lengthy periods when he found himself feuding constantly with his parents or, alternately, not speaking to them at all (Bergman, *Images* 17). In response to those unpleasant realities and others, young Ingmar would occasionally act out, such as when he tried to murder his young sister out of jealousy or a friend who betrayed his confidence, or when he physically assaulted a girl he was dating, as the pressures from the parsonage became too much for him to bear (Bergman, *Magic* 2, 12, 116).

It is to be expected, therefore, that during his childhood Ingmar sought out distinct ways to make his daily existence more tolerable. For example, he enjoyed hours of release in fantasy, which were provided by viewing images with his cinematograph or creating new worlds with his puppet playhouse (Bergman, *Magic* 16). About such experiences he has expressed, "My imagination and senses were given nourishment, and I remember nothing dull, in fact the days and hours kept exploding with wonders, unexpected sights and magical moments" (Bergman, *Magic* 13). When those approaches failed to adequately distract him, however, he found himself fantasizing about running away from home to join the circus.

Bergman's early love of the circus was fostered by a rich woman, whom his family referred to as Aunt Anna, who took him each year to the premiere performance of the Schumann Circus on the island of Djurgården. As he explains:

> This event drove me into a state of feverish excitement: the car journey with Aunt Anna's uniformed chauffeur, going into the huge brightly lit wooden building, the secret smells, Aunt Anna's voluminous hat, the blaring orchestra, the magic of the preparations and the roaring of lions and tigers behind the red draperies of the circus entrance [Bergman, *Magic* 11].

An image from one performance particularly stood out to him, after his attention was seized by some vibrant music: "a young woman was riding around on a huge black stallion" (Bergman, *Magic* 11). He recalls that, at the age of seven, he was overcome with emotion for this woman and increasingly included her in his fantasy games, referring to her as "Esmeralda" (Bergman, *Magic* 11). It was not long before he lied to a male classmate, under an oath of secrecy, that his parents had sold him to the Schumann Circus and that he would soon be trained to perform as an acrobat with Esmeralda, whom he considered to be the world's most beautiful woman (Bergman, *Magic* 11).

Given such fond recollections, it is perhaps entirely unsurprising that Bergman opted to write and direct a circus-themed film early in his career with 1953's *Sawdust and Tinsel*, the first cinematic offering that garnered early international attention for him. What *is* surprising, however, is the degree to which his overall negative representation of circus life—in this serious art film exploring adult themes—differs so substantially from the far more positive recollections he has shared from his childhood.

Ingmar Bergman Makes a Circus Movie

During the second half of the 20th century, Ingmar Bergman consistently utilized the medium of film to wrestle with his personal issues and demons as he created a series of movies that explore (among other topics) memories and fantasies from his childhood, humiliation experienced by artists of various kinds, and the complexity of romantic and sexual relationships involving heterosexual women and men (Hart 107). Impressively, all three of those common themes from the director's oeuvre are already being explored in *Sawdust and Tinsel*, which focuses on the actions and interactions of Albert Johansson (played by Åke Grönberg), the aging owner of the Cirkus Alberti, who finds himself inexorably torn between: his longtime love of the traveling circus life; the affection he feels for his mistress, Anne (played by Harriet Andersson), who travels and performs with him; and his competing desire to return to the more stable life he abandoned when he left his wife and young sons behind years earlier.

In contrast to his childhood reflections on the circus as being a place of excitement, magic, wonder, and joy, Bergman's representation of circus life in *Sawdust and Tinsel* is far more dreary and depressing. It soon becomes quite evident that Bergman is indeed exploring the theme of memories and fantasies from his childhood in the film, yet from the more realistic perspective of a grown man rather than that of a wide-eyed, mesmerized boy. This distinction is immediately suggested by the starkly contrasting notes evident in the music accompanying the film's opening credits, which shift quickly from spirited and whimsical to menacing and dramatic. Immediately thereafter, black-and-white images from this cinematic creation start flashing across the screen: somber gray skies; dramatic silhouettes; a caravan of horses and trailers squeaking their way through a silent, sleeping world. As a coachman begins to wail a particularly eerie tune while leading the wagons across the vast countryside to their next destination, it is clear that Bergman's approach to depicting circus life in this film will be quite unlike the way he experienced circus realities as a child.

It is particularly telling that, when the circus caravan reaches the town of its next performance, the coachman's wailing fades as rain begins to fall. The scene transforms into a torrential downpour at the same moment that props must be unloaded, animals tended to, and the big top erected by all of the male and female circus workers and performers as Albert looks on, grimacing. It is not long before the tired performers begin to reveal the ongoing realities of their circus-based existence. In addition to currently being quite cold and wet, none of them have been paid recently and they have nothing to eat. They had to leave half of their costumes behind (presumably sold to obtain some money to help keep the circus financially afloat awhile longer) in the last town. Several of their accompanying children have worms. Their wagons are infested with fleas. The performing bear has been ill for some time and appears to be on the brink of death.

To make himself feel less of a failure and fire up his circus colleagues,

Albert suggests that they collaboratively lead a parade through town to generate interest in their upcoming performance. He inspires them with visions of bands playing, elephants trumpeting, and cheering people lining the streets, and instructs them to make some promotional posters, assemble the horses and wagons, don the best costumes they have left, put on their biggest smiles, and immediately depart. At this point, the workers' spirits have been lifted and the sun has begun to shine. Playful music fills their campsite. As they begin to encounter the townsfolk on their journey, they are an enthusiastic, eye-catching lot, promising a dazzling evening filled with beauty, thrills, magnificent costumes and sets, and endless laughter to all who choose to attend. Their animated promotional efforts are immediately halted, however, by a group of police officials who point out that their permit-less parade is illegal, order them back to the fairground to practice their "art," and seize their horses for twenty-four hours to teach them a lesson. The members of the crowd chuckle as the circus performers begin pushing their carriage out of town. It is evident that the "damned carnies" (as one of the officials refers to them) are not particularly welcome in respectable society.

Although early in the film Albert assures Anne he has a feeling the circus's luck is bound to change, little hope exists that this will occur anytime soon. When Anne visits an actor at a local theater, he points out that she reeks of cheap perfume, stables, and sweat. About the same time, Albert expresses his ever-growing desire to sell the circus tent, horses, and costumes in order to begin a new chapter of his life. It is not long before Albert admits to Anne that, with their vagabond existence, they are stuck together in hell, and he confesses to one of the clowns how desperately he wants out of the circus business. Before the film concludes, and at the end of an emotionally draining day, Albert's growing sense of desperation motivates him to hold a loaded pistol to his head and pull the trigger; however, there is no bullet in the selected chamber, so he is left to continue on in his everyday circus life. (He does successfully end up firing one bullet into a nearby mirror and two more into the sick bear, in order to put at least one of the circus performers out of its ongoing misery.)

The theme of humiliation experienced by artists of various kinds is explored most directly in the film during a scene that contrasts stage actors with circus performers. Just prior to the circus parade through town, Albert and Anne visit the local theater director, Sjuberg (played by Gunnar Björnstrand), with the goal of borrowing some fancy costumes for their upcoming performance. The two don their finest fashions (which nevertheless look quite garish when compared to those of the local townspeople), hoping to make the most positive impression possible. Upon their arrival at the theater, Albert instructs Anne to simply smile, look pretty, and show off her bosom and legs and let him do all the talking. Offended that anyone has interrupted one of his rehearsals, Sjuberg immediately orders an underling to tell his unexpected visitors to go to hell. Seconds later and apparently a bit amused, however, he reverses that decision and feigns excitement to meet them. Albert attempts to depart gracefully, but he and Anne are quickly led into the director's presence.

After introducing himself to Sjuberg and (falsely) claiming that Anne is his wife, Albert requests, while adding that he and Sjuberg are professional colleagues of sorts, that the circus be lent an assortment of trousers, capes, and hats. He seems entirely unprepared for Sjuberg's insulting response, which suggests that any costumes borrowed would ultimately be returned infested with lice, scabies, and strange diseases. Sjuberg emphasizes that he has never dealt with the likes of circus performers before, and that doing so now would likely be a dreadful decision. He proceeds to make Albert grovel after forcing him to admit that he is unable to provide any sort of payment in return. Rubbing additional salt into Albert's wounds, Sjuberg notes that although theater and circus folks are certainly both artists of sorts, the former make art while the latter deal in artifice, and "the lowest of us would spit on the best of you." Nevertheless, while staring directly into Anne's bosom as he speaks, Sjuberg instructs Albert to borrow whatever costumes he desires on the condition that his theater troupe be invited to attend the evening's circus performance for free.

Without question, the theme of the complexity of romantic and sexual relationships involving heterosexual women and men is quite prominent in *Sawdust and Tinsel*. For example, viewers learn early in the film that, because he has been traveling so extensively with his circus, it has been three years since Albert has last seen his wife and sons. That situation is about to change, however, because the troupe has now returned temporarily to the town where his family resides. Realizing that Albert plans to visit his wife and children, Anne immediately becomes insecure and begs him to never leave her. As he prepares for his impetuous reunion, Albert admonishes Anne for drinking in the morning in an attempt to quell her insecurities; in return, she calls Albert an "old buzzard" who is rickety, scared, and hoping to reunite with his wife and family, with the aim of putting circus life behind him forever. Although he assures Anne that he loves her and will be back in time for the evening's show, she threatens to no longer be around by the time he returns.

When Albert visits his wife's tobacco shop and attached home, he is disappointed that his nine-year-old son does not recognize him and expresses he would never be interested in joining the circus. Agda (played by Annika Tretow), his spouse, generously feeds him lunch, provides him with a drink of brandy, sews a button on his jacket, and offers to loan him money if he needs it. During this same interaction, Agda emphasizes that she found peace when Albert left, discovering what it is like to have a life of her own—and one that thankfully is entirely devoid of people shouting and swearing, always being on the road, lice, disease, misery, and hard years when she was constantly freezing and afraid. As a result, she has no interest in his giving up the circus lifestyle so they might one day be together again.

During Albert and Anne's visit to Sjuberg to borrow costumes, Anne had locked eyes with the attractively effeminate actor named Frans (played by Hasse Ekman), who immediately expresses his desire to sleep with her. Anne discourages his advances, instructing him not to speak disparagingly about her "husband" Albert or to touch her without her approval; she ends up biting Frans on the face to halt his unwanted advances when he attempts to take her by force. Frans then insults her by asking her price, suggesting that she is a prostitute. Anne retorts, noting that he is as pretty as a girl and, as a result, has likely never actually satisfied a woman. "You're not so pretty with red ears. Touch me and I'll bite that mouth to shreds," Anne cautions. "I'll make mincemeat of it." Although Frans begs her forgiveness, she departs after giving the man one momentary peck on the lips. However, out of jealousy that Albert has gone to visit his wife and will likely abandon her, Anne returns to the theater later that day in search of the actor. During this latter interaction, she approaches Frans in his dressing room, expressing that she wants to leave the circus and have him take care of her. She appears much more open to the prospect of seduction and fails to take offense when Frans offers to "lick [her] clean like a dog." She suggests that they arm wrestle, which leads to him telling her she is locked in his room until he gets what he wants. To make her more amenable to his sexual proposition, he promises to provide her with both the key to the locked door and a valuable amulet—which he claims she can live on for an entire year once it is hers—upon the conclusion of their tryst. Perhaps unsurprisingly, Anne soon learns that the amulet is worthless and, without any other viable options in sight, returns to the circus to be with Albert.

When they are reunited, Anne is unaware that Albert witnessed her in town earlier as she attempted to sell the amulet to the local goldsmith, so he strongly suspects that she has been unfaithful. Although she initially (and repeatedly) denies her infidelity, Anne eventually admits what she has done. "Want to know what I think?" Albert responds. "I think you went to see him because you're as sick of the circus and me as I am of the circus and you." Nevertheless, and despite everything they have been through in the preceding twenty-four hours, at the film's end the two choose to walk together in the night behind the circus carriages, off to their next destination.

Analyzing Sawdust and Tinsel

The only aspect of Bergman's childhood circus recollections that appears to have made it into *Sawdust and Tinsel* in relatively pure form is the director's aforementioned affection for the extremely beautiful, horse-riding "Esmeralda," whom he portrays in this film through the role of Anne. During the work's concluding circus performance, Albert introduces Anne to the crowd as "the highlight of the evening: a fiery Spanish rider astride an Andalusian thoroughbred" and "an act you'll never forget"; earlier on, Anne brags to Frans that she is the circus' "Spanish señorita" capable of riding "great geldings bareback at a full gallop, holding on with just [her] thighs." Other than Anne/Esmerelda, however, as noted above the circus-based film Bergman opted to create as an adult differs substantially from the one he would likely have made as a child. In fact, the contents of this film are so mature in their themes and representational approaches that it was released in the United States with the alternate (and intentionally more salacious) title *The Naked Night*, rather than *Sawdust and Tinsel*.

After starting off with a series of shots in the present, *Sawdust and Tinsel* cuts immediately to a flashback scene from seven years earlier that tells "the story of Poor Old Frost." As Bergman states in his book *Images: My Life in Film*: "The drama [of *Sawdust and Tinsel*] had its origin in a dream. I depicted the dream in the flashback about Frost and [his wife] Alma" (184). During this powerful flashback sequence, the character named Frost learns that his wife is swimming nude in front of a group of soldiers, who have paid her to do so. He rushes to the scene, pulls her from the water, and begins to slowly carry her home, amid jeers and laughter, past soldiers and phallic weaponry. A close-up of Frost's face reveals pained eyes, troubled lines, and plenty of chalky white makeup, i.e., he is a clown, albeit a tragic one.[1] As he walks, Frost struggles, stumbles, and then ultimately falls to the ground, unable (or perhaps unwilling) to rise. As the dreamlike sequence draws to a close, Frost is represented as a humiliated, heartbroken figure.

It is noteworthy that several of the central women in *Sawdust and Tinsel* are portrayed as being superior in both spirit and resourcefulness to the men who surround them. Take Agda and Anne, the two women of central importance in Albert's life, for example. While Albert has barely been able to survive on the meager profits generated by his circus, his wife Agda has, in his absence, managed to establish and maintain a comfortable lifestyle for herself and their sons by working as a tobacconist. While Albert feels the need to cling to one of these women or the other, his mistress Anne musters the courage to try to leave him and his circus forever, selling herself to the highest bidder (the actor Frans) in an attempt to control her own destiny. It comes as little surprise that Bergman would create such strong female characters, however, considering that much of his inspiration for such characters was derived from observing and interacting with his own mother, whom he regarded as being a strong female role model even though he did not particularly like her.

Sadistic tendencies (i.e., the inclination to derive pleasure from inflicting physical or psychological pain on another) also rise to the surface in Bergman's intriguing representation of circus life. In the world of *Sawdust and Tinsel*, it is the character Frans who experiences noteworthy moments of sadistic euphoria. After Anne revisits the actor and confesses that she wants to leave the circus, their initially innocent arm-wrestling match escalates into a take-it-or-leave-it sexual proposition that appears to hold the key to Anne's ultimate freedom as Frans cockily dangles what he claims to be the precious amulet before Anne, her "reward" should she choose to give in and allow him to use her body sexually. The corresponding sexual act which begins on screen is remarkably painful without being physically abusive; Frans savors every second of the encounter, while Anne's face reveals coldness, emotional detachment, psychological distance. As if forcing Anne to prostitute herself for a chance at freedom was not stimulating enough, Frans is able to maximize his sadistic pleasure during the encounter with his knowledge that the "precious" amulet is actually worthless. But even *that* is not enough for the actor. Hours later, Frans attends the evening's circus performance with an attractive woman by his side. When Anne appears on horseback during the show, he proceeds to derive additional sadistic pleasure by shouting to her, "Feel all right after our adventure, sweetheart? How about another ride tonight?" The entire audience, along with Albert and all of Anne's fellow performers, understands fully the implication of his taunts. Anne is mortified; Frans gleams with pleasure, self-satisfaction, pride. Yet because such complex physical and psychological dynamics were common in Bergman's own life as he matured, it seems only natural that they would rise to the surface in one of his early creative works. For example, thinking back to the time when he attempted to murder his baby sister, Bergman writes, "I recall that the deed itself was associated with acute pleasure that rapidly turned into terror" (*Magic* 3). And reflecting on the variety of punishments that were so common during his developmental years, he explains, "I can't maintain that it hurt all that much. The ritual and the humiliation were what was so painful.... After the strokes had been administered, you had to kiss Father's hand, at which forgiveness was declared and the burden of sin fell away, deliverance and grace ensued" (Bergman, *Magic* 8).

A final aspect of note is that Albert's circular exploration path in *Sawdust and Tinsel* leads the protagonist both nowhere and everywhere at once. From beginning to end, *Sawdust and Tinsel* is a spectacle-filled journey film. On an explicit level, it presents the most recent chapter in the continuing journey of circus owner Albert Johansson, his mistress Anne, Frost the Clown, and the rest of the traveling performers. On a more implicit level, it presents the at-times-painful journey of a man passing through a yet-appealing past on his way to perpetual tomorrows. Relatedly, a theme quite evident in *Sawdust and Tinsel* is the longing of a central character for a return to the "good old days," even though such days were less than fully appreciated at the moment they originally occurred. When Albert visits his wife, Agda, and their sons for the first time in several years, he finds that going back can sometimes seem remarkably appealing. Upon his arrival, Albert begins to revel in the security of his wife's daily setting—which stands in dramatic contrast to his everyday vagabond lifestyle—until he is denied the opportunity to remain there indefinitely by an independent woman who is determined to retain her freedom and peace of mind. As Bergman sums it up in *Images*, "Albert Johansson, the circus owner, loves both Anne and his chaotic life in the circus. And yet, he is strongly drawn toward the bourgeois security he had in life with his now-abandoned wife. To put it briefly: he is a walking chaos of conflicting emotions" (185). Nevertheless, although it becomes evident that Albert is longing for a place where life is simpler and trouble-free, he ultimately recommits himself to his vagabond circus lifestyle after exploring potential detours. At the same time, however, Albert does not return to the precise point where he began his cinematic journey even though, geographically speaking, he may at first glance appear to do so. At the film's end, as Bergman himself has noted, "The circus hits the road again. Anne meets [Albert], and the two walk behind the circus trailers, heading for the next stop. The circus rolls onward. On and on forever" (Bergman, *Images* 400). Accordingly, Albert ultimately emerges on a brand new journey stemming from, yet not simply remaining equivalent to, the continuation of another.

Concluding Observations

As Bergman matured, he reached a point in his adult life when he realized he was losing his "joy" and simply "drying up inside" (*Magic* 43). Perhaps that serves to explain, at least in part, why his overall representation of circus life in *Sawdust and Tinsel* differs so substantially from the way that he personally anticipated and experienced the circus as a child.

Without question, *Sawdust and Tinsel* provides a unique and noteworthy depiction of circus life in an earlier historical era, one that is much darker and more serious than viewers might typically expect from a circus-themed media offering. In an interview years later, the director recalled that at the time he made the film, he was well aware that both actors and circus performers were regarded in society as being "scum" (Björkman et al. 83). Nevertheless, about the various appeals of Bergman's complex cinematic vision, critic John Simon has emphasized:

> Here were real people, their lives expressionistically intensified. Along with camera work that boldly made things paler or darker (and richer in chiaroscuro than we were used to at the time), *Sawdust and Tinsel* boasted earthy yet somehow charged, poetically heightened dialogue, alternated with achingly eloquent sequences, all of which would become part of the trademark Bergman style [5].

When all is said and done, it is yet another notable film within which the director offers an intense drama about "desperate or guilt-ridden intimates [who] discover ugly truths about themselves and each other" (Cohen 171). In those regards and related others, the film offers glimpses into a challenging and intriguing world from which Albert verbalizes that he wishes to escape yet finds himself ill-equipped to ever actually do so. For as Bergman himself explains, "He has been so thoroughly poisoned by his own sort of life, where everything is in ceaseless motion. For him, silence is emptiness. For him, everything must keep moving, always" (Björkman et al. 86).

For Albert Johansson and his colleagues in *Sawdust and Tinsel*, daily life is composed of intriguing interactions and journeys that offer a wide range of appealing spectacles, sights, and sounds, including alluring outfits with eye-catching splashes of brilliant color, awe-inspiring exhibitions of strength and skill, and occasional jaw-dropping demonstrations of courage. As a result, the film influences the ways its viewers think about and perceive individual and cultural differences, gender ideologies, and conceptions of human identity by setting its unfolding developments in a unique cinematic world that ends up normalizing atypicality and fueling human fantasies. Ultimately, however, Bergman's cinematic creation utilizes its intimate and somewhat unpredictable atmosphere of glamour and glitz to reveal and explore the widely shared human desire for conventional domesticity, in whatever forms it may be possible to approximate or achieve. In the end, one thing becomes remarkably clear: Albert Johansson truly *is* at home in the environment where *Sawdust and Tinsel* begins, with his loved ones and chosen family members surrounding him, even though it takes his attempts to escape this environment in order for him to achieve this important realization. For Albert, and arguably for Bergman, the circus has finally come home.

NOTE

1. Although I knew *Sawdust and Tinsel* revolved around the traveling Cirkus Alberti and could tell that Frost was a circus performer of some kind, it never dawned on me that Frost was a clown. It was not until much later that this realization was achieved. (I did, however, realize that there were *other* clowns in the film.) This reality is what perplexes me the most about my initial *Sawdust and Tinsel* viewing experience. How could I *not* have made the connection? Maybe it is because Frost the Clown is such a sad, almost tragic figure. Perhaps it is because while Frost's is supposed to resemble a clown's face, there is consistently so much grief and sorrow showing through.

WORKS CITED

Bergman, Ingmar. *Images: My Life in Film*. Translated by Marianne Ruth. Arcade Publishing, 1994.
____. *The Magic Lantern*. Translated by Joan Tate. Penguin, 1988.
Björkman, Stig, Torsten Manns, and Jonas Sima. *Bergman on Bergman: Interviews with Ingmar Bergman*. Translated by Paul Britten Austin. Touchstone, 1973.
Cohen, Hubert. *Ingmar Bergman: The Art of Confession*. Twayne, 1993.
Hart, Kylo-Patrick R. "The Auteur Filmmaker as Star: Reading the Films of Ingmar Bergman as Autobiographical Acts." *Film and Television Stardom*, edited by Kylo-Patrick R. Hart, Cambridge Scholars Publishing, 2008.
Sawdust and Tinsel. Directed by Ingmar Bergman, performances by Harriet Andersson, Gunnar Björnstrand, Hasse Ekman, Åke Grönberg, and Annika Tretow. Sandrews, 1953.
Simon, John. "The Lower Depths." *Sawdust and Tinsel DVD Insert*. Criterion Collection, 2007, pp. 4–11.

Dumbo and the Circus of Childhood

MICHAEL CHARLTON

Dumbo never speaks a single word. Everyone around him is as loud and bustling as the circus itself—the loving mother who gets thrown in a cage for defending her son against taunts and insults, the gossiping matrons who mock him and treat him as a freak, the ringmaster who thrusts him into the spotlight to be embarrassed and ridiculed by the crowd, the clowns who use him as a prop for their antics, the crows who mock him but then give him the secret to his triumph, even the motor-mouthed mouse who takes the place of his absent father. The big top is motion, color, and noise but he is clumsy, gray, and mute. The simplest explanation for his silence is his infancy but he is an anomaly even among his kind. Other classic Disney films from *Bambi* (1942) to *101 Dalmatians* (1961) and modern hits like *The Lion King* (1994) and *Zootopia* (2016) feature young animal protagonists who invariably talk. So why is Dumbo the flying elephant silent?

In many ways *Dumbo* (1941) is an unlikely classic. It was based on a long-forgotten children's story by Helen Aberson and Harold Pearl, made on an intentionally tight budget, and at 64 minutes barely runs to feature length (Maltin 49–53).[1] In addition to the oddity of a non-speaking, almost completely passive main character, the film is highly unconventional in structure. It begins before the protagonist's birth, lacks a real villain, contains the barest bones of a plot in Dumbo's search for a successful circus act, does not introduce the character's defining characteristic of flight until it is nearly over, and has at least one sequence ("Pink Elephants on Parade") which famously departs from the tone of everything else. The main speaking role of Timothy Mouse never even has his name spoken out loud. Yet it was a box office hit, won an Oscar for its score, was reissued to theaters at least four times, spawned a television show and popular theme park attractions around the world, and Tim Burton's remake was released in 2019. This odd little story has been one of the definitive images of the circus for generations of children. What is it that has made *Dumbo* endure? Perhaps part of the answer is that it takes two strange states of being—the circus and childhood—and embraces their oddness.

Depictions of the circus have often presented it as a place of fun and wonder for children. "Running away to join the circus" is the cultural cliché for escaping the ordinary world for one of excitement and splendor. This idea of the circus as an escape connects to theorist Mikhail Bakhtin's concept of the carnival or the carnivalesque. Lachmann summarizes what the carnival means in these terms:

> in the carnivalesque game of inverting social values [Bakhtin] sees the anticipation of another, utopian world in which anti-hierarchism, relativity of values, questioning of authority, openness, joyous anarchy, and the ridiculing of all dogmas hold sway, a world in which syncretism and a myriad of differing perspectives are permitted [118].

In other words, the carnival is a space where accepted social behaviors and values are challenged, thrown out the window, or turned upside down, and the act of mocking these social behaviors and values becomes liberating and allows for different voices. Bakhtin saw this topsy-turvy world of the carnival in all sorts of folk traditions, from the mockery of fools to the games played at fairs to the birth of the novel itself. As Carmeli has noted, the circus is a classic example of this type of isolated world where participants and spectators alike play with the idea of being on the margins of normal society (176). It is a world ruled by clowns where anarchy and fun are valued over obedience and work. As such, it also participates in this carnivalesque kind of social critique.

Objections to this idea have been raised. For example, Kwint has argued that the circus largely abandoned any real social critique in exchange for greater legitimacy as a socially acceptable pastime—clowns may mock but mostly the ringmaster himself or herself, not anyone in an actual position of power (107). *Dumbo* is even more detached from "real" critique; while many cinematic depictions of the circus have little to do with representing an actual or documentary view of the circus as it is actually performed, *Dumbo*'s depiction is intentionally fantastical, with talking animals and magical feats. Loo and Strange acknowledge that the modern circus mostly lacks anything truly subversive but argue that the act of trying to enforce hypocritical, moralistic municipal regulations on the circus in the 19th and early 20th centuries had the ironic effect of creating an identity for circus performers: "Unlike other outsiders … troupers and carnies celebrated and reveled in their status as outsiders, constructing their difference as a source of superiority rather than inferiority" (663). The circus is a strange space, outside of everyday life and with the potential for wild flights of fancy but also subject to many of the same rules as everywhere else. Even the power of claiming an outsider status as a member of the circus comes at the price of being seen as a freak by the world.

Children have also had a peculiar relationship with the circus. West points out that it is a mistake to assume that children have always been a primary audience for circuses given their popularity with modern juvenile audiences; in fact, prior to the 20th century many children were banned from attending due to the presumed "corruptive influence" of the form, and advertising for circuses was rarely aimed at them (265–6). However, the continued status of the circus not just as a performance in itself but as a perennial setting for children's books, movies, television shows, educational materials, and video games suggests a vital link between the circus and childhood. One study of hospitalized children interacting with clowns described the relationship as being "fantasy in reality"—"a world that was not the real one, but one in which the children were seen and acknowledged in an atmosphere of joy" (Linge 6). Engaging with these acts helps some children to work through anxieties and issues in a space apart from the real world. Seymour and Wise chronicled a similar phenomenon with a program that encouraged autistic children to interact with the circus, arguing that it is a place which values difference and creativity in ways that help children to develop community.

For a film of its undoubted popularity, there has been surprisingly little critical scholarship around *Dumbo*. Langer's analysis focuses on how the film is broken down into distinct and almost standalone sequences rather than a more traditional narrative and how these sequences show the differing influences of the animators. It receives passing mentions in other examinations of the Disney films, such as Watts' examination of animation and populism or Ohmer's discussion of the use of animal companions in *Cinderella* (1950). Jenkins, Best and Lowney, and Lutts describe it only as being famous for making audiences sad. Scholars such as Siegesmund and Flory have placed the film within a disgraceful history of African American stereotypes in visual media. Maltin's survey of the Disney canon praises *Dumbo* for its visual inventiveness and "warmth and empathy" but also stresses on more than one occasion that the story is deliberately "simple" (51). Animators Frank Thomas and Ollie Johnston's classic *The Illusion of Life* uses the same terms to discuss the film, praising the tearjerker scenes between Dumbo and his mother and the creativity of the "Pink Elephants" sequence (499, 522–4). However, thematic criticisms of the film, including its unusual depiction of both the circus and childhood, are uncommon.

Dumbo is less a traditional three act story than a series of individual sequences loosely tied together. The same could be said for the type of circus represented by the film, which has a unifying character in the form of the ringmaster but is mostly a series of individual acts that build on or contrast with each other. *Dumbo* proceeds through radically different acts of performance, with different sequences borrowing their tone or content from the circus itself—the advertising extravaganza of arriving in town, the gala display of putting up the tent, the parade, the animal acts, the freak show, and the clowns, with the songs providing acts of sentimentality and nostalgia ("Baby Mine"), comical absurdity ("Pink Elephants on Parade"), and even deeply problematic overtones of the minstrel show ("When I See an Elephant Fly"). It all ends with the ultimate flying act, in which Dumbo is able to perform aerial stunts as the new star of the show. The film is disjointed in many ways because the circus itself is disjointed in many ways—a planned, deliberate succession of individual bits and pieces that ultimately create a carnival atmosphere of joy and chaos.

The opening instantly invites the viewer into the world of circus, with stylized credits that evoke posters for various circus acts, boisterous brass band and calliope music. It comes as a surprise, then, when the actual first shot of the film is a bleak, windswept vista of snow and sleet. A narrator (who never reappears) talks about the weather in highly dramatic fashion, stressing the fortitude and determination of an unknown character who will perform his job whatever the obstacles. In a more traditional story, this character would be the protagonist, braving the odds to achieve success. This expectation is immediately undercut by the reveal that the intrepid hero is actually a group of storks carrying bundles with babies in them and accompanied by a bouncy tune. The reveal of the circus is done almost as an aside, with the parachute-clad bundles of joy drifting into what a cartoonish map labels as the winter quarters. What follows is a quick montage of circus animals, from bears to kangaroos to hippos and more, receiving their new children. At the end Mrs. Jumbo, Dumbo's mother, falls into a deep sorrow after not getting her own child. This bizarre opening, which first misleads the viewer about the hero of the story and then instantly goes from bleak to joyful and back again, actually does an excellent job setting up the film's perception of the circus. It is a place of misdirection but also of exotic animals and fun; here characters change at a moment's notice from contentment to anxiety, much like the powerful mood swings of childhood.

The "Casey Jr." sequence which immediately follows repeats the same pattern, with the song celebrating the determination of a character who is still not the actual hero and contrasting the spectacle of a circus train being loaded and the delight of the young animals at being part of this world with the dejected, bullied state of Mrs. Jumbo. Here is one of the interesting peculiarities of the film, which from the very beginning contrasts the childhood joys of the circus world—noise, play, color, time with loving parents—with anxieties about being outcast, neglected, or abandoned. This is the world of the carnival, in which expectations are turned upside down and inside out, and also the world described in therapeutic studies of clowning, in which circus acts become a place to work out negative feelings precisely because they represent something both fantastical and part of the sadder, more complicated real world.

Dumbo, the titular hero, has still not made an appearance even after these two major sequences. The first actual dialogue in the film, other than a few scattered bits from the ringmaster and the train itself, and the monologue of the bumbling stork, comes from the four elephants who will be the main antagonists to Mrs. Jumbo and her son. Here, too, the film subverts expectations, presenting these performing animals not as joyous and playful but as gossiping, humorless scolds keen to put people in their rightful place. In many ways they come to represent the darker side of the circus—the one in which social values are not mocked but reinforced, the one in which difference is not celebrated but derided. This becomes clear once Dumbo is finally delivered by the stork and revealed to have his infamously enormous ears. While Mrs. Jumbo treats her son's oddity with instant love and acceptance, the other four elephants recoil in horror at something beyond the norms they accept after initially cooing over him as adorable. They hasten to reassure each other that their cruelty is perfectly acceptable, and they give the newly born and named Jumbo Jr. the insulting nickname that will stick with him throughout the film—Dumbo. Dumbo is such a creature of the circus that everyone calls him by his stage name. However, even in this traumatic scene there are hints of the lighter, more liberating aspects of this world. Mrs. Jumbo uses his supposed deformity, his enormous ears, to swaddle him like a blanket and draw him closer to her. The thing that marks him as an outcast in a world of outcasts is also his first source of comfort.

The next major sequence returns the story to the circus train Casey Jr., as he pulls into a dark, rainy town filled with sagging, decaying buildings before workers and the elephants walk out into the storm to erect the tent. Visually the scene is interesting for making a connection between the gray, sad world outside of the circus and the hard work and toil that go into making the circus a contrasting world of color and fun. As always, there is a suggestion that a certain amount of unhappiness is part of both worlds. The above-it-all elephant matrons are forced into labor. The song's insistence that the roustabouts are "happy" in their lives is undercut by the gloomy images of faceless workers in a downpour. Dumbo's first real actions are to imitate playfully the hammering, pulling, and tying of his elders. This is not the normal depiction of the child or work in the circus and suggests that even the most powerful and biggest members of this world are still a type of lower class.

As viewers have probably come to expect at this point, this image is immediately juxtaposed with a colorful, serene shot of the assembled circus in bright daylight and the frivolity and splendor of the parade through town. This situation has reversed again—now the audience is faceless while the animals are seen in close-up, still tired from their travels and labor. This is also the first time the film depicts the lunacy and riot of the clowns, who will come to stand for the circus as a whole in the second half in both good ways and bad. Here is the world of the circus as it is usually represented in children's toys or films—bright, bouncy, carefree.

Dumbo, who is at the very end of the parade, seems to belong to this world for a moment, enjoying the cheering and happiness of the crowds before stumbling into mud and being mocked. This transitions into what may be the most unapologetically sweet scene in the film, where Mrs. Jumbo gives her son a bath to clean him up from the parade and make him presentable to the coming audience. Not by coincidence, this is also one of the few scenes in the film where Dumbo makes any real noise, playfully imitating his mother's toots. At the end, the world of the circus intrudes itself in the form of a carnival barker, calliope music, and shots of other animals and crowds. This will be the last moment Dumbo and Mrs. Jumbo are really allowed to be free and together until the end. The audience comes into the tent and a child begins to mock and taunt Dumbo, who at first enjoys the attention before realizing that it is negative. Notably, the child who mocks Dumbo and whom Mrs. Jumbo assaults has the same physical oddity—large ears. Being part of the circus spectacle, however, marks Dumbo as an object to be ridiculed. His mother's defense violates the rules of this supposedly rule-free environment; though she is a major attraction herself, she is simply to accept whatever the audience does rather than protect a loved one. She is whipped and caged for showing normal parental protectiveness. The children in the paying audience experience freedom while the child in the circus experiences a sudden loss of affection and security. Rather than the fantasy of escaping his restrictive parents by running away to join the riotous circus, Dumbo is born into the circus and loses his parent to the iron fist of circus discipline. His mother goes into a truly frightening frenzy, completing the transformation of their sweet bonding moment into a traumatic moment of abandonment. The scene ends on a mirror image, with the ringmaster being thrust into the bathtub where Dumbo was nurtured. The topsy-turvy world again reveals the anxieties beneath the joy.

Without his mother, Dumbo becomes even more of an outcast. The elephants side with the human masters of the circus over Mrs. Jumbo, and treat parent and child as a disgrace to their good names. The film then introduces the one true spot of hope Dumbo experiences between his mother's imprisonment and his final flight. This comes in the form of Timothy Mouse, who will become the elephant's friend and takes the place of the father whose absence goes unexplained. Timothy is another piece of oddity in this odd film.[2] As noted before, his is the major speaking role but his name is never spoken. Arguably he is the closest thing the film has to a traditional protagonist—his decision to help Dumbo and his schemes to make him a star are what move the plot forward from this point on—but he is not introduced until a third of the way through the runtime. Like the carnival of the circus itself, Timothy turns expectations upside down. His friendship with Dumbo is a deliberate mockery of the old folkloric belief that elephants and mice share a mutual hatred. He is clearly part of the circus, complete with his ever-present circus costume, and yet the film gives no indication of what his job is supposed to be or what he is supposed to do. He sincerely longs to help but his schemes are invariably badly thought out and disastrous. The scheme that finally works—the feather—comes from the crows, not from him.

One possible reading of Timothy is that he is the embodiment of the joyous but comical side of the circus—tiny in body but big-hearted, surrogate father to his natural enemy, loving but unwise when it comes to children. He has no patience for the darker and more rule-bound aspects of the circus, telling off the elephants at the top of the social food chain for making Dumbo an outcast, and refusing to accept the role of clowns on the bottom rung. He first befriends the elephant not *despite* his perceived physical oddity but because of it, declaring that his big ears (which are not unlike his own) are cute, and rejecting the label of freak. While the orchestral score and songs like "Baby Mine" stand in for the sad part of Dumbo's voice, Timothy provides the happier, more confident part. His mockery of the elephants for "picking on little guys"—getting them to abandon their stern, correct demeanor for panicked flight at the sight of him—is the first real injection of the circus/carnival atmosphere since Mrs. Jumbo's breakdown. It is also noticeable that Timothy, who only ever tries to be supportive to the elephant, insists on calling him Dumbo rather than his given name. This is in keeping with his role as the positive side of the circus, embracing the cruelly meant stage name not as a taunt but as part of the fame and success to come. What others perceive as unnatural or ugly he calls "beautiful" and "decorative." With Timothy, as with many children, the circus is a dream world in which the outcast can become the star. He first speaks to the ringmaster about Dumbo in the form of a dream, convincing him that his friend will make the perfect "climax" to his vision of an elephant pyramid. This is a realm in which the small can become big, as Timothy often does in the shadows he casts on tent walls or as he intends to do with what he calls the "world's mightiest midget."

The pyramid is a disaster, of course, as all of Timothy's schemes will be. He fails to take into account the contempt of the elephants not only for the ringmaster (whom they disdain as a "stuffed shirt" who does no real work) but for each other, as well as Dumbo's clumsiness. Seeing the child's ears as positive rather than freakish, he is unable to understand that they actually are a barrier to the grace and agility expected by the circus. Loving as he is, he is also unwilling to foresee that the crowd will see Dumbo not as the sweet, curious child Timothy knows him to be but just another physical oddity to be laughed at and jeered. Dumbo brings the big top down in a painfully literal way and winds up more of an outcast among the elephants than ever, who scorn him for becoming the most disgraceful thing imaginable—a clown. Landing among the intentionally ridiculous does not help him. More concerned with their own goofy pratfalls than his safety, the clowns treat him as a prop in a dangerous act involving fire and heights. He is a freak to the freaks and good for nothing but visual gags. Throughout the sequence Dumbo is terrified and anxious. They stoop to mocking his loving, absent mother in the form of a clown in a dress and elephant mask. Timothy tries to make the best of it, telling him that he is a big success, but knows that his friend continues to be alone and dejected.

The clowns toast his humiliation while the film heads into the painful reunion of mother and child through prison bars. In a story filled with sharp juxtapositions between the joyous and frightening aspects of the circus this might be the sharpest. "Baby Mine" is such a famously tear-jerking sequence, with its bittersweet song accompanied by contrasting visuals of Dumbo being cradled with his mother's trunk while other children nestle close to their parents, that it can seem almost detached from the rest of the film. However, it is thematically aligned with the ongoing depiction of the circus as a place of both happiness and anxiety, freedom and captivity. It is a symbolic playground where children are cherished and indulged as well as cast aside and punished. Moments after Dumbo is tearfully separated from his mother a supposedly fun clown declares that "elephants ain't got no feelings."

"Pink Elephants on Parade" is a sequence that its own animators seemed to regard as a strange, almost psychedelic departure from the rest of the film. It follows closely on the heels of the lachrymose "Baby Mine" and is a startling shift in tone and animation. However, it could be seen as not a detached, if admittedly brilliant, piece of experimentation but as a sequence closely aligned to the ongoing depiction of the circus as both childhood carnival and childhood nightmare. Unwittingly drunk, Timothy and Dumbo see bizarre, surrealistic images of marching, dividing, exploding, and swarming elephants while the music warns them to "look out" for danger. These frightening specters start by imitating the parade from earlier in the film. If Timothy represents the positive aspects of the circus as a place of freedom and joy, these images represent the ultimate, almost ghoulish extension of these traits—totally free to change their shape, size, and appearance, and therefore terrifying. What seems to frighten Dumbo most is the circus itself, embodied by these elephants and their chaotic parody of everything from trains to skaters.

Reading the film as a depiction of a child's attempt to work through psychological issues and anxieties around abandonment and being a social outsider in the form of the joyful-yet-frightening circus world makes the otherwise jarring transition between "Pink Elephants on Parade" and the introduction of the crows seem more natural. "Pink Elephants" becomes the culmination of Dumbo's fears about the chaos and pain in his life. Only after he works through those feelings can he finally embrace the positive aspects of the circus as a carnival atmosphere—its embrace of oddity, its ability to lift the outcast to star status. The film's most famous twist, his ability to fly, is not even hinted at much more than ten minutes from the end. This is because he has to learn to embrace the circus through failure, rejection, and nightmares. His entire encounter with the crows repeats this film-long cycle of mockery followed by acceptance. They start by ridiculing the very idea of his talent ("When I See an Elephant Fly") and end by giving him the key to his success in the form of the feather. Fittingly, this acceptance comes from fellow outsiders—the only talking animals in the film beside the stork to live outside of the circus. In a sense, they are the first circus audience Dumbo wins over.

The final sequence returns the viewer to the initial question. Why doesn't Dumbo talk? In a typical underdog story, the protagonist gains confidence, overcomes obstacles, and speaks up for himself or herself. This is certainly the trajectory Dumbo follows, climaxing in his realization that his talent lies within himself rather than in the feather. Yet he continues to say nothing. "The very things that held you down are going to carry you up and up and up," Timothy tells him, finishing his role as the positive spirit of the circus by telling him to embrace the carnival's love of oddness—the eccentricity and individuality which marks him as an outcast is also what makes him a spectacle worth seeing. On one level Dumbo as a character works through his pain to become the embodiment of the circus, which in this film is a world where pain and pleasure are inevitable companions. He is a wonderful impossibility, a melding of rejection and joy who triumphs precisely because he started out on the bottom. Like many children, he matures into confidence only by first facing fear and anxiety. The circus is the fantastic space where he can both fall and fly. Once airborne, he embraces the carnivalesque language of the circus by turning the world topsy-turvy—dive-bombing those who mocked him, peppering the matrons with peanuts, unmasking the clown dressed as Mrs. Jumbo. The disjointed structure of both the circus and his life climax in a grand finale which provides both closure and anticipation for future shows and future triumphs. He lands in a world where talent and joy speak louder than words ever could and so is finally in the embrace of his mother again. The child following Dumbo's journey and identifying with him through his ups and downs is given images and experiences which mirror his or her own anxieties and which offer tools with which to talk about them. Dumbo may not speak, but his life in the circus space encourages the children who love him to speak for themselves.

NOTES

1. For more information on the original book, see animation historian Michael Barrier's essay "The Mysterious *Dumbo* Roll-a-Book."

2. Timothy Mouse does not appear in the original book, where Dumbo's friend is a bird. Timothy makes an interesting contrast with Disney's most famous mouse as the equally kind-hearted but far more boisterous and aggressive cousin to Mickey, who had hosted his own circus in a 1936 short supervised by Dumbo's future director. "Mickey's Circus" has a much more antic and slapstick view of the big top, with Mickey and Donald Duck tormented by a group of unruly orphans as they try to control an act of performing seals, get shot out of a cannon, and do an accidental high wire routine.

WORKS CITED

Bakhtin, Mikhail. *Rabelais and His World*. Translated by Helene Iswolsky, Indiana UP, 2009.

Bambi. Directed by David Hand. Disney, 1942.

Barrier, Michael. "The Mysterious *Dumbo* Roll-a-Book." MichaelBarrier.com, 20 Oct. 2011, www.michaelbarrier.com/Essays/DumboRollABook/DumboRollABook.html.

Best, Joel, and Kathleen S. Lowney. "The Disadvantage of a Good Reputation: Disney as a Target for Social Problems Claims." *The Sociological Quarterly*, vol. 50, no. 3, 2009, pp. 431–449.

Carmeli, Yoram S. "Text, Traces, and the Reification of Totality: The Case of Popular Circus Literature." *New Literary History*, vol. 25, no. 1, 1994, pp. 175–205.

Church, David. "Freakery, Cult Films, and the Problem of Ambivalence." *Journal of Film and Video*, vol. 63, no. 1, 2011, pp. 03–17.

Cinderella. Directed by Clyde Geronimi, Wilfred Jackson, and Hamilton Luske. Disney, 1950.

Dumbo. Directed by Ben Sharpsteen. Disney, 1941.

Flory, Dan. "Race, Rationality, and Melodrama: Aesthetic Response and the Case of Oscar Micheaux." *The Journal of Aesthetics and Art Criticism*, vol. 63, no. 4, 2005, pp. 327–338.

Jenkins, Eric S. "Another *Punctum*: Animation, Affect, and Ideology." *Critical Inquiry*, vol. 39, no. 3, 2013, pp. 575–591.

Kwint, Marius. "The Legitimization of the Circus in Late Georgian England." *Past & Present*, no. 174, 2002, pp. 72–115.

Lachmann, Renate. "Bakhtin and Carnival: Culture as Counter-Culture." *Cultural Critique*, no. 11, 1988, pp. 115–152.

Langer, Mark. "Regionalism in Disney Animation: Pink Elephants and *Dumbo*." *Film History*, vol. 4, no. 4, 1990, pp. 305–321.

Linge, Lotta. "Magical Attachment: Children in Magical Relations with Hospital Clowns." *International Journal of Qualitative Studies on Health & Well-Being*, vol. 7, Mar. 2012, pp. 1–12.

The Lion King. Directed by Roger Allers and Rob Minkoff. Disney, 1994.

Loo, Tina, and Carolyn Strange. "The Traveling Show Menace: Contested Regulation in Turn-of-the-Century Ontario." *Law & Society Review*, vol. 29, no. 4, 1995, pp. 639–667.

Lutts, Ralph H. "The Trouble with Bambi: Walt Disney's *Bambi* and the American Vision of Nature." *Forest & Conservation History*, vol. 36, no. 4, 1992, pp. 160–171.

Maltin, Leonard. *The Disney Films*. 3d ed. Hyperion, 1995.

"Mickey's Circus." Directed by Ben Sharpsteen. Disney, 1936.

Ohmer, Susan. "'That Rags to Riches Stuff': Disney's *Cinderella* and the Cultural Space of Animation." *Film History*, vol. 5, no. 2, 1993, pp. 231–249.

101 Dalmatians. Directed by Clyde Geronimi, Hamilton Luske, and Wolfgang Reitherman. Disney, 1961.

Seymour, Kristy, and Patricia Wise. "Circus Training for Autistic Children: Difference, Creativity, and Community." *New Theatre Quarterly*, vol. 33, no. 1, Feb. 2017, pp. 78–90.

Siegesmund, Richard. "On the Persistence of Memory: The Legacy of Visual African-American Stereotypes." *Studies in Art Education*, vol. 48, no. 3, 2007, pp. 323–328.

Thomas, Frank, and Ollie Johnston. *The Illusion of Life: Disney Animation*. Disney Editions, 1995.

Watts, Steven. "Walt Disney: Art and Politics in the American Century." *The Journal of American History*, vol. 82, no. 1, 1995, pp. 84–110.

West, Mark Irwin. "A Spectrum of Spectators: Circus Audiences in Nineteenth-Century America." *Journal of Social History*, vol. 15, no. 2, 1981, pp. 265–270.

Zootopia. Directed by Byron Howard and Rich Moore. Disney, 2016.

Problematic Participants and Circus Ethics

The Human/Nonhuman Concurrence
of Jacob and Rosie in Water for Elephants

RACHEL L. CARAZO

Introduction

Many modern circus productions, such as Cirque du Soleil, have removed elements of the non-human animal[1] from the performance, a "[symptom] of a deep shift in attitude toward animal life which ultimately tends to integrate animals into the democratic process of the civil, and, probably, specifically urban society which projects its views and values toward the rest of the world in the name of globalization" (Bouissac, *Multimodal*, 113). Instead, these circuses focus on human-centered bonds, creativity, and efficiency. Even though for scholars Norma M. Rantisi and Deborah Leslie choices similar to those made by the Cirque du Soleil have created translation zones, spaces where incoming participants (actants) (151) both fuse with show traditions and then negotiate their own places within them in creative ways (148), the lack of animals in these zones indicates that an important element, essential to the circus in its original form, is missing. Interviews of Brazilian circus performers mention a similar absence of animals, claiming that "Soleil is always mentioned with negative associations and its name is used to qualify absence, inefficiency, and something lacking" (Aguiar, Carrieri, and Souza 14). While these opinions are not fact, they do show that even great performances do not have everything: in this case, they do not have animals.

However, in many circus films, the importance of having animals in a human network often reappears with significant consequences. In Francis Lawrence's *Water for Elephants* (2011),[2] both Jacob (a human) and Rosie (an elephant) serve as problematic participants; the two, whose human and animal statuses equalize the shifting nature of the boundaries of circus networks, demonstrate how even though the friction in Rantisi and Leslie's translation zones is successful in a positive way (148), the problematic participants in the film are necessary to establish a *universal* circus ethics. By adding "controversial" characters, whose beliefs or social statuses force the other circus members to consider new ideas, the boundaries of star, home, power (social), violence, and ethical networks shift in a more positive direction, demonstrating that even though human-only circuses like the Cirque du Soleil are magnificent and entertaining (Rantisi and Leslie 148), the most inclusive ethics between performers will still not appear viable until a problematic human participant *and* a problematic animal participant join the company.

Circus Abuses and Shifting Boundaries

To understand the impact of activism toward non-human animals in films about the circus, a "locus of mythical, transcendental experiences," a brief mention of abuses against animals in real-life circuses in necessary (Bouissac, *Multimodal*, 161). Abuses existed as early as Ancient Rome (Simon 13–15), but the mistreatment involved during modern capture,[3] maintenance,[4] and performance, the latter of which moved animals from their menageries[5] and was highly engineered by Isaac Van Amburgh (Neumann 169), is much better documented.[6] Despite the efforts of writers and philosophers, like Hornaday and Bouissac, who have argued for the right of animals to perform,[7] several recent bans[8] have been implemented on wild animal performances, which have resulted in the demise of the circus as it has been known until the present, for now many circuses with animals, like Ringling Bros. and Barnum & Bailey circus, are removing them from the show and, as a business, are ceasing to exist (Nir and Schweber 1).

Together, these philosophies, documented abuses, and efforts at activism also demonstrate how the boundaries of animal ethics shift. For example, during performances, the human and animal elements are often blurred. Janet M. Davis writes: "With their blurring of male and female bodies, circus acts flattened sexual differences, and went so far as to challenge the distinction between human and animal. Trapeze artists and acrobats became birds and butterflies, while the "Learned Pig" solved simple math problems, and elephants, tigers, and bears danced upright" (Davis 27). Instead of becoming immutable, these are ethical processes "enrolled in the creation [and now limitations] of a contemporary circus performance" and they will continue to change over time (Rantisi and Leslie 147).

Nevertheless, when examining these ethical changes, it is important to remember they have only developed because *humans have interacted with animals*. Animals, then, have not existed in the circus separate from humans; the two groups share space and experiences, as occurs in *Water for Elephants*, and these interactions make the progress toward a universal ethics, in whatever form, more likely. Thus, even if current proponents for animal rights continue these bans and, fearfully for other people, aim to have "no animals anywhere in our lives—no circus animals, no pets, all animal products off the menu" (Abel 34), the centuries-long efforts of animal rights philosophies demonstrate that goals will still change, creating one of Rantisi and Leslie's "politicized" (Barry 2013) translation zones, "one that is contested, shifting, and always open to invention" (Rantisi and Leslie 150).

Jacob and Rosie in *Water for Elephants* exemplify how network boundaries shift and blur in the cinematic world as well, especially when humans and animals interact and strive to gain similar rights in a single contested space. However, as should be most apparent from the film, these translation zones (Rantisi and Leslie 148) would not produce as effective results without the transacting presence of *both* humans and animals in similar situations, a reality that animal rights activists cannot ignore for fear of creating "some unbridgeable cognitive gulf dividing humans and other animals" even if certain abuses are justifiably removed from the circus ring (DeGrazia 6).

Water for Elephants: *Jacob and Rosie as Problematic Participants*

Jacob (Robert Pattinson) and Rosie spend time together in *Water for Elephants*. Even though August is a cruel circus impresario, Jacob cares greatly for Rosie and spends a lot of time bonding with her during the course of the film.

In the film *Water for Elephants*, which comprises an older Jacob's (Hal Holbrook) narration of his past circus life to a modern-day circus manager named Charlie (Paul Schneider), young Jacob (Robert Pattinson) and Rosie (Tai) become problematic participants in the Benzini Brothers Circus. This notion of creating a translation zone, in which new elements are creatively integrated (Rantisi and Leslie 148), does include three circus perspectives—the trainer (August, the circus's violent impresario, and Jacob), the non-human animal (Rosie and Silver Star) and the audience (Marlena, the performers, and the audiences within and without the film) (Bouissac, *Semiotics*, 52); however, unlike the human-only Cirque du Soleil, in which the participants are only mildly disruptive before assimilation, Jacob and Rosie are never truly integrated into the Benzini Brothers' system (Rantisi and Leslie 148). Instead, they eventually create a new translation zone, away from August (Christoph Waltz). Thus, Jacob and Rosie are complex participants because the friction that their entrance into Benzini Brothers causes results in the creation of an entirely new system, keeping the notion of the creative from Rantisi and Leslie but overturning the idea of eventual accommodation (148).

Part of the dysfunction of August's regime as impresario is symbolic; it references the clown acts of classic circus traditions. In fact, August's name links him to a complicated aspect of circus culture. A certain type of clown, "an awkward, sloppily dressed, and foul-mouthed partner who displays a heavily colored make-up ... became known through the generic name of 'august,' a name that probably originated in a sarcastic term of address since his persona evokes anything but imperial distinction and poise" (Bouissac, *Semiotics*, 104). In the film, August is certainly not a clown; he has fancier clothes and serves in a leadership position. Nevertheless, like august clowns, his demeanor is disagreeable and his lack of ethical consideration for humans and animals places him in *opposition* to the other performers, acts that mirror those of august clowns. Unlike the classic august, who generally succeeds against his circus fellows, August does not win. However, Jacob, Rosie, and Marlena (Reese Witherspoon) prevail *because* they have respect for humans *and* animals.

Jacob and Rosie are problematic participants because their differences from the Benzini culture, coupled with their complementary, mirror-like attributes, create a newer, more ethical circus system regarding the treatment of circus performers. Consequently, humans and animals must be present for this translation zone to appear (Rantisi and Leslie 148); otherwise, the ethics and circus culture created would be closer to that of Cirque du Soleil, which, while having its own sense of splendor, misses the universal nature of human *and* animal collaboration and how such forces can overcome the *iconization* of certain circus aspects (Bouissac, *Semiotics*, 36).

First and foremost, Jacob is controversial because of his Polish heritage and Cornell background, setting him apart from the other Benzini perform-ers. Even though he befriends Camel (Jim Norton), who is also Polish, eth-nicity, at the time in which the film is set, was perceived as "racial difference," adding to their general surprise when Rosie responds to commands in Polish and exhibits a similar "racial" background as Jacob (Davis 26). Thus, the her-itage that complicates communication with Jacob and Rosie makes them communicate effectively with each other. Rosie's first caretaker (James Frain) complains about her, demonstrating this divide. He tells Jacob: "You see this animal? This here is the stupidest goddamn animal on the face of God's good earth. Here's your bull hook. You're gonna need it. Good luck to you. If I don't ever see another dumb bull in my life, it'll be too soon" (*Water*). Rosie is not stupid; she is just another symbol of the Polish Other, and once Jacob discovers their affinity, an unshakeable bond with his animal "mirror" leads to his later success.

Second, Jacob is problematic because of his loving background. His par-ents mortgaged their house to pay for his education, and Jacob is so attached to his home that, after his parents' tragic deaths, he remarks: "I remember walking out the front door and forcing myself not to look back. I couldn't stay where everything reminded me of the life that was gone. And I didn't see the point in going back to school" (*Water*). His education is also a part of this "loving" background since being a vet helps him self-actualize and help animals. His subsequent position as Benzini's veterinarian becomes problematized because he is a pioneer in this role; August even confirms that Ringling Brothers does not have its own vet. Yet Jacob's formal education should not prevent him from communicating effectively with other perform-ers. However, August comments: "Yeah, I could use an educated man around here. Gets pretty tiring talking to my menagerie of trained seals" (*Water*). August makes two important distinctions here concerning Jacob's placement within Benzini; he unwittingly connects humans and animals, as Davis does (27), supporting the position of Jacob and Rosie as reflections of each other; and then places Jacob in theoretical opposition to the regular circus perform-ers, who follow August's rules, ensuring that Jacob will remain a part of the circus but still somehow outside of it.

Lastly, both Jacob and Rosie love Marlena, unlike August, who is married to her. This complicates the nature of human relationships and suggests that certain kinds of love can function differently for different species, proving that the "love" promoted by August is dysfunctional and unaccommodating, unlike the translation zones in Rantisi and Leslie's examination of Cirque du Soleil (148). Rosie's main "problematic" attribute is being an elephant. Accord-ing to Bouissac, "More is going on in elephant acts than meets the eye. These animals are highly social and, if let alone, they constantly test and reinforce their relationships with each other. They have friends and foes. They tussle for ranking in the group. They hold grudges" (*Multimodal*, 38). Rosie is controversial for being herself as well as for being a mirror of Jacob. Rosie may understand Polish as a language, but she recognizes the language of love that Jacob and Marlena have for her. When Jacob and Marlena first meet Rosie, they seem to discuss the name of a song, but underlying their dialogue is an early avowal of romantic love, which they are finally starting to articulate because of the appearance of Rosie, another object of affection.

> MARLENA: I think she likes music. It is a lovely song.
> JACOB: I'm confessing that I love you.
> MARLENA: Hmm?
> JACOB: Uh, it's the name of the song.
> MARLENA: [Chuckles] Oh, right, of course. Louis Armstrong [*Water*].

In addition to this affective revelation between humans and animals, Rosie also tests her boundaries, as an elephant, within their human social group. She holds a grudge against August and she fears him when he holds the bull hook. Yet she recognizes the "authority" of Jacob and Marlena when they ask her to perform, for they provide her with care and affection. Thus, at the end of the film, when August tries to strangle Marlena with the bull hook, Rosie saves Marlena and kills August. In effect, Rosie can respond to human speech, albeit without words, confounding the human hold on communication in circus translation zones and thus further demonstrating how Rosie is a problematic participant in the August-centered culture (Rantisi and Leslie 148). Together, Jacob and Rosie generate a "conversation" in this circus space that develops a new sense of ethical behavior within star, home, social/power, and

Jacob (Robert Pattinson) and Marlena (Reese Witherspoon) bond with Rosie after Rosie first comes to Benzini Brothers Circus (*Water for Elephants*). The connection between Jacob and Rosie becomes a way for Jacob and Marlena to also become better acquainted with each other. As music about love plays, the three characters begin to understand their deep caring for one another.

violence networks, resulting in a new translation zone (148), where humans and animals have more *equal consideration* in the circus (Singer 2).

Circus Networks and Ethics

The star network in *Water for Elephants* is the first aspect of the circus to be problematized by the appearances of Jacob and Rosie. When Jacob works as a roustabout, Marlena and her liberty horses are the star attractions. Yet there remains a sense of separation between Marlena and the rest of the performers until Jacob appears. At first, when he sees her horse Silver Star's hurt leg (laminitis), Jacob asks to examine it. Marlena wordlessly assents, but she is called to the ring and abruptly leaves Jacob before he can finish. Her refusal to speak to Jacob supports what Camel later tells Jacob about her.

> JACOB: Hey, Camel, who's the woman who works with the horses?
> CAMEL: [Shushes] That ain't no woman. That's the boss's wife, Marlena. She's a star attraction. And she don't talk to nobody, and you don't talk to her. She'll just high-hat you anyway [*Water*].

Jacob's immediate interest in Marlena is obvious. As he watches her perform, he remarks: "She didn't seem real to me at first. The way she looked inside that big top under those lights. I thought I'd go blind from the shine" (*Water*). Marlena and the four horses are stars; the side-by-side association of human and animal stars is an important theme in the film, and the eventual merging of Marlena with Rosie and Jacob demonstrates the adaptability of star networks.

Jacob's "star" ethics, though, oppose August's ethics from the beginning. Upon hiring Jacob, August specifies: "My star attraction is limping and I can't get a new liberty horse midseason. So you make sure the horse performs, and the job is yours" (*Water*). Jacob insists on putting Silver Star down, despite August's desire for the horse to perform until he dies, and as Marlena begins to speak to Jacob, even she challenges August's ethics by confirming their dysfunctionality, for even the star performers are not treated well.

> MARLENA: I should have taken him out of the show.
> JACOB: It's not your fault. It happens. It's not uncommon, but he is suffering. And the pain is only gonna get worse. The right thing to do would be to put him down.
> MARLENA: That's not going to happen, is it? Not when August can get a few more shows out of him. Around here, everybody works till they're run into the ground. Nobody stops, nobody dies until August says so [*Water*].

Now that Marlena and Jacob have problematized August's star network, whose sole interest is profit, not their welfare, a channel of communication opens between them.

With Rosie's appearance, the star network again changes, acknowledging the increased importance of animal performers. Even August aligns, for once, with this notion, when he declares of Rosie: "Children, meet out salvation! We got ourselves a guaranteed sell-out, crowd-cheering bull! Her name is Rosie, she's fifty-three, and she's brilliant" (*Water*). August certainly does not consider Rosie an equal, but he does see her as an equal component of the star act, especially since he knows that her presence will be profitable. What August does not realize, though, is how Jacob and Rosie are already complicating his simple image of star and profit, for even Jacob is becoming a star in this developing network. He is serving in a novel role, as vet and bull man, and his connection to Rosie, initially through the Polish language, trumps that of August's language of greed. Jacob and Rosie become stars together, with the slow integration of Marlena, which allows their new network to flourish.

Rosie is a star in and of herself as well. When August abuses her, she chooses which commands to follow; her star act then demands the creation of a new circus ethics for animals. Unlike the liberty horses, whose mistreatment nevertheless sparks the idea that star networks should not function this way, Rosie is less passive about her role as a star. Rosie, through her refusals to listen to August, solicits the proper respect and aids in the creation of a new star act comprising her, Jacob, and Marlena. Even the older Jacob, as he ends his narration to Charlie, reveals the absolute cohesion between the three when he tells him, "And with my degree, our animals, and Marlena's act, Ringling got themselves a sweet deal. A sweet deal" (*Water*). Jacob and Rosie challenge the star network of Benzini Brothers so significantly that it ceases to exist, moving the star act to the Ringling network.

The second complex network is the home network, and it relates to the scenario of running away from home to the glamour of the circus (Davis 31). Home, then, only seems important in the peripatetic circus world. Marlena's experiences, until her break with August, epitomize this idea:

> I was born a passenger. They found me wrapped in a newspaper under a seat on the Baltimore and Ohio. I was just three days old. I grew up in foster homes. I'd always daydream about who my parents were. When I was five, for an entire year, I pretended my mom was an Appaloosa mare. I did. And that I was a filly, and that I was just dreaming that I was a girl. And that one day I'd wake up, and I'd run home. One thing was for sure, I was a lot safer in those stables than I ever was in those homes. And then the circus came to town. And there they were, six gorgeous black Friesians with red tassels hanging down their manes. So beautiful. And August was right out front. And as soon as he looked at me, I knew I'd never live with strangers again. So we got married. And where did I end up? Living on a train. It's the only real home I've ever known. And you know, I'm a star attraction. Out there, I got nothing just like everybody else.

Marlena's idea of a stable home seems incompatible to the allure of the circus. She believes that she can only have one or the other, not both.

Jacob, though, defies this assumption. Jacob loves and idealizes his original home. Yet his experiences with Benzini Brothers lead him to consider aspects of the circus as home. To the circus, Jacob brings his original values, questioning August's feeding of the "cats," refusing to allow Silver Star to suffer, and fighting for Marlena and the rights of the other performers. Jacob also opposes August's idea that national values do not apply to them. August comments: "You must learn, my dear boy, that the rules of these United States of Suckers do not apply to us. To talent and illusion!" (*Water*). Clearly, when Jacob defies August and supports the ethics that he learned before his circus life, he is demonstrating that August's "power" is an illusion. Thus, Jacob's first home network never disappears; the Polish heritage of Camel and Rosie reminds him of his former life, keeping the "home" network problematized and always in flux, unlike the eventual accommodation of Rantisi and Leslie's Cirque du Soleil translation zones (148). Even his initial encounter with the circus illustrates this, and problematizes home, when Jacob wonders at the beginning of the film: "Now, I don't know if I picked that train, or that train picked me. But something told me my mother and my father sent it my way. I'd like to think that anyway" (*Water*). His parents seem to send him to the circus, and when the circus no longer remains his home, Jacob is able to move back to a less peripatetic life without losing the loves that he gained from it. Rosie and Marlena accompany him to Ringling, where they perform together, as a human/animal team. Jacob then works at the Albany Zoo and "bought some property so [h]e could keep the horses, Rosie, and then five kids" (*Water*). Jacob finds comfort in both places, contesting the simple idea that he will be happier away from home and in the circus. Yet home changes for the older Jacob after he loses Rosie and Marlena. Having no permanent place again, Jacob finds himself back at the modern circus and petitioning Charlie for a job.

> JACOB: I won't argue. You won't be sorry.
> CHARLIE: Yeah, we'll get you in the record books. "Oldest man that ever ran away with the circus."
> JACOB: [Laughs] I'm not running away. I'm coming home [*Water*].

At the end, Jacob again alters the notion of home. After he loses so much in the beginning, he again finds a sense of belonging in the peripatetic life of the circus, where, unlike the running away of other performers, he feels that he is returning to another aspect of his life. Thus, Rosie and Jacob problematize home networks by demonstrating that "home" is not a simple concept, and that it can exist in both places, especially when part of it includes being around humans *and* animals that love one another. Jacob is at home wherever

Marlena and Rosie are, and even after they (or his parents) are gone, he still feels a connection to the places where he lived with them. The circus, then, is a home because it is both moveable and immobile; it implies an absence of certain things (August) and the presence of both humans and animals in equal consideration (Singer 2).

The third major network problematized by Jacob and Rosie is the social/power network of Benzini Brothers. On the macro level, the circus, although it has its own culture (Bouissac, *Multimodal*, 11), still tends to represent the basic social structures of the nation (Davis xii). In the United States during the Depression, class and ethnic differences were extremely important to the traveling circus, and this fact does not change for the members of Benzini Brothers. When Jacob questions Camel about taking him to see August in the middle of the night, Camel replies: "The only time circus people live, even the boss. See, musicians and sideshow people are above us roustabouts, but below the specialty acts, which, of course, are below the ring stock animals. And everybody, everybody, is below the bosses. Don't ever forget that" (*Water*). Even though August claims that "the rules of these United States of Suckers do not apply to us" and Camel calls August "the Lord and Master of the Known and the Unknown Universe himself," society still functions in the circus largely as it does in the United States (*Water*).

The fact that status remains relevant to August is evident when he first meets Jacob, in a discussion that demonstrates how controversial Jacob is to him.

AUGUST: Why would a college boy dirty his hands as a filthy roustabout?

JACOB: I guess because out of all that dirt and sweat, working with these fellows you wouldn't want to be caught dead in the daylight with, comes so much beauty.

AUGUST: You grandstanding me, kid?

JACOB: No. No, sir.

AUGUST: That was beautifully put. Yet you ride my train, you eat my food without my permission while hard-working men labor all day for the same privileges. And these filthy roustabouts are my family. You, you are an intruder. Next stop, throw him off. Probably studied poetry.

JACOB: I studied veterinary science, not poetry. And I can tell you one thing. That star attraction horse of yours? It's not gonna be walking in a few weeks, let alone performing.

AUGUST: Earl? Wait. Veterinary sciences? What school?

JACOB: Cornell.

AUGUST: You're a Cornell graduate? [*Water*].

August sees himself as the ultimate authority in his world, even though, during their conversation, Jacob is able to question and check his power. Jacob problematizes the social and power networks of Benzini Brothers because he is Polish, which, for the time, is technically a "lower" status, while he is also

Ivy League educated, giving him a higher status. Jacob therefore begins to integrate himself into Benzini Brothers by outwitting the "Master" and using his own bag of tricks, to which August and Marlena later refer at dinner while celebrating Rosie's arrival.

> JACOB: I'm not licensed.
> AUGUST: Jacob, do you think Lucinda the Fat Lady weights eight-hundred pounds?
> MARLENA: [Laughs] She's four hundred tops.
> AUGUST: Do you think the Tattooed Woman was tattooed by headhunters in Borneo?
> MARLENA: She's from Pittsburgh! It took her nine years to ink herself. Tell him about the hippo, darling.
> AUGUST: When she died, we swapped out her water for formaldehyde, kept showing her. For two weeks we travelled with a pickled hippo! Jacob, the world's run on tricks. Everyone plays. But it's having a true talent, a gift born within, something no degree can give you…. You have such a talent [*Water*].

Jacob understands his contradictory nature, as he serves as a licensed vet without having passed his final exams. Yet, at this moment, August accepts this dual nature, not realizing that these tricks, as he calls them, will carry over into other networks and translation zones of his circus (Rantisi and Leslie 148).

Rosie benefits from the same kind of social power when she is integrated into Benzini Brothers. She was trained in Polish, effectively giving her the same "low" status as Jacob. However, she is also the star attraction, which gives her a certain power over *all* of the humans and animals there, including August. Rosie's intelligence is undeniable, and she uses it to overturn August's power as well, killing him with a stake. Rosie, then, ends up having the ultimate power over everyone's circus life. Her triumph with Jacob and Marlena forces Benzini into bankruptcy; however, she also allows Marlena and Jacob to have a new, more fulfilling life at Ringling, where she *does* appear to recognize the new social/power network. Consequently, Linda Simon's idea of the myth of the circus has merit when she writes: "The myth of the circus as a site of freedom, power and enchantment contradicts the hard reality of circus life. Although artists and writers imagine the circus as a challenge to bourgeois values, a rejection of the commodification of culture, in fact the circus is a business, always precarious, subject to financial pressures and its audience's fickle desires" (Simon 26). August's Benzini Brothers relates directly to the myth of the glamorous circus. Yet his power, contrary to his beliefs, is not absolute. Just as adding the "problematic" characteristics of gender, race, and being an animal can inspire change, so too can August be overcome by Jacob and Rosie, who simultaneously exhibit both "low" and "high" statuses.

With these changes comes the complication of the violence network in *Water for Elephants*. Violence and the circus have a shared history since, as Peta Tait relates, "a range of human fighting practices coincided with animal exhibition and animal presence in public entertainment that spread globally. From staged enactments of power and nationhood to spontaneous offstage physical fights in menageries, animals were surrounded by notions of fighting that were formal and informal, orchestrated and accidental" (xi-xii). As a result, violence, in and of itself, is a complex issue in the film. It remains an ethical dilemma, especially when done by August, who red-lights performers (throwing them off a moving train) because he cannot pay them or because they refuse to yield to him. In fact, August threatens to red-light Jacob after he puts down Silver Star. August claims: "This circus, my circus, is a sovereign nation. You break my law, you have to pay a penalty. I tell you to fix a horse, you shoot it? That's breaking my law. The penalty is red-lighting. You need to get off the train. Except we don't stop the train. There's a chance you might survive, although unlikely" (*Water*). August is aware of the violence inherent in his actions. He knows that someone could die from the fall, as occurs later when he red-lights Walter, Camel, Wade (Stephen Monroe Taylor), and Grady (Richard Brake). Marlena recounts to Jacob: "He had Blackie red-lighting men all night. Wade and Grady hit soft ground, and they found Walter and Camel. They had hit the rocks. They didn't make it. Wade and Grady are gonna take August down. I don't know how, but you have to get out of here" (*Water*). This red-lighting fits with Janet M. Davis's revelations that Bailey (Barnum & Bailey) red-lighted performers in Argentina—albeit not as violently—and that:

> Pronounced forms of employee resistance were risky because workers had little recourse for airing their grievances. Employees remained without a union until 1937. At the turn of the century, circus contracts absolved proprietors and railroad companies of any liability for employees who were killed or injured during the show season. If workers were injured on the job or became ill during the season, they received no wages or sick-time benefits while they were unable to work. Occasionally, a circus short on cash would "red-light," or strand, its workers without pay or transportation back home [Davis 80].

August makes himself master and "ethical leader" on the train, which fits into the history of certain abusive circuses impresarios.

However, this violent regime becomes problematized by Jacob and Rosie, who resist August's violence and, in turn, challenge the film audience's ethical response to violence as well. Jacob's honesty about Silver Star and the cats' poor diet leads to an early outburst from August, who grabs Jacob aggressively and states:

> Does it hurt? Like this? Your gut tells you to shoot my star attraction? No treatment, no hoof tester, just your Cornell gut. You know how a circus survives? You said it

yourself, kid. On blood, sweat, pain and shit. When a circus begins to die and animals eat garbage, you know what men eat? Nothing. Your heart goes out to an animal suffering. Well, that's noble, and that's good, but all that tells me is that you never saw men suffer. So before I get back from town, you do whatever it is they taught you in that Ivy League sandbox to get that horse ready for the parade. As long as we can walk, we play [*Water*].

August is not afraid to impose his will on Jacob, who nevertheless finds ways to resist him.

Then, with the appearance of Rosie, the network of violence and opposition escalates quickly, for even though August's violence against humans is disturbing, his repeated acts of violence against Rosie are even worse. August beats Rosie with the bull hook and tries to justify his treatment, saying: "I saw the bull rear up and run away with her [Marlena], and I lost my mind. That's no excuse. I know that. I've spent all that money on that bull. I need to pay the workmen. I have debts to pay" (*Water*). August blames his actions on fear for his wife and his business, but he only cares that he injured Rosie because she is a profitable investment.

These beatings enrage Jacob so much that he prepares to enact his own violence against August. He carries the bull hook into August's room, but ultimately resists this urge to use it. Later, when Jacob and Camel take care of Rosie's injuries, they discuss August's nature, especially his atrocities against animals.

JACOB: He'll kill her next time.
CAMEL: There's nothing you can do. A man like that. He throws men off a moving train so he doesn't have to pay. You think he thinks twice about killing one of God's innocent creatures? [*Water*].

Camel sees the situation as fixed, even though it is wrong. Yet Jacob, who is not so easily manipulated, has a rebellious attitude despite his own earlier temptation to commit violence.

The final scenes of violence culminate after August, accusing them of having an affair, slaps Marlena in front of Jacob. Jacob is fired for his aggressive response; he tries to flee with Marlena, but he must chase her back once she is seized by August's men. Jacob returns to August's car with a knife, again ready to end August's reign. However, Marlena shakes her head and implores him not to strike. August's end only comes when he tries to strangle Marlena in the circus ring, after chaos erupts. Rosie takes the step that Jacob could (or would) not. The elephant lifts a stake and strikes August, killing him. The older Jacob then relays this part of the story to Charlie, the modern-day circus manager. He states: "The official report said August had been trampled to death. Blackie was never seen again after Wade and Grady dragged him out of that tent. And no one was charged with letting the animals out of those cages. To the police, it could have been anyone" (*Water*). Yet the violence against August was not random or committed by *anyone*. It was done by Rosie, and there are few viewers who would see this act of violence as regrettable. Not only does Rosie's killing of August demonstrate how "animals were not passive in this process or in lives lived in captivity," but it also reveals how "[a]nimal shows repeatedly demonstrated emotionally conflicted human–animal and human–social relations" (Tait xii). The reality that the viewers can easily accept this violence does in fact problematize violence in the circus network. Most people would feel that Rosie is justified since she saves multiple lives in the process. And no one would think that Rosie deserves execution, which occurred on several occasions in circus history (Davis 162). Yet she does commit violence, making the audience accept it and changing the way that violence functions. In many ways, she resembles Jacob, but she is also different because she does what he does not. Since both Jacob and Rosie are perceived as heroes in the film, it is clear how fluid the borders are in this translation zone (Rantisi and Leslie 151). Specifically, "the creation process depends on the work of many actors. With ANT [actor network theory], actors (termed *actants* [by Callon and Latour]) are not only human, but also nonhuman, including objects and nature (Callon 1986; Latour 1987, 2005). No one actant has complete control. Rather, each is either modifying or strengthening an initial idea or artifact" (151). Rosie's final decision to kill August adds to Jacob's earlier violent temptations, and it does not matter that Rosie is an animal because she is still an important actant, like he is, in the story. Together, the efforts of the human/animal pair highlight how "[e]xotic animals in the 19th century became a metaphoric part of narratives of overt and covert human violence," which symbolized social issues outside of the circus as well (Tait xv).

The ethical changes in the Benzini network are therefore obvious and far-reaching. Jacob and Rosie are problematic participants because they are moral beings[9] who challenge August's rule. When Jacob sees how poorly the cats are fed, he shares this concern with August. August does not care, even if he knows that the animals are malnourished. Jacob, though, does care, and he defies August in this and in his decision about Silver Star. Rosie resists August by refusing to acknowledge his violent authority. This shared heroism between Jacob and Rosie gives credence to Bouissac's comment: "Heroes, antiheroes, and animal actors are mutually defined with respect to the system of the modalities of actions" (Bouissac, *Multimodal* 103). Both Jacob and Rosie are moral beings, but they cannot mutually create an ethical system until they *interact* with each other and became a part of that system.

A similar notion is true for creating a more universal ethics in the circus, a move in the film that resembles Peter Singer's *equal consideration* principle. At the end, Jacob comments: "Benzini Brothers was officially belly up, property of Altoona, Pennsylvania. Shows on the road would get the scent soon enough and come to pick off our bones. I wouldn't leave Rosie to that. I wasn't gonna let anybody touch her with that hook again. So like I planned, I took my finals" (*Water*). Jacob leaves with Marlena *and* Rosie, the human and the animal, giving both equal consideration over the importance of their futures. The fact that Jacob cares for them both, as they care for him until their deaths, attests to the formalizing of this new circus ethics. Rosie's particular influence is noted at her death; Jacob recounts: "So then it was just Rosie and us. When Rosie passed on, Marlena cried for days. We owed Rosie our whole lives" (*Water*). This final statement, of what two humans owe to an animal, says a great deal about the critical element of having animal ethics not only in the circus but also in other aspects of life.

However, animals *must* be present and able to *interact* with humans in some form or fashion for this ethics to function. This notion goes against some of the interaction bans between humans and exotic animals, but clearly not *all* interactions between humans and animals are inherently bad (Neumann 185). Even though Tait posits that "[h]uman–animal proximity and tamer handling [...] carried the misconception of compatibility between humans and wild animals," collaboration between certain humans and

Jacob (Robert Pattinson), Marlena (Reese Witherspoon), and Rosie leave Benzini Brothers in *Water for Elephants*. After the demise of August and the Benzini Brothers Circus, Jacob, Marlena, and Rosie leave and prepare to begin a new life together.

wild/exotic animals *is* possible. Jacob and Rosie create a better situation for each other because they work together, and even if the animals' future is not in the circus, a future of some kind *together* is better than a separation that prevents such ethical gains from enduring or progressing. Thus, when some zookeepers or animal activists comment, "I *know* this elephant" (Abel 34), they are acknowledging a familiarity with animals in an equal capacity to that of humans (Singer 2), demonstrating that a viable path toward the creation of a universal ethics between humans and animals is to have *ethical* interactions between the two groups, just as Jacob and Rosie do in the film.

Conclusion

According to Linda Simon, "E.E. Cummings once declared that 'a periodic and highly concentrated dose of wild animals—elephants, tigers, lions, leopards, jaguars, bears, wolves, giraffes, kangaroos, zebras, horned horses, camels, hyenas, rhinoceri and at least one hippopotamus—is indispensable to the happiness of all mature civilized human beings," and from the example of the interactions between Jacob and Rosie in *Water for Elephants*, this advice has merit (Simon, 177). Because Jacob and Rosie are problematic participants in a circus translation zone—affecting star, home, social/power, violence, and ethical networks—*with* non-human animals, unlike the human-only zones of Cirque du Soleil, a more universal ethics that includes animals can develop (Rantisi and Leslie 148). And even if future circuses will no longer include animals, there is a sense of *inclusion* in this *exclusion* since the rights of animals are still being *included* and deemed important, suggesting that humans and animals must still interact to keep this ethical progress alive, whether within the circus, or outside (Bouissac, *Multimodal*, 195).

NOTES

1. The accepted term is *non-human animal*; however, in order to facilitate the flow of the essay, the term *animal* will predominate.

2. *Water for Elephants*, Benzini Brothers, and Rosie are representations of the circus, and as such, no claim is being made that the film portrays a real circus or that real elephants act this way.

3. Animals (and humans) died during capture; Charles Mayer captured 60 elephants under the Malay Sultan, but he also lost 3 Malay men (Davis 155); W.C. Coup, who worked for the Reiche Brothers, helped natives maim and kill mother elephants so that they could take their calves; the local leader did not care when humans died in the process (Davis 196).

4. Once the animals reached the circus, their situations did not improve. Philip Astley whipped humans and animals (Simon 35). George Conklin shot blanks near his "cats" to agitate them (Simon 159). Animal performers were often overfed to make them docile, and most horribly, several circus elephants were publicly executed. For more details about the execution of elephants (Albert, Tip, and Chief Forepaugh), see Davis 162.

5. P.T. Barnum also referred to these exhibitions as "human menagerie[s]" since humans were sometimes kept in cages for the benefit of spectators (Davis 10). These activities helped

to inaugurate modern activism, for both caged groups endured abuses and had inadequate keepers.

6. Activists have documented measurable abuses, such as how long animals spend in confinement ("Enjoy" 1), or qualitative abuses, such as biologically unintended circus movements ("Circuses" 1), a sense of mastery, imperialism (Davis 160), or even orientalism (Said 2) associated with exotic animals, and determining the fates of rescued animal performers (Christian 54). These acts, plus the perceived subjugation of the animal spirit (Simon 174) and the cage "becom[ing] a site of anxiety" (Simon 175), are just a few examples of the mistreatment of circus animals that have inspired activism.

7. For example, one of the strongest rationales remains the equalizing of the experience of humans with animals. Dr. William J. Hornaday wrote a "Wild Animals' Bill of Rights" and it asserts: "A wild animal has no more inherent right to live a life of lazy and luxurious ease, and freedom from all care, than a man or woman has to live without work or family cares.... Human beings who sanely work are much happier per capita than those who do nothing but grouch.... [I]t is no more wrong or wicked for a horse to work for his living—of course, on a human basis—either on the stage or on the street, than it is for a coal carrier, a foundry-man, a farmer, a bookkeeper, a schoolteacher or a housewife to do the day's work" (Davis 69). Hornaday's, purposeful, work on a philosophy toward non-human animals is supported by many veterinarians and zoologists who generally find that "circus animals are well taken care of by their owners who have a vested interest in their well-being, and that the training methods are ethnically appropriate to the natural behavior of the wild species concerned" (Bouissac, *Multimodal*, 189). These assessments do not deny the abuses that have occurred and that may still occur, but they at least present the other side of the argument about animals in the circus and the practice of the "kindness method" (Davis 159). In addition, Paul Bouissac, an avid circus scholar whose association with Alexander Lacey, a trainer whose "cats" seek kisses as ultimate rewards, offers great support for the care, respect, and love that non-human animal circus performers do receive (*Multimodal*, 126). His mention of the Roman *mansuetarii* (*mansuetas* means accustomed to the hand), "wild-animal trainers who used nonviolent methods to tame their animals and were performing tricks in close contact with them," also supports having animal performers (Bouissac, *Multimodal*, v).

8. For example, avid activism has resulted in the Traveling Exotic Animal Protection Act ("TEAPA") and the Animal Welfare Act ("AWA") (Neumann 178). In addition, non-human animals are now completely banned from circus performances in Austria and Bolivia (Bouissac, *Multimodal*, 188). Bans also exist in Irvine and Pasadena (California) and Boulder (Colorado) (Neumann 184), and in "Belgium, [the] Czech Republic, Denmark, Estonia, Finland, Greece, Italy, Malta, Poland, Slovakia, Spain, and Sweden" (Neumann 189).

9. Attributing moral dimension to Rosie and her actions is problematic; I have chosen to do so here based on her apparent recognition of August's attempt on Marlena's life, and her subsequent actions. Without this moral dimension, this argument is still valid.

Works Cited

Abel, Allen. "The Elephant's Final Bow: After a Long Battle with Animal Rights Groups, the Era of the Circus Elephant Is Coming to a Bitter Close." *Maclean's* vol. 17, 2016, pp. 33–35.

Aguiar, Ana Rosa Camillo, Alexandre de Pádua Carrieri, and Eloisio Moulin de Souza. "The Wonderful, Magnanimous, Spectacular and Possible World of Traveling Circuses in Brazil." *Brazilian Administration Review,* vol. 13, no.3, July/Sept 2016, pp. 1–19.

Bouissac, Paul. *Circus as Multimodal Discourse: Performance, Meaning, and Ritual.* London: Bloomsbury Academic, 2012.

_____. *Semiotics at the Circus.* Berlin: De Gruyter Mouton, 2010. Semiotics, Communication and Cognition.

Christian, Sena. "Beasts Under the Big Top: Government Bans on Circus Animals Are Leaving Rare Creatures Such as Lions and Monkeys Without a Home." *Newsweek,* vol. 52, 2015, pp. 52–54.

"Circuses." *PETA.org.* 2017.

Davis, Janet M. *The Circus Age: Culture and Society Under the American Big Top.* U of North Carolina P, 2002.

DeGrazia, David. *Animal Rights: A Very Short Introduction.* Oxford UP, 2002.

"Enjoy the Circus? The Animals Don't." *PAWS.org.* 2017.

Neumann, Jacqueline. "Redefining the Modern Circus: A Comparative Look at the Regulations Governing Circus Animal Treatment and America's Neglect of Circus Animal Welfare." *Whittier Law Review,* vol. 167, 2014–2015, pp. 167–194.

Nir, Sarah Maslin, and Nate Schweber. "After 146 Years, Ringling Brothers Circus Takes Its Final Bow." NYTimes.com. 21 May 2017.

Rantisi, Norma M. and Deborah Leslie. "Circus in Action: Exploring the Role of a Translation Zone in the Cirque du Soleil's Creative Practices." *Economic Geography,* vol. 91, no. 2, 2014, pp. 147–164.

Said, Edward. W. *Orientalism.* Vintage Books, 1978.

Simon, Linda. *The Greatest Shows on Earth: A History of the Circus.* Reaktion Books, 2014.

Singer, Peter. *Animal Liberation: The Definitive Classic of the Animal Movement—Updated Edition.* HarperCollins, 2009.

Tait, Peta. *Fighting Nature: Travelling Menageries, Animal Acts, and War Shows.* Sydney UP, 2016.

Water for Elephants. Directed by Francis Lawrence, performances by Reese Witherspoon, Robert Pattinson, and Christoph Waltz. Twentieth Century–Fox, 2011.

Under the Bi(g) Top

AYAL C. PROUSER

"You should make every man want to be you and every woman want to be with you." This sentence has been said to countless young men in performance arts, whether it be theatre, dance, music, or the like. The inverse has also been taught to young women in an attempt to teach them how to harness a demanding presence. It does not take deep analysis to identify the heteronormativity in this statement and this is a beneficial starting point to problematize specific theory structures in spectator theory and in binary approaches to gender, sex, and sexuality.

The focus of this essay is on the potentiality of a "bisexual vantage, whose presence within a text catalyzes spectators to see the world as bisexuals," as theorized by Elisabeth Daumer (Daumer, 98) through a lens which deconstructs socially confining and oppressive constructs. The "bisexual vantage" is contingent upon the identification of a tripartite constellation. The first prerequisite is an eroticized, shared discourse that manifests through a communal skill or community activity. This discourse must be equally shared by all members of the community regardless of sex or gender. The second and third prerequisites are partnered points: the second is discerned by identifying that the text (understood here to mean film) allows the viewer to align themselves with people of different genders at once, both as the "one you want to be" and the "one you want to be with"; and the third element is the equal eroticizing of different genders, or of people of different genders, simultaneously without a hierarchy. The "bisexual vantage" can be identified as ubiquitous across circus arts.

Both words of the term "bisexual vantage" were carefully chosen. Though at first it may seem that a Mulveyian-esque "gaze" is the natural term to use, "vantage" is a preferable term for reasons beyond simple nomenclature (and the fact that bisexual gaze is perhaps a misleading homophone). Daumer argued that bisexuality should not be understood within typical structures

of sex, gender, and sexual orientation, e.g., the gay/straight binary, man/
woman binary, or male/female binary. For her, bisexuality is a *vantage* point
from which to deconstruct these confining binaries (*ibid.*). Whereas the male
gaze situates an, ostensibly, man in the perspective of a sexual, gendered hierarchy, a position of power, the "bisexual vantage" is an equalizing agent. It
catalyzes a spectatorial experience wherein one is forced to deconstruct confining understandings of sexuality and gender by affirming and rejecting the
binaries associated therewith. The equalizing non-hierarchical nature of the
"bisexual vantage" is why the word "gaze" is inaccurate.

At first glance, the deconstruction of binaries as seen in this essay may
seem to fall within the realm of contemporary trans and gender queer theory;
this, however, would be inaccurate. This essay is specifically discussing spectatorship, aesthetics, and desire as opposed to identity. Bisexuality is theorized
as a sexuality rooted in relation to the de-gendering of the *beheld*, not the
self. The two, of course, are not mutually exclusive. This essay should also
not be understood as a rejection or denial of fluidity in regard to sexuality;
it is simply working within a different paradigm. This theorization of bisexuality assumes a permanence in sexuality. For example, when a bisexual man
has sex or falls in love with another man, it is not homosexuality, when a
bisexual man has sex or falls in love with a woman it is not heterosexuality;
both are still *bisexuality*.

This discussion has parallels to an area of scholarship from early feminist
film theory that sought to de-gender certain theorizations of spectatorship.
The "bisexual vantage" problematizes certain of these theories but should be
read in conjunction with feminist film theory. Despite the parallels, bisexuality is a more precise and correct categorization over feminist film theory.
Bisexual theorist Clare Hemmings articulates that gender belongs to the field
of feminism, and sexuality belongs to the field of queer studies. Bisexuality
requires the theorization of both. Hemmings further speculates that this
binary approach to scholarship is one of the causes of the lack of theorization
of bisexuality (Hemmings 37). I intend to assist in rectifying this scarcity,
and in bringing the B back into LGBTQIA studies.

The 1952 classic circus film *The Greatest Show on Earth* can serve as a
case study for both circus and cinema. While *Greatest Show* displays the mul-
tifarious performative elements of circus, and they are all complex issues
demanding extensive and thorough exploration, this essay specifically focuses
on aerial arts and only glances at equilibristics and acrobatics. One last note
is that I specifically analyze unique spectatorial aesthetic aspects of traditional
circus, and make no attempt to explicate the artistic intentionality of circus
artists or of the filmmakers. Moreover, there is no attempt to deny inequalities,
bigotries or oppressive structures found in the circus industry.

A–E, LGBTQIA: On the Film Selection

Though circus and cinema share a long history, their relationship has been insufficiently explored from a theoretical perspective. Circus and acrobatic skills were seen in early motion pictures, such as *Trapeze Disrobing Act* (1901). Helen Stoddart, on the subject of the long history of circus and cinema, found that early in film history, screenings occurred on circus lots. They were found, however, to be too dangerous, given how flammable both film and circus tents were (Stoddart 27). Sergei Eisenstein, noted film/art theorist as well as director, found inspiration for his noted "Montage of Attractions" at the fairground, which shares many performative elements with the circus (Eisenstein 33–39). And the circus has been used as a setting or plot device throughout cinema history in films including *The Circus* (1928), *At the Circus* (1939), *Dumbo* (1941), *3 Ring Circus* (1959), *Billy Rose's Jumbo* (1962), through today in *Water for Elephants* (2011) and *The Greatest Showman* (2017)—and many more.

This long and intertwined history provides a rich selection of motion pictures to choose from. *The Greatest Show on Earth* was not chosen at random. First, it is within the paradigm of what will be understood as "circus cinema" which consists of motion pictures that contain elements of circus, and that, through analysis, reveal a similar ethos or internal logic as the circus does, i.e., the presence of the "bisexual vantage." Moreover, circus films contain a demonstrable connection to the actual circus. For example *The Greatest Show on Earth* very clearly had connections to the Ringling Bros. and Barnum & Bailey Circus. *Trapeze* (1956), another example of circus cinema, starred Burt Lancaster, a former circus acrobat. On the other hand, *Big Fish* (2003), though it has circus elements, would not be considered a circus film for my analysis because it uses the circus as simply a plot device; *Circus World* (1964), though set at a circus, has been cited by Peta Tait as so against the internal logic of circus, given its aggressive masculinity, that it cannot be considered as truly representative (Tait, 111). While there are clearly many movies to choose from, *Greatest Show* was found to be a fruitful vehicle for this exploration.

Before entering deeply into the analysis, certain theoretical aspects pertaining to the presence of the "bisexual vantage" in a film must be understood, specifically as they apply to the selection of *Greatest Show*. As stated, the "bisexual vantage" is a spectatorial experience in which one is *situated* to perceive the world through a bisexual lens. The "bisexual vantage" does not assume that bisexuality is present in the text. Bisexuality in a text neither asserts nor negates that the text contains the "bisexual vantage." In fact, *Greatest Show*'s seeming heteronormativity is part of why it was selected for this analysis. While pedagogic texts can easily be identified in art cinema and the avant-garde, identifying a film that triggers one to begin deconstructing societal confines in Hollywood is rarer.

An intersection of specific theories on the subject of queer cinema postulated by Richard Dyer, and Comolli and Narboni's essay "Cinema/Ideology/Criticism" (CIC), helps to explicate the idiosyncratic space that Hollywood films containing the "bisexual vantage" occupy.

For Dyer, queer cinema is defined neither by the sexuality of the filmmaker nor the subject of the film. It is defined by a change in cinematic grammar and aesthetic that is rooted in the filmmaker's access to queer discourse, regardless of their sexuality (Dyer 188). CIC specifies five categories of nondocumentary film and labels them A–E. Each is defined by its form and content and how it furthers or counters mainstream ideology. Whereas Comolli and Narboni were discussing an Althusserian approach, and thus were discussing film from a leftist political perspective, for this essay, "counter-ideological" is replaced with queer.

Of course it is difficult, if not impossible, to create a media taxonomy without flaws, especially one that compares itself to a "scientific" approach (Comolli and Narboni 479–480). Taxonomies, however, can be beneficial for helping to process and synthesize texts in new capacities. For example, appropriating Comolli and Narboni's categories into a Dyerian approach to queer cinema leads to new analyses for the "bisexual vantage," as well as helps to process the place of queerness in Hollywood.

In CIC, Category A consists of films that are part of the dominant ideology in both form and content. For this analysis Category A includes films that are not queer in both form and content. Category B is the inverse; such films attack ideology and the apparatus through both form and content, the "signified and signifier," and includes films that are queer in both form and content. Category C are films whose content is part of dominant ideology but whose form is not. For the sake of the appropriated taxonomy, it refers to films that are queer in form but not in content. Category D is the opposite, in that its content is counter-ideological but its form is not. This includes films that are queer in content but not in form; this is the most problematic for this version of the taxonomy.[1]

Category E is the most difficult to identify; it includes films that appear to belong in category A, but are riddled with "cracks" that reveal them as subtly counter-ideological. Cracks should be seen as an internal and reflexive criticism of the dominant ideology that the film is deceptively not furthering. With enough cracks present, the film tears itself open, revealing its true and counter-ideological nature. For this taxonomy, the "bisexual vantage" is a potential example of Category E, which reveals further nuances of the "bisexual vantage." While it is generally easier to identify the "bisexual vantage" in films that might be considered Category B or C, its presence in a film that appears to be Category A relegates that film to Category E. For example, *Greatest Show* appears to be a typical Hollywood film in regard to form and content; it is a typical heterosexual love story[2] and appears to be made in the typical Hollywood problematic mode. However, it situates the viewer to deconstruct exactly these problematic roots through a bisexual lens, which should be understood as a queer experience. For a film that was made in the 1950s,[3] an anti-queer and aggressively gendered time, the concept of a queering catalyst as a form of entertainment is fascinating and is exactly those "cracks."

Circus cinema should be understood as riddled with more "cracks" than live circus. The circus has a long history as being understood as transgressive. This is partially rooted in its acceptance and celebration of difference and the other, albeit in a sometimes exploitative manner. One could argue that this status is what allows people to not recognize the queer moment they are having publicly as iconoclastic to their beliefs, or even "legitimate"—*they are at a circus, after all.* Hollywood cinema, however, is understood as a site of identification with, as well as a site of reflection for, society at large. This is why those queer "cracks" loom larger—they are closer to home. Thus circus cinema typically fits into Category E. While these films seem to fit into the heteronormative, heterosexist mode of production suffused throughout Hollywood, they are actually generating a queer experience in which one questions societal givens.

The Backlot: Fundamental Theory for Understanding the "Bisexual Vantage"

The first point of the tripartite constellation of a "bisexual vantage" is an eroticized, shared discourse that manifests through a communal skill or community activity, and stands on an understanding of Michel Foucault's approach to sexuality. In *The History of Sexuality*, Foucault, posits sexuality is the discourse behind the physical act of sex. For him, sex and sexuality are two separate concepts. One's personal sexuality, as well as societal sexuality, determines how one might approach and perform sex (Foucault 68).

Sexuality should not specifically be understood as orientation; it is related to identity. The distinction lies in that, for Foucault, "sexuality" is identified by a state of otherness. Foucault discusses the etymology of the word heterosexual as a response to the creation of the word homosexual. Since heterosexuality was assumed, it did not need a word. This same concept applies to sexuality; it is only one's sexuality if it is considered different from what is deemed typical (an idea explicated below). Any sort of queer, however, can become a part of your identity. In fact, given that it is an area of oppressions and being other, it often becomes an important aspect of one's identity. In an ideal world all orientations and sexuality would be completely separate, but alas that is not the case.

To understand the connection between Foucault's theory and circus arts, certain cultural understandings of circus are required; it too is an othered, shared discourse that manifests in an erotic action. In an interview I conducted with Troy Wunderle, noted clown and circus director, he articulated the reality of a circus life. "Traditional circus was built upon the backs of circus families that passed their trade and talents down through the generations … [and that] traditional circus was for a lifetime" (Wunderle). Beyond trade and talents, so, too, were culture and lore bequeathed from generation to generation. This would include, for example, certain lexiconic traditions such as never saying "goodbye" at the end of a contract but saying "see you down the road." Since the circus is such an insular community and people stayed in the community for their whole lives, paths would naturally cross time and time again. What is also passed on with the peripatetic life is an impression of being outside of traditional society. Rob Mermin, former dean of Ringling Brothers Clown College who now lectures on the circus, discusses that a common result of this migratory lifestyle includes a feeling of continued otherness, and living outside of the law. Mermin and Wunderle discuss living a "circus life" from the standpoint of the artists, claiming that it is separate from the general public. Moreover, as will be discussed in more detail shortly, the physical act of circus, the act connected to these details, is quite erotic. The discourses behind this identity of otherness should be understood as the "sexuality" to the "sex," the physical act of circus. This same concept applies to *Greatest Show* where the shared discourse is the same circus sexuality. For the sake of *Greatest Show*, the shared discourse is circus. This will be explicated further, below.

For the second and third points of the "bisexual vantage," a detailed understanding of specific theories regarding sex, gender, and sexuality are required. As stated above, Elisabeth Daumer argued that bisexuality should not be understood within typical structures of sex, gender and sexual orientation, e.g., the gay/straight binary, man/woman binary, or male/female binary. For her, bisexuality is a *vantage* point from which to deconstruct these confining binaries that have become presumed societal "truths." She argues that these "truths" are too deeply rooted both in the queer community as well as the heterosexual community (Daumer 98). It is best to understand these "truths" through the Foucauldian approach to biological sex, sexuality, and the physical act of sex. Foucault traces the confining definitions of "acceptable" sex and sexuality back to the Catholic Church. He states that the advent of confession created a culture in which people sought inner truths in regard to self, philosophy, and society (Foucault 59). This led to seeking a truth in sexuality as well, whether it was a "proper" age, location, or practice. As for biological sex, Foucault discusses in "Herculin Barbin" the understanding of a binary as a relatively late onset, after much social constriction. There was a time when one was not expected by the Church, and thus by an ideologically dependent public, to fall within a sex binary. With exceptions, of course, Foucault identified an overall[4] surprisingly liberal approach to intersex people. In the Middle Ages, however, a patriarch would have to decide on behalf of an intersex person what their "true" sex was, and even later, a trained professional was the only one equipped to find the hidden truths of an intersex child. During these times it was also "acceptable" for one to change their gender performance in pursuit of their "true" sex (Foucault, V–IX). These "truths" of sex, sexuality, and gender identified by Foucault begin to illuminate the sites of deconstruction that Daumer identified. Building on Daumer's theory, it is not only that bisexuality can be described neither in terms of gender, sex, or sexuality, nor as a vantage point from which to undo associated structures, but even more that bisexuality is grounded in one's sexuality, affirming and rejecting such binaries. It is here that the "bi," the duality of the sexuality, is present.

As for sexuality itself, this seeming paradox of affirmation and rejection is explored in the work of Clare Hemmings. She articulates that bisexuality is the only sexuality where the object of desire cannot all at once signify. For instance, the homosexual's desired articulates their sexuality. For a bisexual, it is rare for a single partner to, all at once, represent their sexuality (Hemmings 24). Hemmings cites philosopher and theorist Jonathan Dollimore who discusses the overwhelming experience for a bisexual man who, while in a threesome, sees a man and a woman having sex. Dollimore theorizes that the bisexual viewer would want to perform both positions—to be the man having sex with the woman and be the woman who is having sex with the man. In other words, he is conflating the "one you want" to be and the "one you want to be with." Dollimore continues that the man is not confused or undecided. He also does not describe this as an oscillation (Dollimore 33), an idea that will be discussed momentarily. For Dollimore, the bisexual person is desiring both at once, and this is beyond the constraints of "typical" desire (*Ibid.*). This is easily transitioned to a spectatorial phenomenological understanding, especially in regard to desire and voyeurism, or even simply spectatorship. There is no longer the performer the spectator "wants to be" and the performer the spectator "wants to be with," they are one and the same, and each is a manifestation of both.

While the dualities of bisexuality are one reason why one's partner most often does not represent the sexuality of the beheld, it is also contingent on the fact that bisexuality stands to reject typical readings of sex, gender, and sexuality. In terms of the affirmation and rejection of gender and biological sex, this can be understood via two distinct manifestations of bisexuality. The attraction to more than one gender, or the "same and the different" is a common understanding of bisexuality, though I would include attraction to androgyny as well. Androgyny, in this case, has two separate definitions. The first connotes a person who reads as completely non-gendered or unsexed. An example of this would include early punk, where people of all genders would wear the same slim fitting pants, shredded t-shirts and big hair. Concerts would easily turn into a sea of blacks and neutrals where neither sex nor gender were deeply signified. The second definition of androgyny indicates an appearance that reads as a complete conflation of genders. David Bowie and his space oddity character Ziggy Stardust exemplifies this category. Queer theorist Chris Straayer discusses this androgynous demographic, referring to them as "she-male" which is "a fully functioning figure signifying both man and woman." (Straayer 94) He clarifies that such people do not use their femininity as a source of comedy, but as a vehicle for enhancing their sexuality and appeal. The former of the two categories of bisexuality affirms that gender is a construct that is within the sexuality of the beholder. It simultaneously, however, rejects assumptions that genders have any inherence, especially in regard to sexuality. Moreover, by recognizing androgyny, one is acknowledging that such people use sex as a perceived sign system, although the androgynous person rejects that same binary and the gender and sexuality associations therein. A "bisexual vantage" rejects that the gender or secondary sex traits of one's partner can be used to read the sexuality, or identity, of a person. It is an equalizing vantage that, when in action, disarms hierarchy.

The eroticizing of people of different genders without hierarchy or roles based on gender performance should be understood as the textual manifestation of the duality of being attracted to more than one gender. Similarly, the eroticizing of androgyny, or the feminizing of men and masculinizing of women, is a direct correlation to the attraction to the two categories of androgyny. It is for this reason that the "bisexual vantage" should be seen in response to, or as problematizing, Laura Mulvey's spectatorial transvestism. Mulvey postulates that her monumental essay, "Visual Pleasure and Narrative Cinema," which triggered the theorization of the male gaze, required further nuance. She furthers her original argument by theorizing a spectatorial transvestism wherein women may identify with the masculine perspective and men may identify with the feminine perspective, and moreover that one can oscillate between the two. She discusses this as a fluctuation in sexuality with women as active and men self-relegating into passivity (Mulvey 127). It is this binary approach to sexuality in spectatorship that the "bisexual vantage" problematizes. Why is it a fluctuation when it can be men and women, or anyone at all, fulfilling both roles of the "want to be" and the "want to be with" all at once? This is exactly the second point of the "bisexual vantage."

This directly relates to the third element within the tripartite constellation, the eroticizing of people of more than one gender as well as androgyny, all without a hierarchy. These can all be identified in *The Greatest Show on Earth*.

In the First Ring: The Greatest Show on Earth *and the First Point of the "Bisexual Vantage" Constellation*

In *The Greatest Show on Earth*, the shared, eroticized discourse is identifiable from the very beginning of the film. The monologue which accompanies the opening montage follows.

> We bring you the circus, pied piper whose magic tunes greet children of all ages, from six to sixty, into a tinsel and spun-candy world of reckless beauty and mounting laughter and whirling thrills; of rhythm, excitement and grace; of blaring and daring and dance; of high-stepping horses and high-flying stars. But behind all this, the circus is a massive machine whose very life depends on discipline and motion and speed. A mechanized army on wheels, that rolls over any obstacle in its path, that meets calamity again and again, but always comes up smiling. A place where disaster and tragedy stalk the big top, haunt the backyard, and ride the circus train. Where death is constantly watching for one frayed rope, one weak link, or one trace of fear. A fierce, primitive fighting force that smashes relentlessly forward against impossible odds. That is the circus. And this is the story of the biggest of the big tops, and of the men and women who fight to make it "The Greatest Show on Earth."

While this monologue, which is read over a near military-esque march, serves to catch the audience's attention, it also helps to identify the existence as well as specific aspects of the discourse behind the physical act of circus, that is the discourse to the practice—the sexuality to the sex of circus. The circus is not just a "world of reckless beauty and mounting laughter and whirling thrills; of rhythm, excitement and grace; of blaring and daring and dance; of high-stepping horses and high-flying stars," but is a community with a shared discourse behind those performative aspects. Beyond the aforementioned discourses, the aspects of the discourse readily identifiable in this march include, but are not limited to, facing, curbing, and mastering danger, maintaining discipline in training as well as performance, and abiding by the signature line of show business, "the show must go on." When the opening march cites the circus as "a fierce, primitive fighting force that smashes relentlessly forward against impossible odds," it is to this mentality that they are referring. These are all aspects of the discourse, the sexuality, of circus, that manifest in the physical act, the Foucauldian "sex" of circus.

The last line of the march, "And this is the story of the biggest of the big tops, and of the men and women who fight to make it 'The Greatest Show on Earth,'" not only stands to introduce the film, but states that the discourses, the sexuality, behind the circus, is shared by men and women equally. While this is verbalized with a measure of subtlety, its cinematic depiction is more explicit and comprehensive. During the montage which accompanies this monologue and march, there is limited distinction between the responsibilities and roles of men and women except in costuming, which will be discussed below. For instance, when the voiceover says "A place where disaster and tragedy stalk the big top," these words are accompanied first by seeing an injured man on the floor, presumably after a circus accident, then a cut to a woman walking up a guy-rope on the outside of the tent at a dangerous level. Both men and women risk their bodies and lives in the name of circus.

This reading is further corroborated through a close reading of the circus arts themselves. One of the two flying trapeze tricks is a passing leap, one of the very few tricks typically seen in flying trapeze shows that require two flyers to participate, crossing in midair as one is caught and one returns to the bar. It is common to see this move executed with two men, two women, or mixed with either man or woman in either position. In this shared trick there is no hierarchy; it is a triad with complete equality. The equality of the circus discourse is further depicted when the voiceover says, "Where death is constantly watching for one frayed rope, one weak link." This is accompanied by a woman spinning on a Spanish web, an act that, for the time of the film's production, was most associated with showgirls or those who are to be looked at, a passive allocation. This clip, however, cuts to a scene of a woman hanging from a cradle, holding another woman, who hangs from a neckloop and is in turn basing (supporting) a man lying on her feet. One name[5] for a person lying on another's feet while on an aerial apparatus is a "Sleeping Beauty," which nicely articulates the passivity of the pose—especially of the one being held. The man in this case, the "beauty" as it were, is in the passive, to-be-looked at, position, while the woman is in the strong, what might be described as masculine, muscular pose—an idea which will be returned to below. Men and women in this montage are depicted filmically, performativity, and verbally, without a hierarchy and they fulfill the roles of both passive and active, portraying them as equals and without gender assumptions. This can be understood as a physical manifestation of their equally shared discourse or of their equality; that equality is part of the discourse—a necessary element in the presence of the "bisexual vantage."

The "bisexual vantage" does not only require that the discourse be equally shared but that it is eroticized as well. In the next subsection, circus will be discussed as having a near-inherent erotics as part of its performativity; *Greatest Show* filmically accentuates the eroticism all the more. In the scene where the performers Sebastian and Holly are competing on their trapezes (which will be deeply analyzed below), it is not just a friendly competition but an erotic back and forth of showmanship. They are trying to seduce each other; Sebastian even goes so far as to tap his leg when he is balancing on top of the chair placed on his Washington trapeze to gesture "come sit on my lap." In a different scene, as a means of flirting, albeit a risky one, Sebastian without announcement replaces the regular catcher in the flying trapeze act that Holly flies in. During this act Sebastian pulls Holly up from underneath him and asks her for a kiss mid-swing. It is another attempt at explicitly adding erotics to a near-inherent erotic moment.

Overall, in fact, sexuality is a motif throughout *Greatest Show*, especially in regard to Sebastian. Before Sebastian even arrives on the circus lot, a businessman in a meeting discussing the future of the circus says, in regard to Sebastian, "He may be a god in the air but he's a devil on the ground" to which another businessman responds "You mean with women?" This should be understood as conflating his circus self and his sexuality. From the very beginning of the film, the audience is taught that Sebastian's impressive aerial and acrobatic feats should reflect his sexuality and that both together should be seen as a repeated syntagm within the suffused sexuality paradigm.

An outright declaration of his "sexiness," which should be seen in conjunction with all the discussion of sexuality thus far, comes from other circus performers. When Sebastian walks by Phyllis (Dorothy Lamour), one of the other circus performers who is having her hair washed, she states "why is it whenever he's around I'm all wet." Birdie (Julia Faye), a friend and colleague, replies "in more ways than one." While this dialogue is surprisingly vulgar for a film from the 1950s, it is highlighting the sexuality of Phyllis while also highlighting the sexiness of Sebastian. This should be seen as, explicitly, sexuality in the Foucauldian sense, because of the vulgarity for such a prudish time. With a reading of *Greatest Show* in regard to the second and third points of the "bisexual vantage" the erotics will become clearer.

In the Far Rings: The Greatest Show and the Second and Third Points of the "Bisexual Vantage" Constellation

The third point of the bisexual vantage—the equal eroticizing of people regardless of gender and without hierarchy—should already be understood as present within the text to some extent. Reading the film with the theory previously put forth, in conjunction with specific circus studies theories, will help to display both of the final points more clearly. Peta Tait, one of the leading scholars in the burgeoning field of circus studies, identifies a unique mode of communication in the circus between performer and audience. Specifically, she theorizes a body-to-body form of communication.[6] She argues that the extreme, seemingly death-defying feats that circus artists produce with their bodies trigger a bodily reaction from the audience. She marks this primarily in the form of members of the audience holding their breath, though she also talks about jumps in moments of surprise, and visceral anxiety. She discusses further that a circus act is structured for the maximum bodily reactions from the audience (Tait 142–143).

In the aforementioned scene in which Sebastian and Holly try to one-up each other, they visually articulate this unique communication. With both artists on their Washington trapezes, they perform acts of human exceptionalism with their bodies, forcing the audience to have bodily responses. When Sebastian is first seen leaning in his chair on top of his trapeze, it is a low angle shot, as if from the audience's perspective. The audience, in return, is shot from a high angle, as if they are being seen from either Holly or Sebastian's perspective. The audience members from the beginning are all fidgeting in their seats. Even though the bodily exceptionalism from Sebastian and Holly had just begun, the body-to-body communication is already present. This shot/reverse shot display of communication continues throughout the scene and, as the tricks become bigger, that is, as the bodily declarations to the audience intensify, so, too, do the bodily reactions from the audience. As the contentious effort to demonstrate superiority continues, when Sebastian stands on the chair, the audience's fidgets become full body gazing and squirming. When Holly handstands on top of the chair, the culmination of the affecting, bodily exceptionalism, Brad (Charlton Heston) and Buttons (James Stewart), stand up in worry. When she slips, though she is safe, the audience jumps to their feet. The audience, as well as Brad and Buttons, jumping to their feet displays the culmination of their bodies' ability to react, as a result of Holly surpassing her body's ability to display within safe boundaries. A bodily reaction from the audience could only get bigger if it erupted in a Stravinsky-esque riot, though, of course, that was not as a result of body-to-body communication.

Low angle shots of the performers not only make the viewer of the film watch the performance from the position of the diegetic audience, but make the spectators of *Greatest Show* participants in the body-to-body communication. The spectators are forced by the shot to make the bodies of both the male and female performers our spectatorial focus—which in turn gives rise to bodily reactions, just like the diegetic audience. Though this is not a typical erotic act, arguably, a spectator having a bodily reaction as a result of pleasurable viewing of someone else using their body to actively cause the spectator a body-based pleasure is erotic. Most importantly to the "bisexual vantage," it is an erotic act that does not mark for sex or gender. This should be read also as corroborating, and as a fundamental backdrop for, the argument that the shared discourse of circus is eroticized. This is also directly connected to the conflation of the "one you want to be" and "the one you want to be with." Sebastian and Holly in this context should be understood as the two people in Dollimore's threesome. They are giving both the audience and each other an erotic experience. The idea of the audience being able to identify with one, and see the other as the beheld, due to the unique bodily spectatorial and erotic experience, is fading away. This conflation, and the sexualizing of people of different genders without hierarchy, is further emphasized by the costuming within *Greatest Show*. Sebastian, at any time of performance, and often out of the ring, wears his green tights and no shirt. Tait discusses male aerialists' costuming, noting that it is common for them to wear slimming costuming so as to emphasize their dancer-like bodies. These costumes elongate the aerialists' legs and make them appear petite. She notes one exception; trapeze catchers typically wear costumes that emphasize their large chests and shoulders. The marked difference, however, further emphasizes the feminizing of the other aerialist men.

Women, on the other hand, as evinced by the spaghetti strap leotard worn by Holly, or the bikinis worn by aerialists and showgirls in the opening march, at first glance appear to wear overly gendering and objectifyingly revealing costumes. Tait suggests that these revealing costumes are not a vehicle of objectification but the exact opposite. For Tait, the muscular build of women acrobats is unyielding to being objectified (Tait 39). It is important here to understand that Tait is talking from a spectatorial standpoint; neither she nor this article is attempting to disregard the feelings of performers put into such costuming, or disregarding the problematic source of asking women to wear such costumes. The costuming from a spectatorial standpoint, however, does stand to emphasize these women's muscularity, which connotes activity, and given the lack of differentiation in the tasks of both men and women, the activity it connotes is bodily exceptionalism, impressive feats, and de-gendered erotics.

This feminizing of men and masculinizing of women, especially in regard to body-to-body communication, should be understood as the textual manifestation of attraction to androgyny. This is due to the fact that the characters at times read as more than one, and no gender simultaneously. Moreover, the standard circus ring is 42 feet in diameter and performing in the air only adds further distance; thus due to the distance of the circus, the audience loses the ability to use secondary sex traits to identify a performer's sex. Additionally, this disassembling of gender and sex-based visual cues should be understood in conjunction with the allocation of both men and women in the place of "to be looked at," all at once, as a textual equivalent of attraction to more than one gender. These two together represent the two types of bisexuality and should be understood in that same affirmation and rejection of a correlation between gender performance, secondary sex traits, and sexuality.

To call on the language of the "bisexual vantage," what this further accomplishes is the conflation of the "one you want to be" and the "one you want to be with."

In this contentious act, with no differentiation between active and passive and with both performers executing incredible feats, there is no way to deduce with which we are intended to identify. Moreover, with the erotic act that does not mark for gender, one cannot identify a single performer as the erotic focus. In the case of Holly and Sebastian, both are both, all at once. They personify the second and third points of the "bisexual vantage."

Conclusion

With this understanding of bisexuality and its role within the circus and *The Greatest Show on Earth*, one can more fully understand the "bisexual vantage." The presence of the "bisexual vantage" constellation in a text forces the reader to affirm and yet reject societal, confining understandings of sex, sexuality, and gender which have come to be understood as "truths." This theorization is rooted in Elizabeth Daumer's understanding of bisexuality wherein it is a vantage point to deconstruct such truths. This affirmation and rejection will occur when all three points of the "bisexual vantage" are present. The first prerequisite is an eroticized, shared discourse that manifests through a communal skill or community activity. The second prerequisite is that the text allows the viewer to align themselves with people of different genders at once, both as the "one you want to be" and the "one you want to be with." Lastly, the third prerequisite is that men are eroticized simultaneously or equally to other genders. While these are ubiquitous across circus arts, The *Greatest Show on Earth* filmically accentuates each point.

Circus and cinema have a long history together, and this relationship deserves to be more deeply theorized. Moreover, it is important that circus be understood, discussed, and theorized to the same degree as other arts. At the same time, the circus is a live art form that should be enjoyed as such. To paraphrase Friedrich Nietzsche discussing a high wire walker: "we have heard enough of circus artists, now let's watch them" (Nietzsche 7).

GLOSSARY

Base—The title in partner or group acrobatics/aerials that refers to the acrobat who supports/lifts/throws/balances other acrobat(s) (see flyer)

Catcher—One of the two main positions in flying trapeze (see flyer). The catcher for the most part stays on their catch trap (see catch trapeze) and catches the flyers who perform tricks.

Cradle—An aerial apparatus in which a performer hangs by their knees from one side of a rectangular frame and tucks their feet under the other side. This hooking provides extra security for the base which allows for more dynamic tricks. A cradle is often used in place of a Spanish trapeze (*see catch trap*) in flying trapeze.

Flyer—The position in partner or group acrobatics/aerials that refers to the acrobat who is supported/lifted/thrown/balanced by other acrobat(s). Also refers to the performer in flying trapeze who performs the trick that is caught by the catcher (*see catcher*).

Flying trapeze—The iconic circus spectacle that involves an aerial acrobat swinging on a trapeze, performing a trick, and then either being caught by another acrobat (see catcher) or grabbing on to another bar.

Guy rope—A rope on the outside of a structure (like a circus tent) that anchors it to the ground for further support.

High wire—A tight wire rigged at a great height.

Spanish web—A vertical rope, with a loop attached, so that aerialists can secure themselves as they are spun in circles by a fellow performer.

Static trapeze—Static in aerial terminology conveys that the bars and ropes for the most part do not swing. It is common for the ropes on static apparatuses to be padded.

Traditional circus—A retrospective term applied to a specific style and form of circus, at the advent of the *cirque nouveau* movement in the 1970s. A bill passed by the House of Representatives in 1910 on the topic of how expensive a license tax should be for circuses aptly begins a discussion on the ontology of traditional circus. The bill reads that a circus is defined as:

> Every building, tent, space or area, where feats of horsemanship, or acrobatic sports, or theatrical performances pertaining to or being part thereof, are exhibited, including shows or exhibitions of horsemanship, marksmanship and the like, depicting tribal scenes costumes, or costumes and the like, commonly knows as wild west shows, and exhibitions commonly known as dog and pony shows or the like, shall be regarded as a circus.

One can deduce from this definition that a (traditional) circus is a performance where feats of acrobatics and equestrianship are performed in conjunction with displays of skills and animal training. There are some defining factors that this bill has left out. For instance, a staple of traditional circus is the longstanding tradition of circus families, where technique together with insider lore and culture are transmitted from generation to generation.

Trapeze—A category of aerial apparatus which consists of a metal or wooden horizontal bar that hangs from ropes, cables or chains.

Washington trapeze—A type of trapeze often wider and flatter than a traditional trapeze bar. The flat surface allows for the performance of balance-based tricks.

NOTES

1. Category A, whether it was for CIC or this queer appropriation of the taxonomy, consists of most Hollywood films. Examples of Category A for both are *American Pie* (1999), or *Transformers* (2007). In CIC, feminist avant-garde films, such as early Sally Potter films, e.g., *Thriller* (1979), or *The Gold Diggers* (1983), or Marxist cinema such as Vertov's *Man with a Movie Camera* (1929), would be Category B, albeit for different political and formal reasons. For queer cinema, Category B would not only include queer experimental film, but also "Dyerian" queer films, with queer content. *Velvet Goldmine* (1998), for example, is formally not as jarring as Sally Potter's films, but has an arguably queer aesthetic, and certainly has queer content (as well as a queer director). Category C might include films such as *Two-Lane Blacktop* (1971). Category D is complicated in the queer rendition of this taxonomy and is an example of how taxonomies can help one ask questions. For a heterosexist/sexist system such as Hollywood, can a Category D film exist? Will the juxtaposition of the queer characters, viewed through a heteronormative and gender role-asserting lens only stand to articulate that queerness is other? Is *Brokeback Mountain* (2005) an example of Category D? Or perhaps does *Brokeback Mountain* contain a subtle change in cinematic grammar, thus making it Category B? This is an example of where taxonomies can be flawed, and how subjectivity can become a factor. Simultaneously, however, this Category D tension in regard to queer cinema under Hollywood helps us recognize aspects of queer cinema that may not always be on the forefront of theory. While this can all be further developed, it is beyond the scope of this essay.

2. Though, of course, a love-triangle is a source of its own for queer analysis.

3. This is all the more fascinating given the abundance of circus films made in the 1950s.

4. He notes that there were hate crimes and legal ramifications for some but they were exceptions.

5. I say "a name" because, unlike gymnastics where names of skills and techniques are canonized, the names of circus tricks are different for different people. When I was in Circus Smirkus, a traveling youth circus based in New England, I was in a partner acrobatic act with six people from five different schools. We renamed many tricks because there was confusion as to which trick we were referring to, and that interfered with training.

6. While Tait discusses this as unique to circus, I believe it can also be identified in the work of specific post-modern choreographers such as Elizabeth Streb and Trisha Brown. The work of both of these choreographers have similarities to circus given the use of apparatuses; choreographed works that can be compared to aerial dance. Streb's work is also very acrobatic.

WORKS CITED

At the Circus. Directed by Edward Buzzell. Metro-Goldwyn-Mayer, 1939.
Billy Rose's Jumbo. Directed by Charles Walters. Metro-Goldwyn-Mayer, 1962.
The Circus. Directed by Charlie Chaplin. United Artists, 1928.
Comolli, Jean-Louis, and Narboni Jean. "Cinema/Ideology/Criticism." *Critical Visions in Film Theory*, edited by Timothy Corrigan, Patricia White, and Meta Mazaj, Bedford/St. Martin's, 2011, pp. 478–86.
Daumer, Elisabeth. "34 Queer Ethics; or, the Challenge of Bisexuality to Lesbian Ethics." *Hypaptia: A Journal of Feminist Philosophy* 7.4 (1992).
Dumbo. Directed by Ben Sharpsteen. Walt Disney Productions, 1941.
Dyer, Richard. *The Culture of Queers*. Routledge Taylor & Francis Group, 2012.
Eisenstein, Sergei. "The Montage of Attractions." *S.M Eisenstein: Selected Readings*. BFI, 1988, pp. 33–39.
Foucault, Michel. *The History of Sexuality, Volume I*. Translated by Robert Hurley. Penguin, 1990.
_____, and Herculine Barbin. *Herculine Barbin: Being the Recently Discovered Memoirs of a Nineteenth-Century French Hermaphrodite*. Vintage, 2010.
The Gold Diggers. Directed by Sally Potter. BFI Production Board, 1983.

The Greatest Showman. Directed by Michael Gracey. 20th Century–Fox, 2017.

Hemmings, Clare. *Bisexual Spaces: A Geography of Sexuality and Gender.* Routledge, 2002.

Mulvey, Laura. *Afterthoughts on "Visual Pleasure and Narrative Cinema" Inspired by* Duel in the Sun. Routledge, 1990.

Nietzsche, Friedrich. *Thus Spoke Zarathustra,* edited by Adrien Del Caro and Robert Pippin, Cambridge UP, 2006.

Stoddart, Helen. *Rings of Desire: Circus History and Representation.* Manchester UP, 2000.

Straayer, Chris. *Deviant eyes, Deviant Bodies: Sexual Re-orientations in Film and Video.* Columbia UP, 1996.

Tait, Peta. *Circus Bodies: Cultural Identity in Aerial Performance.* Routledge, 2005.

3 Ring Circus. Directed by Joseph Pevney. Paramount, 1959.

Thriller. Directed by Sally Potter. Arts Council of Great Britain, 1979.

Trapeze Disrobing Act. Directed by Thomas Edison. 1901.

Velvet Goldmine. Directed by Todd Haynes. Film Four International, 1998.

Water for Elephants. Directed by Francis Lawrence. 20th Century–Fox, 2011.

Wunderle, Troy. "Circus Interview." Email interview. 12 Dec. 2016.

Liminal Spaces and Identity in *MirrorMask*

Teresa Cutler-Broyles

The circus, in real life and on-screen, is ideally positioned to create a liminal space that allows for a shedding of inhibitions, a place in which immersion in and viewing of spectacle is the main point, and a space of possibility in which anything might happen. Entering the gates of the circus means leaving behind one's daily routine, sense of propriety, and understanding of reality, and consenting to having one's expectations confounded. In no small part this is due to the presence of elements of the carnivalesque. Mikhail Bakhtin defined the carnivalesque as, in part, an inversion of political, legal and ideological authority that allowed for liberation, for freedom of movement and action, and for a questioning of assumed hierarchies, established ways of doing things, and even identity. With the freak show where humans sometimes seem animalistic to the animals that walk like humans, from the contortionists whose bodies seem unhinged to the stiff-legged stilt-walkers, and from the trapeze artists—humans who can fly—to the masked clowns who seemingly defy physics as they pile into cars far too small to hold even half their number, the circus serves to unsettle audiences. When the show is over, the world has changed, and leaving for one's ordinary home comes with a price. The norm has been subverted, just a bit, and the possibilities for a different sort of world become more real. Perhaps all it would take would be a turning back, a decision to join the circus and accept the topsy-turvy reality that allows for shedding one's self and becoming someone new—or discovering one's true identity.

Circuses in films offer an experience that compounds this carnivalesque element with an extra layer of unreality: the viewing experience itself. Through watching a film, audience members vicariously experience both the point-of-view character's adventures as well as their own reactions, and when the action on screen takes place in a space of already upended expectations, it proves fertile ground for reflection.

One element of the carnivalesque found in the circus in a variety of iterations is the mask, which produces a paradoxical sense of combined freedom and discomfort, depending on which side of it one situates oneself. The word mask as such was first used in English in the early to mid–16th century. It comes from Medieval Latin by way of Italian and Middle French, and in its Latin form it meant "specter" or "nightmare" (a fact that highlights its role in *MirrorMask* (2005) discussed momentarily). Cultures world-wide have created and worn masks for religious, ceremonial, theatrical, nefarious, light-hearted, and other purposes; the only commonality across time and people is the fact that masks allow the wearer to hide him or herself and become someone, or something, else. In other words they, like the circus film itself, allow for transformation. The donning of masks could as well be said to be performative; i.e., putting on a mask is the act that creates the liminal space in which this transformation can take place.

As well, masks interpellate, or invite, others to interact with them in specific, culturally dependent ways. Robin Bernstein, in her work "Dances with Things," posits that certain things have inherent qualities that shape behavior in relation to themselves, and that people who understand those qualities will interact, or "dance" with those things in specific ways that rely on and refer back to those understandings. For instance, a mask's inherent qualities invite certain kinds of behaviors: we pick them up; we put them on; we recoil from them; we laugh; we run away; we see something in them; we see something in ourselves … we see ourselves in them.

The Film, the Mask, the Mirror

Ostensibly a familiar enough coming-of-age tale, *MirrorMask* is about Helena, a girl on the cusp of womanhood who performs as a juggler in the Campbell Family Circus run by her parents, who dreams of running away to join the real world, and whose wish is fulfilled when she has an adventure in a strange world which brings her through a classic coming of age trial to young adulthood. And yet, *MirrorMask* is far more.

Though she lives within a traveling circus, Helena's experience is in other ways familiar to most viewers. She is disgruntled, annoyed at her parents, feels trapped in their world and their rules, and wants to escape. Her "normal world" may be our fantasy, with its juggling gorillas and high-wire acrobats and a father who is ringmaster and paymaster both, but her struggle is one we know. She wants to escape her everyday experience, be her own

Helena Campbell (Stephanie Leonidas) in her trailer on the grounds of the Campbell Family Circus, surrounded by her drawings into which she is about to fall (*MirrorMask*, 2005).

person, and find out who she is when not overshadowed by others'—in her case, her parents'—dreams.

The film starts with Helena in her room in a trailer on the carnival grounds. Its walls are covered with her drawings of a mystical, imaginary world of black and white. When Helena's mother comes knocking—Helena is late for her performance—she resists, ultimately yelling that she wants to run away and join real life. Her mother's response, "I don't think you could handle real life," foreshadows Helena's leaving; what self-respecting 15-year-old wouldn't take that as a dare? When her mother says, "you'll be the death of me" as she walks away, Helena responds "I wish I was," also foreshadowing later events. Her mother falls ill during their evening performance and is taken away by ambulance, and a number of days later once they are all back home, her father tells her that her mother needs an operation. That night Helena has a disjointed, chaotic dream that in essence makes manifest the spectacle that both circuses and circus films embody, makes clear her fear for her mother, and in a significant moment gives us an insight we won't understand until later in the film: at one point Helena stares into a mirror and sees only a caricature of herself, a stick figure with no discernable identifying features. She is not herself; the question of identity is problematic from the start.

All of this unsettles her, and us—but our awareness that it's a dream mitigates the terrifying, disjointed images. When she wakes and goes in search of the source of strange ethereal music she hears, she finds other members of the circus in a darkened courtyard and interacts with them. But they're not quite the people she knows. Something is different.

"What's wrong with your face?" one of them asks when she approaches. What's "wrong" is that she is not wearing a mask and at this point we realize that the others there all are. She is the odd one out and will continue throughout most of the remainder of the film as virtually the only non-masked character. If we hadn't figured out through the title—or the fact that when Helena's mother falls ill and is replaced in the gorilla costume by another circus performer, no one knows—we learn at this moment that masks are the point, and that they are the entry into understanding what this film is about.

Moments after asking Helena the question about her face, the character is killed by a "darkness" that rushes over him, causing him to shatter into thousands of tiny black shards. Helena follows another masked man through a nearby doorway in order to escape the darkness and enters a strange, monochromatic world that looks suspiciously like the one she has drawn and covered her trailer walls with. The extent of this world is revealed when she and her savior take to the skies in a daring escape, and the audience is introduced to the black queen, originator of the deadly darkness and not incidentally a dead ringer for her mother, in an aside that suggests she oversees all. Helena encounters strange, hybrid creatures that for the most part ignore her and her new friend, whose name she learns is Valentine.

Not long after they meet, he asks her: "How do you know if you're happy or sad without a mask ... or angry, or ready for dessert?"

"I've got a *face*," she responds, to which he shrugs.

Without a mask, his question and reaction imply, you can't know anything about your state of being; you can't know anything about *who you are*. This is an intriguing reversal of what masks are generally used for—*hiding those very things from others*. A perceptive viewer will understand that this exchange reveals another central tenet of the film, again as signaled in the title: Helena has entered and needs to learn to nego-

Valentine (Jason Barry) with his mask on in the Mirror World (*MirrorMask*, 2005).

tiate a Mirror world where the reverse of what's expected is often what occurs. And as a consequence of the particular characteristics of this world, faces aren't enough to convey emotion, to identify, or to understand oneself. This is reinforced when Helena is mistaken for the dark queen's daughter, the missing princess, soon after the above conversation, and tries to defend herself against the mistaken identification by claiming what she thinks is her own, fairly evident Self.

"I'm not anyone, I'm just me," she says. She is no one. And while she names herself immediately thereafter, her initial statement is taken as truth. A character much like her father in real life but masked, affirms this when he looks more closely at her naked face and says, "She's not her. I mean, she's not *her.*"

"Who am I meant to be?" Helena asks him, suddenly uncertain.

In a world in which masks identify instead of conceal, Helena has no idea who she is meant to be without one. Amplifying the angst she experiences in the circus space in which she lives in her normal world, this even-more-carnivalesque Mirror world highlights her dilemma: she cannot know what she feels, nor even who she is, without a mask. Even looking in the mirror won't help—she has tried that already. With no other options, and with some prodding, Helena takes on a quest to find a charm stolen by the princess she has been mistaken for, a quest that will save the white queen who looks like a mirror image of the black queen, and much like her own mother. This charm is not just a trinket, however. It is called a mirrormask, potentially the epitome of what the world, the film, and her journey are all about.

"What kind of thing is a mirrormask" she asks Valentine sometime later as they rest. He doesn't know. He can't. A mirrormask should not exist. Like many of the objects and creatures in the dream world, a mirrormask is a hybrid, a melding together of traits and characteristics that blend only superficially and are always in tension. Mirrors reflect and refract, and anyone who looks at one sees themselves; yet the paradox here is that this self is always seen in reverse, producing a kind of uncanny recognition. Masks hide and disguise, and conceal the wearer's true self, yet in this world are essential to knowing one's identity. In a world in which everyone wears a mask to know who they are and how they feel, we begin to understand that it is only by negotiating this tension between self and other that Helena stands a chance of discovering who she is meant to be.

Soon she realizes what we already figured out: the mirror world through which she and Valentine search is her own, drawn—literally and figuratively—from her imagination, and therefore she must be dreaming. She is the source of her own entrapment, this seems to say, and she continues to seek for an exit by looking through various windows they pass on their journey. Windows can generally be looked through without distortion and are often used as metaphors for avenues to enlightenment or clarity; here they are seen as lenses that distort, as barriers that hinder movement.

Through one she sees her own non-dream world, and a girl who looks just like her but is instead a darker, Mirror Helena—the dream world's princess—who has taken her place. The disconnect Helena feels from that person and that world are profound, especially when Mirror Helena acts in ways that run counter to Helena's desires and normal behavior. Though Helena tries to stop her, she cannot reach through the window to her (other) self with either voice or body, and she has no choice but to continue her search for the mirrormask in the hopes that it will save her.

In their search, she and Valentine encounter faceless flying bird-monkey creatures named mostly Bob (and Malcolm) who rescue them from the darkness, and giants who give them a key. As she contemplates this key, Helena has a vision in which she and her sick mother, alternatively dressed as herself and as the sleeping white queen, argue over whose dream they are currently in, and the difficulty Helena is having in finding the mirrormask.

Finally her mother tells her: "You know it's here…. It's probably staring you right in the face." This seemingly throwaway line is in fact crucial, and it is only by finding her way to herself that Helena will find her way home. At her mother's words, Helena claims the dream, symbolically taking control of her life away from her mother and moving one step closer to a return to herself, but her darker, Mirror self has realized that her own existence depends on the destruction of Helena's drawings, i.e., the world of imagination Helena created as an escape and in which she currently wanders. In an effort to hold on to her new freedom, Mirror Helena begins tearing the drawings off the walls of Helena's room, which shakes the foundations of the Mirror World. Helena and Valentine are helpless as this world crumbles around them, dodging falling pieces more or less successfully.

The disarticulation of the dream world Helena created as a way to escape her life signifies the necessary destruction of the fantasy standing between herself and the truth she is seeking. The fact that it is Mirror Helena doing the deconstruction isn't difficult to figure out; *she*, the darker self, is what's standing between Helena and the truth of who she is.

Helena is hurt by falling debris, Valentine sells her out to the dark queen, and finally, in the clutches of self-doubt and despair, Helena descends literally and figuratively into darkness, losing herself completely as she is imprisoned, force-dressed and force-fed, and forced to take the place of the dark queen's daughter. In inhabiting her darker, Mirror Self, she recreates in the dream reality what she had felt in her own world; she literally loses herself in the shadows of her mother's dream. When Valentine returns in a fit of regret, he helps remind her of who she truly is by inviting her to juggle and thereby claim part of the self she rejected early on: her place in her family's circus.

Together they ponder once again the riddle: what kind of thing is a mirrormask? A mask that is also a mirror, an object that conceals and reveals, that reflects and reverses. When Helena peers into the mirror hanging in the room she's been confined to, she sees Mirror Helena destroying the last of her imaginary world and simultaneously remembers her mother's words: "It's probably staring you right in the face."

Indeed. What else does a mirror show us but the obverse of ourselves, staring us right in the face? In a world of masks, the only place a mask that both conceals and reveals could possibly exist is (staring her right in) her face, and (in) her darker self. I.e., the mirror hanging on the wall of Helena's prison, one she has created, offers both mask and deeper insight, and the only avenue to who she is. Through literally facing herself in her own, uncanny reflection, she enacts a return to her own world.

Helena Campbell (Stephanie Leonidas) between worlds, leaving the Mirror World behind and returning to her own (*MirrorMask*, 2005).

The mirror becomes mask, revelation, and portal, and Helena transforms, becoming both someone new, and herself simultaneously. Though Mirror Helena fights this transformation, Helena is successful and she emerges into a new identity, one no longer trapped in a world of others' making. She has fought her way through her own darkness and the masks she didn't know she was wearing to awaken, literally, overlooking a new, brightly colored world that looks a lot like the one she wanted so desperately to escape. But different, of course, because she is different. Cinematically this is made clear as the colors in this, the penultimate scene, are bright and vivid, contrasting with most of the rest of the film which has been strangely monochromatic, punctuated with tinted highlights and straight lines.

Of course her mother recovers, the circus goes on, and Helena takes her place as a new adult in her new, more colorful world. And when she picks up her juggling pins and tosses them into the air in the last scene, she laughs and settles into her new role. She is herself; she is coherent, whole, and no longer desirous of escape.

Film Structure: The Circus as Both Liminal Space and Home

In classical film structure, the characters start in an everyday world, an inciting incident sends them into an adventure in a liminal space in which the main character undergoes conflicts internal and external, overcomes obstacles, often has harrowing escapes, and reaches ultimately some kind of resolution that generally includes a new appreciation for and acceptance of a revised norm(al world). Think of Dorothy's Kansas in *The Wizard of Oz*, the tornado as inciting incident, and Oz as the liminal space in which Dorothy learns about herself, gains confidence as well as friends, and defeats the obstacles that stand between her and her heart's desire.

In *MirrorMask*, the Campbell Family Circus is set up as Helena's normal world. Hence the carnival, generally understood to be a place of carnivalesque, topsy-turvy activity, here is the everyday and sets the rules, and it is the Mirror World Helena discovers which turns her life upside-down. Or, in the parlance of the film, forces her to see the world as it would appear in a mirror. Reflected, almost the same, uncannily different, it is a space of no-space, and anything could happen. More importantly, anyone can transform into someone else—it is as simple as donning a mask, or taking one off. And while some masks are more visible than others, the truth, as Helena discovers, is that the one she wears is just as liberating, and just as restrictive, as any other. She must learn to see herself as more than a reflection; she must answer the question "Who am I meant to be?" And the answer is as easy, or as difficult, as looking in the mirror.

This lesson is not unfamiliar to movie- and circus-goers alike. The circus, and circus films, with their clowns and jugglers and freaks, and their characters who could be us in another world—one we dream of entering—become the mirror in which we find ourselves. In each case, we enter a space of another's making, and we are transformed.

As a space of possibility the circus shakes things up but ultimately, as carnivalesque spaces tend to do, it reinforces the norm from which it deviates. As Helena learns and as we the audience have come to expect, regardless of how many times we pay the admission fee and enter a world that is not our own, when the spectacle is over we quickly return to ourselves.

Works Cited

Bakhtin, Mikhail. *Rabelais and His World.* Translated by Helene Iswolsky. Indiana UP, 2009.
Bernstein, Robin. "Dances with Things: Material Culture and the Performance of Race." *Social Text,* vol. 27, no. 4, 2009, pp. 67–94.
MirrorMask. Directed by Dave McKean. Samuel Goldwyn Films, 2005.

About the Contributors

Lisann **Anders** is a research and teaching assistant at the University of Zurich, Switzerland. Her Ph.D. project focuses on the literary imagination of violence in New York City. Her upcoming publications include articles on the body in Chuck Palahniuk's *Fight Club*, feminism in Disney, and Shakespearean villains.

David **Blanke** is a professor of history at Texas A&M University–Corpus Christi. He has published five scholarly books and numerous articles. His latest book examining the career of Cecil B. DeMille, a noted American film director, was published by Palgrave Macmillan in 2018.

Rachel L. **Carazo** has a graduate degree (M.A. English) from Northwestern State University and is pursuing an MLIS at the University of Southern Mississippi. In addition to a fantasy novel, she has also published four essays regarding topics in literature, television, and pop culture in three edited collections.

Michael **Charlton** is an associate professor in the English and Modern Languages Department at Missouri Western State University, where his research and teaching focus on professional writing, rhetoric, and popular culture.

Teresa **Cutler-Broyles** teaches film and cultural studies in the Cinematic Arts, Architecture, and Freshman Learning Communities departments at the University of New Mexico in Albuquerque and creative nonfiction at the Umbra Institute in Italy. She writes fiction, travel, popular culture and nonfiction, and has been published in numerous academic volumes on a variety of subjects.

Kylo-Patrick R. **Hart** is the chair of the Department of Film, Television and Digital Media at Texas Christian University, where he teaches courses in film and television history, theory, and criticism; popular culture; and queer media studies. He is the author or editor of several books about media.

Whitney S. **May** is pursuing her Ph.D. in American Studies at the University of Texas and is an adjunct lecturer for the Department of English at Texas State University. Her primary research interests include the Gothic and 19th-century horror literature, as well as depictions of the doppelgänger in horror fiction and popular culture. Her related work has been published in *The Edgar Allan Poe Review*, *Gothic Studies*, and *Supernatural Studies*.

Fernando Gabriel **Pagnoni Berns** (Ph.D. student) works as a professor at the Universidad de Buenos Aires (UBA), Facultad de Filosofía y Letras (Argentina). He teaches courses on international horror film and is director of the research group on horror cinema "Grite." His work has been published widely in various collections of essays on film and popular culture.

Ayal C. **Prouser** is a circus artist coach and scholar who focuses primarily on flying trapeze, aerial arts, and acrobatics in all three capacities. He has performed and coached across the United States, as well as in Africa and Asia, and has lectured both domestically and internationally, including Germany and the Czech Republic.

P.A. **Wilder** is a trained clown with an academic background in cultural theory and moving image studies. He is producing a horror film about misogyny.

Jessica L. **Williams** teaches in the English Department at SUNY College at Old Westbury. Her research and teaching interests include multicultural American literature, disability, and popular culture. She is the author of *Media, Performative Identity, and the New American Freak Show*.

Index

www.ingramcontent.com/pod-product-compliance
Lightning Source LLC
Chambersburg PA
CBHW031137270326
41929CB00011B/1656